I0824648

Enter the Villa

Enter the Villa

the (unauthorized) reality behind

Love Island

anna peele

ATRIA BOOKS
New York Amsterdam/Antwerp London
Toronto Sydney/Melbourne New Delhi

An Imprint of Simon & Schuster, LLC
1230 Avenue of the Americas
New York, NY 10020

First Atria Books hardcover edition May 2026

ATRIA BOOKS and colophon are registered trademarks of Simon & Schuster, LLC

Simon & Schuster strongly believes in freedom of expression and stands against censorship in all its forms. For more information, visit BooksBelong.com.

For information about special discounts for bulk purchases, please contact Simon & Schuster Special Sales at 1-866-506-1949 or business@simonandschuster.com.

The Simon & Schuster Speakers Bureau can bring authors to your live event. For more information or to book an event, contact the Simon & Schuster Speakers Bureau at 1-866-248-3049 or visit our website at www.simonspeakers.com.

Interior design by Jill Putorti

Map and archetype diagram design by Ivana Cruz

Manufactured in the United States of America

1 3 5 7 9 10 8 6 4 2

Library of Congress Control Number: 2026934280

ISBN 978-1-6682-0559-4
ISBN 978-1-6682-0561-7 (ebook)

To Alex, my basket

Contents

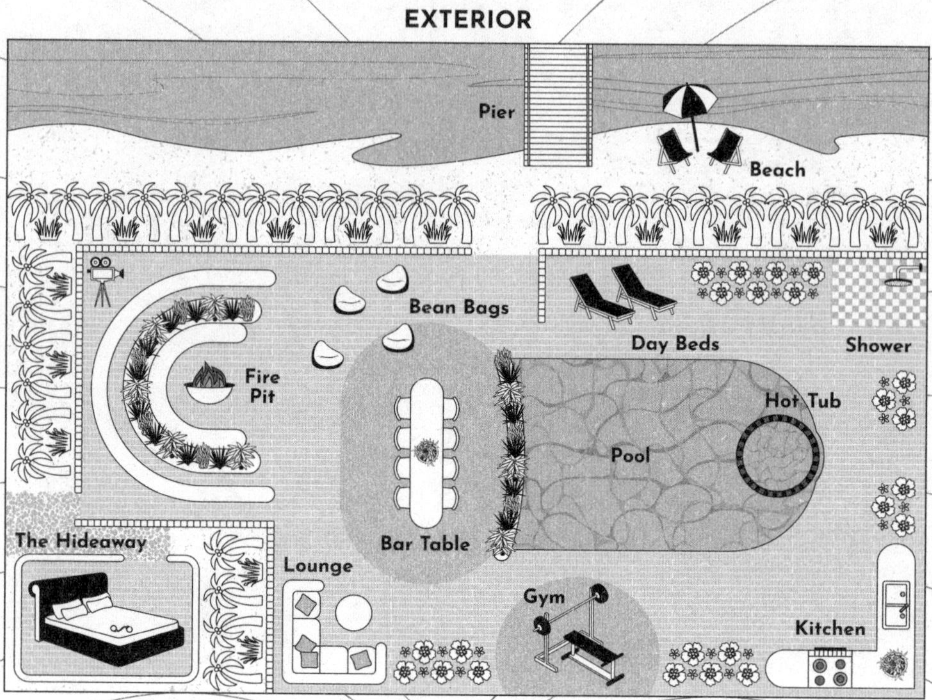
EXTERIOR
Pier
Beach
Bean Bags
Day Beds
Shower
Fire
Pit
Hot Tub
Pool
The Hideaway
Bar Table
Lounge
Gym
Kitchen

The Villa

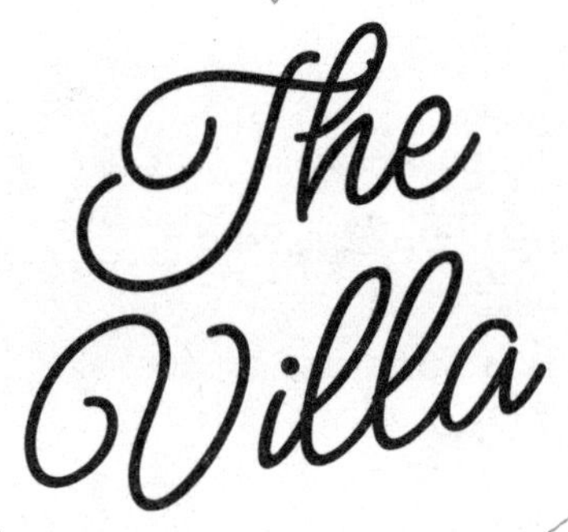

INTERIOR, GROUND FLOOR

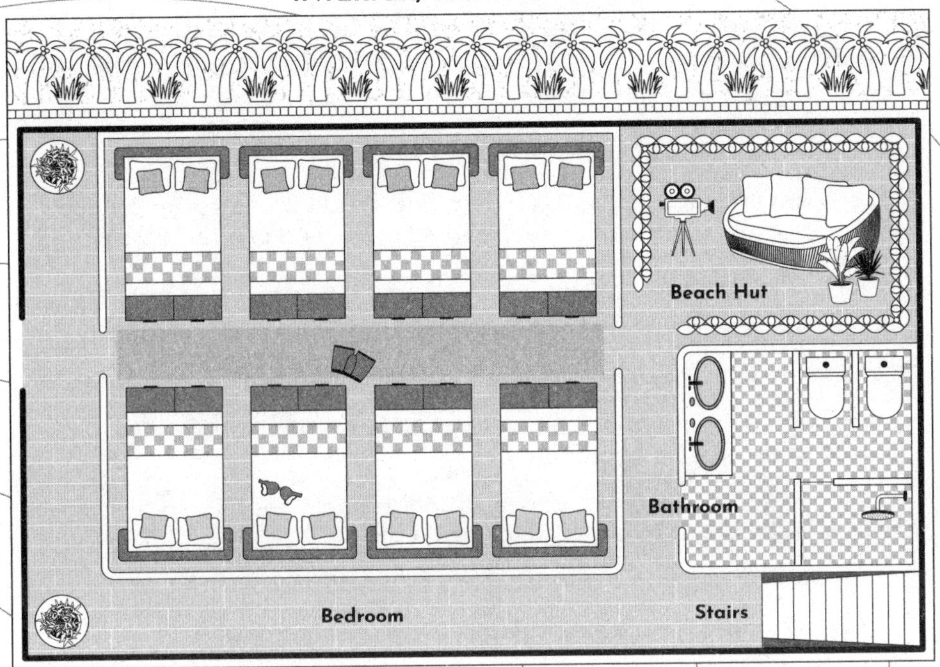

INTERIOR, SECOND FLOOR

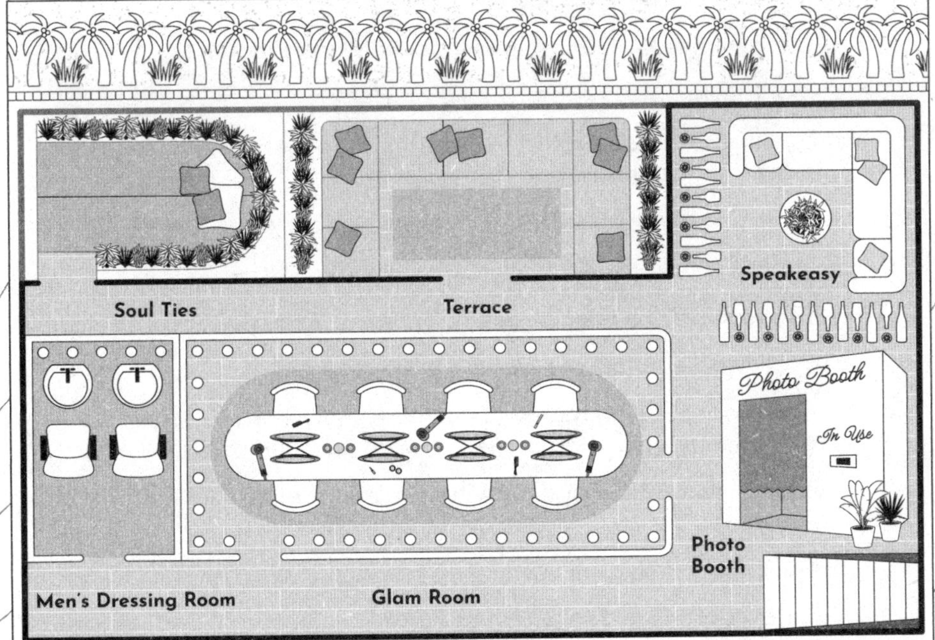

The *Love Island* Glossary

The agg: aggravation (*also: the hump*).

At the end of the day, it is what it is: dejected but brave-faced phrase that indicates a common understanding of the end of a relationship.

Bellend: dickhead.

Bombshell: an Islander who enters at any point after the initial coupling.

Boyfriend/girlfriend: a pairing intended to continue on the outside.

Bruv: term of endearment between men (*also: geez, gaffer, bro; bro can connote passive aggression*).

Can I pull you for a chat?: conversational entrée that could lead to nearly anything, from a snog to a breakup.

Challenge: official game administered by production.

Closed off: romantically entangled via verbal confirmation.

Couple (noun): a show-sanctified pairing.

Couple up (verb): to form a couple (noun) in the first episode, or in subsequent recoupling ceremonies.

Crack on: to mingle, flirt, or otherwise socially animate.

Craic: spark; scintillating camaraderie or rapport.

Crashing out: not in control of one's emotions, generally expressed through tears or inappropriate shouting; spiraling.

Cringe: embarrassing; often connected to self-revelation.

Cwtch: cuddle (*pronounced "cudge"*).

Dead it: verbally end a relationship.

Deep it: take something to heart.

Dumped: the act of being removed from the show; this may also informally refer to someone being broken up with (*also: binned, pied off*).

Early days: too soon to gauge long-term compatibility.

Exclusive: unwilling to consider romantic opportunities outside one's couple.

Fancy (verb): feel sexual attraction toward.

Friendship couple: a pairing for whom there is no chance of romance, entered into for the purposes of staying in the Villa.

Get to know someone: crack on with an understood, if impermanent, intention.

Graft: to try hard to win someone over. If identified by others, the connotation is negative; if identified by oneself, the connotation is neutral.

The ick: unshakable revulsion, typically caused by a benign transgression.

Islander: cast member on *Love Island.*

Lips (verb): kiss.

Melt (noun): person who feels unexpected tenderness.

Missus: woman, usually not present, who holds expectations for the behavior of her partner.

Move mad: to pursue recklessly.

Mug (noun): a person who has been mugged off.

Mugged off: disrespected.

My type on paper: someone fitting an Islander's historic preferences for a partner.

Not bothered: self-declared state of being, indicating a high level of botheredness.

Open: coupled up but unencumbered.

The outside: all areas on Earth excluding the Villa.

Recouple (verb): to affirm one's partnership or form a new couple via ceremony.

Single: unencumbered and imperiled.

Slagged off: (*see: mugged off.*)

Snog: make out.

Test (noun): travail a couple endures to determine viability.

Ticking boxes: signifiers that confirm someone is an Islander's type on paper.

The Villa: the house and garden in which filming takes place.

Where's your head at?: query from a nervous Islander to someone whose interest they're unsure of.

The (Unofficial) Villa Rules

1. Do not kiss outside of a challenge if you're getting to know someone.

2. If you are interested in "getting to know" multiple people, inform all vested parties before you pull someone new for a chat.

3. Recoupling speeches are for publicly affirming one's couple, not verbalizing grudges.

4. Do not crack on with a new partner in front of a previous partner, especially if the coupling ended badly.

5. Bring your partner a coffee in the morning. (This applies to coupled men and grafting women.)

6. Islanders in closed-off couples must sleep on the daybeds during Casa Amor unless expressly permitted by their partners.

7. Follow any Casa Amor misbehavior with a circumspect but Vaseline-lensed accounting of any relevant actions.

8. During the challenge "Snog, Marry, Pie," protocol dictates an Islander "marry" a friend and "snog" their romantic partner. Generally, the recipient of a pie should not be surprised when the dessert hits their face.

9. If you're in a closed-off couple (or would like to be), don't go on the terrace with another Islander you're attracted to.

10. Don't become exclusive if there is any conceivable chance your head could be turned.

11. Don't dump someone from the Villa based on the information you've gleaned about the public's perception of the Islanders.

12. Don't recouple for the purpose of winning.

13. Don't hit relationship milestones for the purpose of winning.

14. Don't talk about winning.

15. Don't try to win.

16. Split the prize money.

17. Don't do anything in the Villa you wouldn't want your grandmother, your employer, or your current significant other to see.

18. No matter what external forces lead to a situation, you are the only person responsible for your actions.

19. If you're on *Love Island*, you're not too good for *Love Island*.

20. Nothing lasts forever, except the decision to go on *Love Island*.

Enter the Villa

Introduction

ROB RAUSCH WAS HIDING in the pool.

The journey had been an unlikely one. After much prodding from a smitten Leah Kateb, the twenty-four-year-old snake wrangler would tell her, through wobbly tears, that she's an amazing woman, just maybe not the right one for him. The twenty-four-year-old college student wasn't a good listener and cut him off in conversation, Rob told her. He mentioned that Leah had once called him a con artist and poured a bucket of water on him. This was all true, though the fact that the teasing had not been received well seemed to shock Leah—with full moon–wide eyes, she blinked at Rob as she took in the news that he didn't find her negging cute.

Then the conversation took a turn toward hell. "I feel like sexually . . ." Rob said, embarking on the thought, then pivoting to a compliment sandwich as he dried his eyes on a towel. "I think you're gorgeous. I think you're sexy as fuck. But I feel like we don't really have a groove." Leah waited until Rob was done talking—he *had* just told her she interrupted him—then responded slowly. "You're allowed to feel the way you feel," she said. Rob, who had been crying for a mucus-inducing length of time, gave his nose a pick and acceded to Leah's request for a hug.

It was tough feedback to get during the breakup, and it would lead to a blowup that would become canon on the reality dating series *Love Island USA*.

Leah went from expressing compassion for the guy she still hoped to keep dating to Chernobyl meltdown. "That is so embarrassing to me," Leah said, starting to cry. "That literally just made me feel so weird." Rob's response to her upset would make the moment eclipse mere breakup. Completely overwhelmed by the conversation, he stripped, starting with the removal of his tank top as he walked down the stairs. Then he jumped into the pool. The puzzled Islanders tried to figure out where he was, but the camera knew: It zoomed in on Rob's reflection as he fled under a temporary deck over the water that he'd noticed earlier. Rob turtled inside the plastic covering while viewers heard a soundtrack of tritely soulful country lyrics about being a house of cards that's about to break. Close-ups of Rob's chlorine-pruned hand and a sliver of his spider tattoo were played so sincerely that it read as comic to viewers.

It was not funny to Rob. "I had a full-on panic attack," Rob says to me nearly a year later. "I uncontrollably couldn't stop crying. I don't even understand how that happened to me."

Rob hadn't been thinking about how his actions would come across to viewers on the reality dating show when he hid in the water, but once he was in there, getting colder and colder, he told himself, "You're so fucking dumb. This is gonna look so fucking dumb."

Neither Leah nor Rob had two other important pieces of information. The first was that Leah, with her beguiling Valley monotone and ardor for a man who cuddled with bugs, was becoming the star of *Love Island USA* season 6. The second was that they had just put the series on a path that would make it one of the biggest television shows in the world.

"When Rob jumped in the pool, I was like, 'Oh, thank God,'" says then–executive producer Simon Thomas. This breakdown reached an ecstatic climax of what the show would be at its most transcendent: absurd, with genuine feeling. "If I write it in a script, you won't believe it," Thomas says of the divinely unscripted moment his team had, if not manufactured, at least created the conditions for. "But if I show you Rob pencil-diving into the pool, it is cinema."

Love Island is the most successful dating series ever created—and, to many, the best. What the show actually is depends on whom you ask. At its core, it's a television program that since its premiere in 2015 has grown from being a lo-fi fantasy about people trapped on vacation to a series that has been viewed billions of times, commissioned franchises in twenty-three countries around the world, spawned an *All Stars* version in the UK and *Love Island Games* in the US, won a BAFTA, and become so culturally ubiquitous that Millie Bobby Brown, Margot Robbie, Kim Kardashian, Kylie and Kendall Jenner, Megan Thee Stallion, Coco Gauff, Bradley Cooper, and Hailey Bieber are vocal fans. It is a show about love, or dating, or competition, or the fleeting glory of warm weather and being young and hot, or insecurity, or conflict, or some sort of combination of all those things. It's an annual televised summer fling. It's communal voyeurism. It forces young adults to put down their phones and engage. It fosters emotional intelligence in the kind of people who would elect to go on a series that almost invariably features more than one wet T-shirt contest. And it has changed the expectations for what a reality show can be: something deserving of our absolute attention nearly every day for months. We invest in *Love Island* because two things are equally true: It's novel to watch people who are foreign to us in appearance and demeanor put themselves in a situation we'd never be in, and there is pathos across that distance; in witnessing every choice they make, we see a reflection of our own lives. We walk alongside them to whatever hell or paradise they wind up at.

Certain elements of *Love Island* are fixed. Each season is usually six to eight weeks, with near nightly episodes in which sexy strangers pair up based on attraction, competing for the love of each other and the viewing public. They play a series of games called "challenges," which are deployed by producers to evoke the trials and tribulations of non-televised long-term relationships in the truncated time span of a TV season. These games often take the form of events that rarely occur in nature, such as squeezing the teats of gigantic fake udders into one's mouth, then transferring the milk to a partner, or humping a balloon until it bursts and doing a dare that was hidden in the latex. Based on their performances in these challenges, as well as the naturally occurring ones that arise from sharing a small space with each other under constant observation, villains and stars are formed as public opinion is formed, then coalesces, then is relitigated as the season progresses. The devotion and caprice of the audience are constantly being triangulated—viewers will embrace someone, and their feelings about that person will either transfer to the object of that Islander's affection or harden into hatred for a cast member whom fans believe has mistreated their favorite. Via viewers' votes—and occasionally the decisions of other castmates—Islanders are dumped from the Villa and watch the rest of the show from "the outside," the show's term for real life beyond the Villa. To make it to the finale, a pairing must be perceived as genuine. The most beloved duo, as ultimately determined by the audience, is named the winner and given £50,000 in the UK or $100,000 in the US, which the couple can choose to share with each other, or not, at the discretion of the Islander who happened to get the envelope with the money. It is understood that splitting the prize is the only acceptable option. Essentially, it's a popularity contest you can win only by not trying to win.

Love Island borrows from classic unscripted tropes: the romantic climax of dating shows; the audience-picks-the-winner finale of competition series; the group debauchery of Bravo's *Vanderpump Rules* and *Summer House*; and the round-the-clock filming and synchronous airing of *Big Brother*. But it also rejects many conventions of reality TV. Unlike *The Bachelor*'s stolid, Christian-tinged plod to the altar, there is no prescribed proposal at the end of a season of *Love Island*, nor a predetermined episode for approved sexual activity. Bravo shoots its shows well before they air, and production typically focuses on preexisting friend groups—or at least location-adjacent, social status proximates. On *American Idol* or *The Voice* or *Dancing with the Stars*, contestants are judged on skill, whereas Islanders garner votes for being themselves. *Survivor* rewards deception and maneuvering, while *Love Island* fosters personal connections beyond alliances.

Love Island became a rare piece of monoculture because of its willingness to forgo the benefits of its peers' and predecessors' formats in exchange for the joyride of immediacy. We're watching people feel in real time; sometimes, as with Leah, these are uncomfortable emotions making a lifetime debut: shame, judgment, rejection. We cheer when an Islander pushes past a pattern of avoidance. We are wounded when they pursue a moment of short-term pleasure that is invariably exposed to the person it will hurt the most. They fight, they fuck, they embarrass themselves, they eke out redemption. They learn faster than they would have if they hadn't been on *Love Island*, stumbling into outsized versions of mistakes and mortifications that everyone who has ever dated has gone through. Our thoughts about them and our votes for or against them impact how producers provoke them, and whether they're given the grace to continue to amuse us on TV at all.

These conditions make *Love Island* as immersive and interactive as a video game. The schematic layout of the Villa, with limited space and no escape for its inhabitants, is a setting in which potential connections are played like levels. If an Islander doesn't advance to the next stage of a relationship, that budding couple dies, and they have to start over from the beginning—unless the audience votes them out, and the game is over for them.

The viewers' influence on the show is thrilling, but our feelings of complicity are soothed by the knowledge that the cast members have elected to be here and the producers are the ones designing this romantic torture chamber—even if those producers insist they're just responding to what the Islanders do. "The train leaves the station on episode one, and we are often just throwing the tracks in front of the train," *USA* showrunner Ben Thursby-Palmer says of the lack of intentional direction.

The show's trick is marrying what cultural critic Walter Benjamin called "cult value" and "exhibition value" in his 1935 essay "The Work of Art in the Age of Mechanical Reproduction."[1] Benjamin believed that cult value—the venerated status of something exclusive and sacred—was diminished by public accessibility. On *Love Island*, intimacy is imbued with meaning by the act of mass observation, whether it's a fondling or an existential crisis. "It turns out Maura has been hiding Jean-Paul Sartre's philosophical classic *Being and Nothingness* inside her copy of *Heat* magazine," narrator Iain Stirling intoned during a *Love Island UK* season 5 moment with cast member Maura Higgins.

"Am I even here?" Maura asked of what felt like her absence, insofar as no one in the Villa was paying attention to her at that moment. She was oblivious to Iain's voice-over as she questioned the impact of perception on her being: "Does anyone even see that I'm here?"

Love Island turns into entertainment the most private physical and emotional moments the kind of person who would volunteer to be an Islander can undergo. And the audience transforms that entertainment into culture by consuming it with the seriousness that the fundamental experiences of being human deserve—and by sharing clips of Rob jumping into the pool.

This book is a love letter to *Love Island*. It is a sociological examination of why we watch and obsess over the show, a process story about the hundreds of thousands of hours of production that have gone into it, and a psychological look at the impact the series has had on the people who cried and came on-screen for our amusement.

My reporting on *Love Island* began in 2021 for a *Vanity Fair* feature that documented the changes made to the show's safety and health protocols following the suicides of three cast members.[2] My goal was to understand the effect of being an Islander and what the people who make the series believe about the morality of the entire endeavor. I wanted to know if it was possible to produce a reality show as great as *Love Island* in a way that didn't hurt people.

But there was so much more to learn about how *Love Island* is conceived and executed, the transformative experience of being in and coming out of the Villa, and what goes on behind the scenes of some of the greatest unscripted television ever created. I needed to know what producers were thinking as the show they'd set up as a Rube Goldberg machine reconfigured its own sequence every episode, and how they reimagined it so the show stayed *Love Island*—by which I mean, remained constantly surprising while hitting the emotional and dramatic notes viewers need to feel sated. I was desperate to get the true story of the reality—and to hear more from the people who had improvised some of the funniest lines in TV history. As Lena Dunham told me last year in an interview for *Rolling Stone*, "If I wrote one line of dialogue as good as anyone on *Love Island*, I'd retire right now."

This book is the result of unprecedented access through almost a thousand hours of research and nearly a hundred interviews with the show's cast members, presenters, producers, creators, executives, fans, and scholars—the only people who could tell the story of *Love Island* and reveal its secrets. I flew to South Africa and visited the Villa in Cape Town, where I sat on the Islanders' beds and went into one of the control rooms where every moment of *Love Island* is streamed and edited as it happens in real time. During an unexpected hug, I accidentally inhaled the scent of UK host Maya Jama's shampoo. (Her hair smells like she looks: luscious.) I talked with Maura Higgins and Ariana Madix about whether Maura is all mouth, learned as Ekin-Su Cülcüloğlu and the stars of *Love Island USA*'s breakout seasons 6 and 7 explained what was going on in their minds during some of the series' most iconic moments, and heard from Charli xcx about why she loves this show. Seeing the work that goes into setting up *Love Island* for the bumbling humanity that blooms inside of it has been the most fascinating discovery of my life. Internalizing the changes it induces in the people who lived in the machine has made me realize my own—and every viewer's—role in the show.

Having studied the series and the conversations of cast members and fans with a Talmudic fervor, I thought I knew *Love Island.* But as the Islanders I spoke with warned me, you can't really understand until you've been in the Villa. So join me in enjoying the explosion of the biggest bombshell ever dropped on reality TV.

1 Early Days

IF YOU CLOSED YOUR eyes and tried to imagine the kind of diabolical deviant who created *Love Island*, you would not see Richard Cowles. Cowles, with his rectangular glasses and frank conversational style, seems more like a lawyer who would dispassionately advise executives at ITV about the liability risks of a reality show than the mastermind behind a series that has found a way to serialize and broadcast multiple sex acts going on in the same room. He is happily married to a wife he met on the set of a different reality series and has two sons, neither of whom he would cast on *Love Island*.

Cowles grew up in Winchmore Hill, a small suburb in North London that was the home of Rod Stewart, The Who drummer Keith Moon, and Spice Girl Emma Bunton. His father was a builder, and his mother owned a haberdashery, leaving Cowles plenty of time for his hobbies: playing Atari and watching TV. In the seventies in the UK, there were four main channels. "Sometimes on a Sunday, there was no television at all," he says. "It was just like it was waiting to happen."

The first reality show Cowles encountered was *The Family*, a 1974 docuseries modeled after the seminal PBS series *An American Family*, which aired a year earlier and documented the implosion of a marriage and the self-mythology of Lance Loud, the family's gay son and the show's breakout star. The heightened characterizations of docu-soaps offered possibility to a boy who would grow up to make TV. Cowles became intrigued by the idea that a program could be sustained by standout personalities, rather than plot.

When Cowles started working in television in 1992, he began producing what was called "factual programming": unscripted shows in mundane, often corporate settings. In 2001 these shows would inspire Ricky Gervais to create *The Office*, set at a paper company in a stark, gray town. "The seed of that was we had ten years of these quaint docu-soaps in the nineties on British TV," Gervais shared on the podcast *Smartless* in 2020.[1] "We had one called [*The*] *Hotel*." Importantly to us, there was also one called *Airline*, on which Richard Cowles was a producer. He spent a year flying back and forth on the budget air shuttle company EasyJet, following everyone from well-steeled pilots to disgruntled passengers to disdainful gate agent Jane Boulton, who has become an unlikely TikTok star nearly three decades later for her blunt interactions with customers. Cowles would frequently fly five routes in a day, spinning in-the-moment storylines out of such scintillating content as the plight of people forgetting their passports.

"It was just normal people [being] filmed, and they'd become sort of stars for ten minutes," Gervais said. "And of course, nowadays, they become stars forever and make millions."

Normal people becoming stars was Cowles's pitch when he proposed bringing back a version of *Celebrity Love Island*, a reality show that Cowles cocreated, which ran for two seasons in 2005 and 2006. *Celebrity Love Island* was filmed in Fiji and featured a production schedule modeled after *Big Brother UK*, on which casts were filmed constantly, with weekly eliminations and almost-daily episodes that were edited and aired shortly after the events took place.

Unlike *Big Brother*, however, an element of romantic coupling was supposedly intended to drive *Celebrity Love Island.* The idea for the show had been sparked by the real relationship between Katie Price and Peter Andre that began on Cowles's *I'm a Celebrity . . . Get Me Out of Here!*, which sees low-end famous people suffer in the wilderness for the privilege of appearing on camera.

In its original incarnation, however, *Love Island* did not fulfill its description as a dating show. "It was good, but it was not about finding love," Cowles admits. Because no viable relationships developed during filming, it focused on what could charitably be described as C-list personalities bumping against each other and playing games. The cast was composed of formers— "former footballer," "former soap actor"—and people like Pierce Brosnan's son Chris, with guest appearances from Dennis Rodman and *Jackass* stuntman Steve-O, who at the time was suffering from a debilitating nitrous oxide addiction. Its only moments of coupling occurred when pairs of Islanders were sent to the Love Shack, a semiprivate space that was ostensibly meant to let contestants get to know each other better but functionally served as a place to take a break from the rest of the cast. The show's game structure was based on whom viewers liked the most. Male and female winners were chosen separately, so contestants only had to be the favorite of their gender group, not the most root-for-able couple. The public bestowed the first season's £100,000 prize on TV presenter Jayne Middlemiss and club owner Fran Cosgrave, then glamour model Bianca Gascoigne and a footballer's son, Calum Best, in the second season, which by then had tellingly dropped the word "Celebrity" from the title.

The show did decently in the ratings, despite the self-own of ITV airing many of the episodes of *Celebrity Love Island* in the same time slot as its inspiration and competitor, *Big Brother*. Louis Staples, author of the forthcoming *Please Do Not Swear: How Reality TV Reinvented Fame*, says the show was seen as "grubby" by a UK populace that was both slightly repressed and full of anger at pop culture's version of nobility—it felt unseemly that celebrities, no matter how grasping and cut-rate, should get a free holiday to pursue potentially prurient activities. At least on *I'm a Celebrity*, cast members had to sleep in the jungle without air-conditioning.

The series was hammered in the higher-end broadsheet papers. "Switch off the box, walk into the garden, and stare at the stars while tears shine in your eyes," wrote *Black Mirror* creator Charlie Brooker in *The Guardian* during the show's first season.[2] "*Celebrity Love Island*: Wish hard enough, and God might make it stop." ITV obliged and the show ended in 2006, which ITV's then–director of television Simon Shaps told Staples was due to "reputational liability" rather than poor ratings.

Eight years later, as Cowles was trying with limited success to pitch another series to networks, the surreal ridiculousness of *Celebrity Love Island* kept coming up in meetings. "I really like *Love Island*," Cowles heard from various executives. "I just don't know why that didn't work, because there was something there."

Dating series were still hugely popular in the US, but the UK hadn't found a fresh way to capitalize on them beyond stunty shows like *Dating in the Dark*, which was a literal interpretation of the title, filming meetups with infrared cameras. It felt like a time to revamp a tired genre. ITV controller of digital channels and acquisitions Angela Jain was looking for a show that would appeal to ITV2's prime demographic of sixteen-to-thirty-four-year-olds while providing the scale and viewer commitment that *Big Brother*'s immersive, circadian construct created. Cowles was savvy and knew how to dismantle the sentiment Jain most hated to hear about her programming: "This is just low-rent television. I get very defensive about that," says Jain, who is now a head of content at Disney+. "Because I think long and hard about everyone that goes in there."

The *Love Island* reboot, then, would not be low-rent television, Cowles convinced Jain—it would be *genius* low-rent television. With executive producers Tom Gould, Sarah Tyekiff, and Andy Cadman, they could find a fix for a failed series with a strong format by refining a silly tone to a self-aware one and reimagining the kind of people who would be cast. Cowles says that like *Celebrity Big Brother* or *I'm a Celebrity*, the thought behind *Celebrity Love Island* was that "celebrities are a shortcut to viewers." He made a sell to Jain that argued the opposite: "We are going to create the stars of tomorrow." Cowles didn't know it in that meeting, but he wasn't bullshitting. Now that the show was greenlit, all he had to do was figure out how to make his prophecy come true.

Eliminating fame as a prerequisite for casting not only had the upside of being cheaper than hiring quasi-famous contestants but also increased the probability that the Islanders might actually wind up in love. Jain says, "I think we always felt that there was something magical about watching real people who don't have any particular artifice to live up to." Put another way: Celebrities are too savvy to have sex on TV, let alone develop deep bonds. Ordinary people would provide more genuine entertainment—albeit the kind of "ordinary" people who get preventative Botox in their early twenties and are not put off by the £500-a-week fee to cover "loss of earnings" because it opens the possibilities of a free vacation, prize money, and becoming a public fixture for little more than being appealing and attractive. Going into this experience without the burden of fame to preserve, in theory with nothing to lose, means they are open enough to form true attachments. *Something* would happen in that Villa between the regular people, Cowles and his cohort were convinced.

Instead of filming in Fiji, which is about ten thousand miles from London and has a twelve-hour time difference, they decided to produce the series in Mallorca, which is only one hour ahead of Greenwich Mean Time and a 2.5-hour air trip. Spanish islands are a popular tourist destination for Brits, and ITV had filmed youth- and sex-centric shows there before for the younger ITV2 audience. The first Villa featured the biggest private pool in the Balearics, but executive Amanda Stavri remembers the design being minimal—they didn't know what *Love Island*'s aesthetic was yet. "It all kind of feels quite basic when you look back," Stavri says. "Astroturf and a bit of trellising." The show's intro music by the brand—not band—agency A-MNEMONIC featured four doinky synth chords, rising and falling for several measures over a simple club beat, which played on-screen as gauzy figures in bathing suits touched each other's tan necks and showed off their body jewelry. As the last "bum bum . . . bum-bum-bum" hit, the show's glitter-filled heart emblem nestled into a seascape that exists in a digital space nowhere near the landlocked Villa.

The team knew it would carry over elements from *Love Island*'s first life: regular coupling ceremonies, challenges, dumpings, and bombshells, who are people sent in at various points throughout the season to either offer a new option for partnership to a single Islander or, more typically, to blow up a couple. "The public want people that can go in and test a relationship," Mike Spencer-Hayter, *Love Island*'s creative director, says of the need for that role.

As for the host, there was never a question of who would lead the Islanders through the bedlam of *Love Island*. "There is only one person who can present this," Jain told a colleague in 2014. "It has to be the Bridget Jones of TV. It has to be Caroline Flack—not only 'cause she's a great presenter, but her love life is always a fucking mess." (Jain does not remember the conversation quite the same way.) The colleague says, "You had somebody who was the living embodiment of the pursuits and search for love."

Caroline was an impeccable fit. She was an identifiable member of the ITV family from her gigs on the talent competition series *The X Factor* and *I'm a Celebrity . . . Get Me Out of Here!* As a host, she projected warmth and brought both authority and childlike effervescence to her role; it led her to pick up even more airtime on the ITV2 spin-off chat show *The Xtra Factor*. Caroline would presage Jimmy Fallon's shtick by playing disarming games with *Xtra Factor* guests, like smashing eggs on each other's faces. She'd clown to the audience, sipping from a flute of champagne or getting a foot massage while chatting about *X Factor* doings.

Moving Caroline to *Love Island* would be invaluable to the show, even if it seemed like a lateral career move for her. By audience vote, she had just won *Strictly Come Dancing*, the UK's version of *Dancing with the Stars*, a coup that underscored her talent and popularity. She had also been commissioned to write a memoir, which would be called *Storm in a C Cup*. As the face of *Love Island*, Caroline would hold up the shambolically glam dating tentpole series concept. Her dating history was chum for Britain's tabloid media, which framed her as simultaneously sexily indefatigable and hapless. The coverage became frenzied when Caroline began dating a member of One Direction.

After his 2010 run on *The X Factor*, a teenage Harry Styles began wooing the then-thirty-one-year-old host in public, if you count doing an interview on the official *X Factor* website as "public"; maybe it was more like writing a note on the teacher's chalkboard before class. Styles said, "If Caroline Flack is reading this, say 'Hi' from me. She is gorgeous!"[3]

Their relationship began after Harry turned seventeen and was no longer an *X Factor* contestant. It wasn't public until Styles was photographed leaving Caroline's home one morning—then came the screaming headlines and rabble. In *Storm in a C Cup*,[4] Caroline described people calling her a pedophile in the streets. Prior to the Styles affair, Caroline had dated Prince Harry—another romance partially scuttled by press intrusion. "Very soon after, they papped me and Flack . . . and those photos set off a frenzy. Within hours a mob was camped outside Flack's parents' house, and all her friends' houses, and her grandmother's house," Harry wrote in his memoir, *Spare*.[5] "She was described in one paper as my 'bit of rough'"—a truly nasty word for a sexual partner of a perceived lower social class—"because she once worked in a factory or something. Jesus, I thought, are we really such a country of insufferable snobs?" (Incidentally, Spencer-Hayter says that, pre–Meghan Markle, Harry would have been the "perfect male Islander.")

The disarray of her romantic dealings was the unspoken—at least in the world of the show—foil to Caroline's on-camera competence. She was caring and assertive, buoyant and prepared in a way that allowed for maximum dexterousness during production. She was beautiful but approachably so. She could deliver a script, wear an earpiece with production feeding her prompts, and improvise banter with the Islander sitting with her, often in front of the audience who were present for the many mid-show live segments that would lard season 1. "To hold the information and make it look completely natural," her colleague says, "her timing was just extraordinary." Caroline's blend of welcoming notoriety and enviable-but-conceivable professional success would become a model for the many Islanders who would dream of gigs as presenters and their own relationships being featured in *The Sun*.

"It's the most relatable show," Spencer-Hayter says of Islanders seeing themselves in Caroline and of viewers seeing themselves in Islanders. "You've all been in that situation. You've all had your heart broken. You've all fallen in love for the first time. You've all picked the wrong guy."

Unlike *Big Brother*'s straightforward, procedural narration, Jain wanted "witty voice-over" for *Love Island*. The choice allows the show to get away with its less prestige qualities—acknowledging the cheesiness of a date staged feet from the Villa with nonalcoholic bubbly and fruit that has been sitting under the Spanish sun for hours, or the fact that a cast member doesn't know the difference between a county and a country.

That is where Iain Stirling comes in. Unlike Caroline, Iain wasn't a known quantity at ITV. He'd been a stand-up comic and then the lead presenter on a kid's show on the BBC Children's network, alongside a puppet of a border terrier named Hacker T Dog. The pair would present games and host interstitial bits in between other CBBC programming, bantering with a chemistry that exceeded anything that had aired on *Celebrity Love Island.*

Since the narrator would largely be an off-screen presence, ITV solicited vocal reels to vet candidates. Iain's stood out. With his fluty, Scottish-accented commentary, Iain would be *Love Island*'s high-status jester, alternating between making fun of himself, the show and its production team, and cast members. The self-flagellating voice-over was meant to marry the anti-self-awareness of most Islanders, which often gave the show a sitcom feel.

Iain's role would also be the ombudsman—if someone was behaving like a dick, he would point it out. "People need someone like that in their lives," Jain says.

With the concept, host, and voice of *Love Island* in place, the show needed people who could conceivably become its protagonists. Hannah Elizabeth was the first Islander the casting team ever met with. Agent Dave Read had previously placed clients on *Celebrity Love Island* and worked with talent from *The Only Way Is Essex* (*TOWIE*), a reality show following the dating lives and intragroup squabbles of a nouveau riche (or at least nouveau middle class) crowd. When ITV decided to run *Love Island* back sans celebrities, executive producer Tom Gould got in touch with Read to see if he had any suitable clients for former *TOWIE* producer Spencer-Hayter, who then worked on the casting team. Read went through his Filofax and scrounged up a dozen-ish sub-famous-but-bikini-ready women to meet with the team, each entering at thirteen-minute intervals to try to impress Spencer-Hayter and his tripod.

Read had to persuade Hannah to audition. "I really think you'd be great on the telly," he told the twenty-five-year-old.

"Oh, I don't think so," she said. "I think I'd make a show of meself." At the time, Hannah was employed as a Page Three girl, so-called because the job entailed posing semi-nude on the third page of tabloid newspapers. She'd also modeled for *Playboy*. Hannah's willingness to show off her breasts was part of her "USP"—the term *Love Island* producers use for cast members who possess a "unique selling point."

Hannah's other USP was her voice. She yells every word of her Liverpool honk at the same astonishing volume, from terms of endearment to antique British insults delivered in her nearly incomprehensible Scouse dialect. ("Talk to a few scruffs in Magaluf, I'll just fuckin' laugh at you, mate!" she would scream on *Love Island* at her partner Jon Clark a few months after she was cast, during a real fight about Hannah flashing her boobs in the Villa that led to her imagining a future fight in which Jon retaliated by flirting with women during a trip to another town in Mallorca.) Hannah had a self-effacing grandeur that embodied what was known in the UK as "hun culture"—the kind of delightfully semi-delusional woman embodied by Patsy and Edina on *Absolutely Fabulous*.

When Hannah walked into ITV's offices for her interview with a blonde blowout even bigger than her bosom, she bellowed at Spencer-Hayter, "Babe! It's me, Hannah! Where are we going, love? Can I have a mug?" gesturing toward a souvenir network cup. Spencer-Hayter couldn't believe it. "Everyone was staring at her," he says. "I just fell in love with Hannah as soon as I met her. I thought, this girl is gorgeous, bold, unapologetic, exciting. And for a new show, you need characters like that." With implants, extensions, filler, and heavy makeup, Hannah would also become a self-presentational touchpoint, setting a bar for cosmetic intervention that many of her successors would endeavor to meet. From the moment Hannah was cast, Spencer-Hayter says, "She has always been our queen."

Hannah wasn't entirely sure she wanted the throne. She'd seen clips of the long-canceled original series and understood the gist, but this show had never been done without celebrities before; what had seemed like the main draw was gone. "Will anyone watch it?" Hannah wondered. "What if it's shit?" After reaching the conclusion that the answer to the first question was "probably not," Hannah decided she wasn't worried about the second.

A few weeks later, Spencer-Hayter asked Read to take him directly to what would become the primordial soup of *Love Island*'s early-season casts: the Sugar Hut, a nightclub featured heavily on *TOWIE*. That night, Read introduced Spencer-Hayter to Hannah's future boyfriend Jon, a twenty-five-year-old builder who embodied the "really funny guy who maybe doesn't have the muscles" role that casting sought. Jon signed his *Love Island* contract without reading it—it sounded good enough when the producers laid it out verbally: "Sexy people looking for love that kind of want the ultimate holiday romance," as Spencer-Hayter sold it. "Big Villa," Jon said of the boxes that were ticked when we spoke in 2021 for *Vanity Fair*.[6] "Pool. Clothes are clean. Food fed. Hot girls. Single guys. It's the perfect recipe to fall in love."

Like Hannah, twenty-two-year-old Jessica Hayes was a glamour model, albeit with slightly less outlandish proportions than the Parton-esque Hannah. Jess had participated in the first of *Love Island*'s trial versions, called the "dry run" or "mock week." Mock week is a miniature, unaired version of *Love Island* with a stand-in slate of Islanders filmed immediately after the Villa is set up and ending a few days before *Love Island* proper begins shooting. For several days, producers get used to the flow of editing in real time and test out challenges and camera angles on cast members who almost never make it on to the actual show. With her cranberry-colored hair and languid flirtatiousness, Jess was so at ease being filmed that producers removed her from the dry run so she could get ready for the real thing. It would be one of only several times in the show's history that a placeholder Islander would graduate to star. "She was much more what I was used to in terms of casting *The Only Way Is*

Essex," Spencer-Hayter says of his gravitation toward Jess. "She was just funny. We thought everyone would fall in love with her."

While some of the casting was typical of a show where hookups were expected, certain Islanders were deliberately off-kilter. Though twenty-four-year-old Zoe Brown was a model, she was also a vocally born-again Christian. Lauren Richardson, meanwhile, began her time on *Love Island* as the Islander everyone was whispering about. The *Daily Mail* accused the twenty-six-year-old phys ed teacher of hooking up with a member of One Direction, based on a photo Lauren posted of herself cuddling Zayn Malik at a club while he was engaged to Little Mix singer Perrie Edwards, several months before *Love Island* premiered.[7] (Lauren denies any contact beyond what was pictured in the photo.)

The lunks who filled in around these women were both awed by Lauren's ability to allegedly pull Malik and boastful about their own lack of interest, as if that made them better than the world-famous boy bander. The opening lineup included twenty-one-year-old joiner Josh Ritchie, as well as twenty-year-old former footballer Luis Morrison and obtrusively tattooed and ear-gauged thirty-one-year-old Jordan Ring, both of whom would pursue Zoe.

The Islander intro videos for the season capture the show's tone: self-mocking—or self-aggrandizing to the degree that it inadvertently swings all the way back around to self-mocking. In the first season's opening number, Caroline "called" the Islanders from Mallorca and told them to come start the best summer of their lives. Each cast member was then presented to the audience in a Technicolor-bright video that showed a pre–*Love Island* life—working as a dental hygienist, for example, or dispensing medication at a pharmacy or lying in bed with a sexy lady. After getting the invitation, viewers saw the person shed their clothes, plaque picks, or last night's sexual partner, and head to the Villa to begin their new life as an Islander.

Zoe received her call from Caroline on a set made to look like a church, then introduced herself: "I'm not your typical Barbie girl. I mean, I've got a big nose." Other Islanders were shown in a room made to like a nineties music video set, dragging their hands up and down their abs with the motion required to grate Parmesan. Some would play with nearly weightless props—bubbles, balloons, feathers—while providing choice sound clips about their astonishment at being single or how high their standards were. ("On a scale of one to ten, how confident am I? Eleven." Or "I literally expect princess treatment or no treatment at all.")

The initial coupling ceremony dropped viewers and Islanders into the show's dynamics like a frigid dunk tank. Caroline had one woman come out at a time and asked the men to step forward if they were attracted to her. The woman could either couple up with a man who picked her (if any did) or reject that act of vulnerability and choose someone she thought was hotter. Then, in an even more humbling moment, Caroline asked why they didn't go with the others. Everyone said a polite version of "Well, Caroline, I do not want to have sex with them." It was like getting chosen last for gym class, if the activity were seven minutes in heaven rather than matball. Even if the person an Islander coupled up with was a consolation prize for their first choice, the backup pair were informed they had to sleep together in the room with all the other people who actually *were* attracted to each other. It was, by design, brutal.

Initially, the plan had been for all the Islanders to come in and mingle, developing a rapport before deciding who to couple with. At the last minute, producers decided to make the choice more instinctual. "It was the best thing we did," says the season's executive producer Gould. "It was the real-life version of Tinder, of swiping left and swiping right." The intention was also to deliberately unsettle the cast so they would expose the tender underbellies hidden beneath their taut stomachs.

On the first day, no one chose Lauren. "It's not nice being the last one," Lauren told Caroline. She was objectively attractive but somehow seemed to break unspoken Villa mores that were being created in the moment with her fair skin and tattoos, which were prevalent on male Islanders but would be almost nonexistent on women throughout the seasons. Lauren spent the summer crying and being paired in a series of sexless "friendship couples" that comprised leftover Islanders who had no plausible romantic connections to pursue, which became more debasing to Lauren with every recoupling ceremony.

After coming into the Villa, Jess was coveted. Then she experienced the status reversal so many subsequent hotties would: She was pied off (ditched) and slagged off (disrespected) by nearly every man she encountered.

Season 1 was sloppy in a way that is disconcerting to revisit. There were many low-res close-ups of sobs filmed from odd angles; when Josh dumped Jess in episode 8, Jon castigated her for being upset and called her a dickhead as the camera on the glam room table captured the underside of Jess's mascara-drenched chin. The conversation in the Villa was often crude and misogynistic: Luis said that Jess "look[ed] like the kind of girl to be slaggy and stuff." (This conjugation of "slag" means "slutty.") Jon said that when he dates, women are not allowed to be in charge of credit cards, shopping, or kids while "thinking they own the relationship, yes," he said before winking. "'*Thinking.*'"

Unrestricted alcohol loosened most Islanders up to the point of drunken hookups and next-morning hangovers. Eye bags were left uncovered, and there was none of the elaborate daytime glam application of later seasons. Hannah often wore curlers in her hair. Max Morley, a twenty-two-year-old professional cricket athlete, threw furniture in the pool. Jess flung makeup around the dressing room. Challenges were sometimes literal trash: One saw the couples make vessels out of mostly single-use plastic items and try to ride across the pool without the floatie falling apart. People were smoking and screaming and talking shit, with minimal—to their bleary, horny eyes—producorial intervention.

In fact, there were hundreds of crew members attempting (if not always succeeding) to manage the madness, working out of modified storage containers called Portakabins and watching footage from dozens of cameras that captured virtually every moment of the Islanders' lives, including showers.

Islanders were frequently called to interview sessions in the Beach Hut. It was a hard stop amid the drama to help Islanders reflect on the happenings of the Villa. Throughout the seasons, these one-sided conversations serve to clarify, for the audience and the Islanders themselves, what they are actually feeling, as the show's pace doesn't always allow for reflection without this forced time-out. Islanders discover previously unknown abilities to introspect with an unseen producer—a priest-like figure who is as likely to hear a dirty joke as a tearful confession.

The Beach Hut producer's physical absence was counterintuitively meant to foster closeness with the Islanders. "There's no science behind it," *Love Island USA* showrunner Ben Thursby-Palmer says of why the to-the-camera interviews are delivered to a person cast members can't look at. "But that voice can be what they need them to be—who they're missing."

The Beach Hut interviewers can elicit any emotion needed to aid exposition. Another type of producing comes from the executive team, who tease out whether it's time to escalate ongoing dynamics, or if someone needs to find out a piece of information that will change their movements. Creating an activity that accomplishes either is delegated to the challenge producers, who execute the gameplay that results in enjoyable friction. Dozens of editors track all the action, each watching several of the eighty-ish live feeds that play in the control room around the clock.

The editors' rough cuts are logged onto whiteboards by story producers, who oversee plotlines. These producers divide each narrative into A, B, and C stories, in order of importance to the episode. These narratives are honed by the editors, then watched by producers and finally network executives, who get a full version of the episode with music at 8:30 a.m. on the airdate. They check to make sure there's no swearing or sex or big fights during the first fifteen minutes of the show and discuss any potential controversies. The creative director flags any moments that might be cut for time or sensitivity. A second afternoon screening is held for any potentially problematic footage, such as a scene in which one party comes across badly, and the team makes sure anything that might make someone look terrible is modulated by context.

Dating shows like *Love Is Blind* have the benefit of creating tension by foreshadowing or misdirecting from an outcome filmed months earlier. *Love Island*'s production schedule means no one knows how the show will end. What might become a season-long A story on the whiteboard can only be guessed at—a slinky smile may be the first moment of connection for a winning couple or an implied "tomorrow on *Love Island*" plot point that is never referenced again. It's a disadvantage that wound up being the show's greatest strength.

"A lot of the decisions we made were made because we were sort of making it up as we went along," executive Jain says of the first season of *Love Island.*

The pull between the structure of the series and the free will of its contestants is what makes it interesting; the show builds off what the Islanders do in response to the stimuli producers present them with. Simon Thomas, who executive produced the first six seasons of *Love Island USA*, references Samuel L. Jackson's line in *Jurassic Park*: "We have all the problems of a major theme park and a major zoo." (And this quote is from the part of the movie *before* the dinosaurs start eating people.) "That is *Love Island*," Thomas says. "You've got all the problems of a live show with all the problems of a reality show."

That instability is also one of the great pleasures of the series for the people who make it. "It's the most enjoyable and satisfying experience as a producer that I've had in my career because you are so reactive,"

Gould says. "I just remember sitting in our executive Portakabin with Richard [Cowles], Sarah Tyekiff, and Andy Cadman, just looking at a blank whiteboard and going, 'What do we do?'" It was as exciting as it was stressful—many times they'd go home after the Islanders went to bed, tucking themselves in on what seemed like an inexorable path forward, at least for that day. When they'd come in the next morning, Gould says, "Everything that you thought was going to happen had completely turned on its head. So then you'd have to go, 'Well, there's no point in us doing this anymore, and there's no point in us doing that. Right. Start again.'"

Executive producers sit down to discuss the many inflection points that occur in just a few hours and think through every tool they have to put Islanders into the most interesting possible positions.

As the people with power decide how the Islanders' past decisions will be presented and what crucibles await them, field producers manage the day-to-day, face-to-face interactions between cast and crew to figure out what Islanders might do (or be nudged to do) next. This team is constantly spurring the Islanders to act, whether that's thinking about whether they want to kiss someone or hydrating enough. "I was a field producer," Thomas says. "We are manipulators." The process of being taken care of by production allowed the season 1 Islanders to relax into the disorientation. "You've got no cares in the world because you've got all these people who are, like, doing your washing, bringing your cigarettes," Hannah says. "You're being looked after like a kid as well. You've got no responsibility."

Islanders are further freed from duty during lunch and their weekly day off. They are segregated by sex and taken off camera, though still mic'd up and monitored to make sure they don't talk about their relationships. This freezing of the couplings and any discussions of them is called "icing"—as in, "putting the content on ice"—so that it stays fresh for when filming resumes and an important conversation doesn't have to be repeated for cameras. "That's just to protect the sanctity of the real," says Thomas. The boys play sports or listen to music, and the women get their nails done, put on face masks, and talk. If the conversation veers to their connections, a voice comes over the intercom and instructs them to change topics. This also happens during filming if the dynamics of the show are discussed openly, such as musing about when a dumping is going to happen, or the prize money is discussed, which came up often in season 1. It made sense that it was a topic of conversation—winning £50,000 was the only significant thing that might happen from being on *Love Island* at that point. Unless, of course, you fell in love.

2

Doing Bits

JON AND HANNAH WERE FUCKING. "Fucking" is a vulgar term, but also the only one that can appropriately describe what was happening when Hannah was bucking atop Jon. It's also a word that meets ITV's standards for content broadcast after 9:15 p.m. in the UK. (Other phrases that could be freely spoken on air at that hour: "slag," "motherfucker," "cocksucker," and a series of words for genitals that shouldn't exist.) The permissive nature of the time slot suggested that what happened within its purview was so barely observed as to be inconsequential. Instead, it created the setting for what would become a historic bang.

In the scene, the couple of three weeks was pictured in bed, somewhat covered by a duvet. The comforter's exaggerated, puffy echoes of the humps beneath it only served to emphasize the obviousness of what was going on, like a fig leaf on a medieval nude announcing "ADAM IS NAKED IN THIS GARDEN!!!" Via the night vision footage, Hannah peeked over her shoulder to check if anyone noticed what was happening. How could they not?

One by one, cast members woke to the sounds of the night. A few hours later, viewers at home were treated to these actions being scored to a song that rode a line between an orchestration for a horror movie and a Looney Tune where Elmer Fudd is stalking Bugs Bunny with a shotgun. The audience watched the Islanders giggle and point as Hannah's thrust rate increased from a lively allegro to a frantic prestissimo. "Oh no," someone murmured.

"I can't stop now, guys, so you're just gonna have to deal with it," Jon barked as Hannah's efforts caused his feet to bounce on the bed. Lauren started to commentate, pointing out to the room that this act was occurring an arm's length away. Without pausing his minimal efforts, Jon chastised her. "Lauren, please, you're making me lose a boner here." While his astonished castmates watched, the off-screen music crescendoed until Jon moaned. *Love Island*, in the premiere season of the greatest reality dating series on television, had reached its first climax.

By the time the infamous sex scene aired, the couple had settled into a primal comfort; in another moment of abandon, Jon punched a hole in a door during the kind of argument that Hannah describes as "having a murder" in her Liverpool slang. For Hannah, this demonstrated the weight of Jon's passion, which was matched by her own eruptive fervor. Before going on the show, Hannah told her agent Read, "There's no way I'm gonna have sex in there." Within a month, they "were pure having loads," as Hannah says. All of it was aired.

The season 1 Islanders didn't know what the show they were living would become, which allowed them to be relaxed about filming. "Maybe the first few days you're in there you're aware of the camera," Hannah says. "Then honestly you do just forget about it and crack on. Like, that's your new little bubble that you're living in and you just kind of forget." Forgetting the cameras—or at least being uninhibited in front of them—created a space for Hannah to believe she was falling in love. "In that moment, I was convinced we were soulmates," Hannah says. "And it was very, very real for me." Hannah loving Jon made viewers love Hannah. They existed in the liminal horny space of not thinking about the fact that they were on TV while also not really believing the network would show how they physically forged their connection. ITV almost didn't.

Then–casting associate Lewis Evans is now the show's executive producer and the only person besides Spencer-Hayter to work on every season. He watched what would become episode 23 from a Portakabin. "I wasn't, like, gobsmacked," Evans says. Because it was Jon and Hannah, who were so unrestrained and outrageous, he thought, "Oh, it's just *them*. They're having sex. It's fine." That Hannah was a nude model and the words that came out of Jon's mouth were more obscene than any televised sex scene rationalized what might have seemed like a déclassé act from a different pair of Islanders. It felt appropriate for these two; Jon had a blue-collar job, and Hannah's diction was laden with "fecks."

In the lean times of season 1 of a show that aired five days a week, Spencer-Hayter was also working late the night Jon and Hannah had public sex. "I don't remember it being kind of scandalous," he says about watching them. "But *Love Island* always took the tone of 'have fun with it.' I think that was probably quite important. And for the younger viewer, I hope it, if anything, normalized sex," the same way *Sex and the City* had for him growing up as a secretly queer kid thinking, "Oh my God, wow. I want to be a gay person. That's fabulous, that life. Come on, be brave. You could do it. You could be one of them."

Around that time, there were other UK-aired TV shows where people were having intercourse or showing nudity on-screen, so it didn't raise an alarm. It did provoke internal debate. If the scene were excised but became important to a plot in a few days, how would the audience understand what was going on? Did cutting to the other Islanders' reactions enhance viewers' understanding of the group? Could a surprising music choice be made? Most importantly, would this actually be funny?

"I won't say [she was] prudish, but she was very squeamish about the idea of us showing sex," Cowles says of Jain, while noting of the especially unerotic coitus: "This wasn't pornography." (After Jon was done, he went to the bathroom to clean up, stopping to jump on another couple's bed and shake his bare ass in their faces.) Jain was eventually convinced.

ITV's commissioning editor Amanda Stavri saw it as a sign of the show's spark. "And that's when you get the little flutter," she says of the under-the-duvet moment. "Okay, we might have something on our hands here." This instinct was confirmed by internal marketing research. "People said that actually it validated the whole process and the relationships," Cowles says. "That's what people do. Why are we pretending it doesn't happen?"

Hannah and Jon's encounter demonstrated a depth of connection that could only be possible because of the circumstances that bred it. "It's easy to get in a bubble," Stavri says of *Love Island*'s synthetic isolation, echoing the word Hannah and so many other Islanders would use to describe the environment. "I suppose they're just young, hot, and horny, aren't they? Good for them!"

Personifying the show wasn't enough to win the season; Jess swooped in with a victory after pairing up with cricketer Max eight days before the finale, at which point the public voted them favorite couple at least partially because they were so relieved she was with someone who didn't seem to openly despise her, and possibly all other women.

Hannah and Jon were named runners-up after Jon proposed, handing her a ring that appeared sourced from a vending machine and telling her, "Loving you makes me feel like a rainbow. Every day you give me the horn, and every day I feel like a unicorn." Hannah was reluctant to leave the Villa and the love that had been enabled by elements that were as likely to be found on the outside as actual unicorns. "You don't want to go back into the real world because it's so cushy in there," she says of her time as an Islander.

When Hannah arrived back in Liverpool, she learned her initial instinct about the show's draw had been wrong; people had watched. Ratings had risen throughout the season, doubling the average viewership of its first week to nearly a million people for the finale. It wasn't a huge number, but *Love Island*'s success was percolating.

In the grocery store, people came up to Hannah crying, proud of their local TV star. She and Jon started doing what are called "PAs," or personal appearances, for a few thousand dollars apiece. An inside feature in *OK! Magazine* earned them about the same.

For Hannah, season 1 of *Love Island* was enough of a boost to maintain a presence in the sidebar of the *Daily Mail* and the aisles of Aldi. For Jon, it earned him a spot on *TOWIE* for a few seasons—after their minor-celebrity-induced breakup. Jon, Hannah says, "got effed up with the whole fame thing. It is really intense, but it just changed him. I think it went to his head."

To his credit, Jon did not disagree when we spoke in 2021."It takes you a bit of time to find your feet in the real world," he said. "You go from being on television and going here, going there, doing this, doing that, money, money, money, money . . ."[1]

The recognition was lasting; people are still discovering season 1 and DMing Jon, imploring him to get back together with Hannah. ("Rather shoot myself," he thinks as he thanks them.) But, Jon said, "You get a realization of going, 'Right, well, there's a big wide world out there, and it doesn't revolve around reality television, having everything done for you, and having storylines.'"

Jon and Hannah were the first couple from *Love Island* to show a glimmer of Cowles's promise that the show would manufacture fame. "There are millions and millions of people now grubbing up, wanting to be on *Love Island*," Jon said, "wishing they could have that experience I had."

3

Once Again with Feeling

SEASON 1 OF *LOVE ISLAND UK* was marked by shock: by an audience who couldn't believe what they were watching on television, by cast members who were surprised to find they'd actually wound up in love, and by producers who realized they'd somehow created a sensation by setting the stage for countless moments they had little control over and then, with fiendish brilliance, capitalizing on them.

Though discussions about whether *Love Island* would return for a second season began immediately, ITV wouldn't make the decision to renew it for a few months. On one hand, viewership had grown over the run, and they had nothing like it in terms of ambition or potential audience buy-in at ITV2; on the other, that ambition was expensive. Cowles and his team came up with a plan to increase the number of digital and interactive elements to further engage viewers; in season 2, the show's Instagram following increased by 430 percent. Crucially, *Love Island* would add episodes, which allowed the network to get more ad revenue without increasing the budget, a cost-saving effort that was also aided by filming at the same Villa and losing the in-show live segments with Caroline. The announcement was timed to Valentine's Day 2016.

"In the first series no one really knew what they were walking into," Jain says. "The innocence of that changes with subsequent stories."

If season 2 couldn't help its loss of innocence, it would compensate by being more intentional; the exchange taking place in the show's expanding social media presence would give ITV a tremendous amount of data about what viewers were liking (or not), which they could incorporate hour by hour. As Jon noted, "I think the producers of *Love Island* realized what they had stumbled upon with my season. It was finding a nugget of reality gold. And all of the kinks that my show did, they ironed out in the second show."

Revisions were made on mundane production issues that would now require enforcement, such as producers beginning to insist that Islanders use the sunscreen that was provided, even if that application sometimes happened after the cast was already suckling-pig red. (In season 1, where sunblock was available but mostly ignored, tanning oil was contraband. Cast members would instead sneak cooking oil to maintain their sun damage levels, often forcing a harried producer to yell, "PUT THE OLIVE OIL DOWN," as a runner would rush into the kitchen to snatch it out of the Islanders' hands.)

They adjusted more major elements of the show, too. Cutting the booze helped stymie the prevalence of slurring and sexist fights while also eliminating the question of whether agreeing to appear on TV applies to behavior filmed when a cast member may be too inebriated to consent in the moment. (This is purely a moral dilemma; legally, once an Islander signs that contract, production is in the clear to show anything they do on camera.)

To accommodate for the missing drunken indiscretion and the fact that cast members now understood the show they were going on and might, subconsciously or intentionally, replicate popular moments or dynamics, casting had to evolve. ITV needed to figure out what it truly meant to be an Islander, since the current definition was someone who had the fortune to be on the first season of a show that could have easily been as forgettable as their Spanish vacation peer series *The Magaluf Weekender*. The process was identifying someone on the outside—show parlance for "the entirety of Earth, exclusive of the Villa"—and successfully guessing how that person, in combination with their new peers, could create the right alchemy for a successful season of *Love Island*. Each Islander would need to be able to function as both a star and an ensemble member, an actor and a foil. This would inform the casting of every subsequent season of the show in the UK and the US.

As a casting producer, Spencer-Hayter had found a higher calling than he'd had on five seasons of *The Only Way Is Essex*. "They have to find love," he says of the Islanders. In fact, almost every producer of *Love Island UK* told me, verbatim, that the top prerequisite for a *Love Island* cast member is "being open to finding love." Not a single UK Islander I spoke with said they were expecting to actually fall in love; nearly all of them did.

In addition to potential cast members having an open heart they might not be aware of yet, Spencer-Hayter was looking for what he calls "the archetype/stereotypes"—personality pots in which people could be sorted to make sure the composition of the cast was correct and its humors perfectly imbalanced for maximum intrigue. That *Love Island* could be a route from dancing at the club to walking down the aisle was a guiding principle, but to fill the different roles Spencer-Hayter envisioned, the team would have to do more than visit the Sugar Hut in Essex.

The process of casting the show takes more than seven months, with tens of thousands of applicants and recruits being pared down to an opening lineup of, usually, ten Islanders. Danielle Gervais is an executive at ITV America and runs casting for *Love Island USA*. "It's like this puzzle that we don't have the pieces to play with just yet," she says of figuring out the initial cast, referred to each season as "the OGs." There are also dozens of bombshells, the fresh cast members who get dropped in when things get too calm. "Okay, we need to bring in someone new because this is getting a bit same-y," Cowles says of the discussions around when to deploy an extra Islander. "There's some people here that don't seem too happy with their relationship. Let's see what happens when a new bombshell comes in." Especially sexy bombshells often come late in the game to turn supposedly steady heads, giving the super-hot their archetypal name: head-turners.

The cast is often not fully set until days before the Islanders begin filming. This is partly logistical but also largely because the pressure of choosing correctly is so great. *Love Island USA* showrunner Ben Thursby-Palmer often thinks about the "sliding doors" aspect of the order of entrance. "It's really interesting where we put people in the run of the show," Thursby-Palmer says. "Like if a person hadn't gone in the very beginning and [instead] had become a bombshell, would their experience be completely different? Would they have still found that person? It always fascinates me to think, if we put all the same cast in a very different order, would we still have the same outcome at the end?"

To be considered for the series, Islanders either submit themselves for contention through a website application, are referred by a previous Islander, or are recruited by a member of production or a casting agent. Cast members are discovered on Instagram, on nights out, at colleges, in gyms, at car shows. Ads are placed in local newspapers; the casting team goes to in-person dating events. (Of the latter: "Those are usually, candidly, a little bit tragic," according to Gervais.) Thursby-Palmer says the most important thing is "authenticity, unfiltered, not perfect, and people that are 'yes, and' people. Like, if I threw you the ball, it's not just gonna bounce off you."

Auditioning cast members fill out a brief form requesting photos, nuts-and-bolts biographical information, and answers to questions like "Why do you think you are currently single?" If they pass that stage, they are approved by groups of increasing import: first casting producers, then executive producers, and finally network executives. Applicants fill out a much longer questionnaire inquiring about everything from body count—how many people they've slept with—to the biggest misconception about themselves. As well as possibly getting them into the Villa, this information can be used to produce them once they get there, and as material for challenges. During interviews, potential cast members are probed on a breadth of topics, including about how they break up with people. "Are you a ghoster?" a producer might ask. "You would make the phone call to break up? You want to do it in person? What's your style?" There is no wrong answer, but a season's cast cannot have too much of any single type.

Once potential Islanders pass this gauntlet, the team awaits the results of aspirants' psychological evaluations that include written and verbal assessments, STI tests, medical exams, and background checks. Sometimes destiny—and, more frequently, mental health concerns—keep would-be Islanders off the show. During a season, multiple cast members might be flown out to Mallorca or Fiji, where *Love Island USA* has filmed four of its seasons, and sent home without ever stepping foot into the Villa if they decide to leave or the show's psych team recommends they need to.

Lineups are often built around anchor personalities; if a specific Islander is not cleared, the opening lineups can entirely change because the mix of personalities and archetypes has to be calibrated.

Spencer-Hayter and Lewis Evans know each season has at least one "cheeky chappy": a man who tends to be rambunctious and puppy-ish, rolling around with his buddies as much as his romantic partners and often adding a charming frisson of homoeroticism to the show that was missing in the noxious cloud of chauvinism that hung over season 1. Season 2's primary cheeky chappy was Nathan Massey, a twenty-three-year-old carpenter from Essex who "fancied the pants" off twenty-five-year-old circus performer Cara De La Hoyde in between ladding around with the guys—and occasionally bringing that boys' club energy into the bedroom, as when he told Cara, "You're the most frigid bird I've ever met in my life."

Another archetype is "edge of fame," which would be known in the US as "celebrity-adjacent." This could be anyone on the periphery of public life. For season 2, Spencer-Hayter would cast two Miss Great Britains: thirty-year-old Sophie Gradon and the reigning titleholder, twenty-year-old Zara Holland.

Every year, Thursby-Palmer prepares for the season ahead by creating a board pinned with forty to fifty headshots of would-be Islanders. (More accurately, every photo includes the person's head, though many also include their mostly unclothed body.) Each auditioning cast member is assigned green, yellow, or red dots to designate how many stages of the vetting process they've completed. Different groupings of ten or so Islanders are moved up and down the board in the order producers think will lead to the lowest chance of inertia.

The accuracy of whom they imagine might get together is never certain. UK producers could recall one lasting couple whom they called from the beginning: season 2's Cara and Nathan. The US team estimates they have about 50 percent accuracy with initial attraction, based on what people say they want. Thursby-Palmer, the rare *Love Island* producer who looks like he could have been an Islander, recapped the kinds of conversations he constantly has with cast members who act counter to their own stated preferences. "Hannah, this guy is everything you described," he will say patiently. "You said you wanted tall. He's tall. You said you wanted blue eyes. He's got blue eyes." He imagines Hannah's response: "Yeah, but I just don't like it."

Gervais says one of the most important elements of casting *Love Island* is determining the ease the men have around women—both their ability to seduce and whether they want to hang out with ones they aren't interested in sexually. A good cast has to have at least one person who isn't smooth, but they also need people who are able to please. During her interview with Thursby-Palmer, *Love Island USA* season 2 star and current *Aftersun* correspondent Cely Vazquez told him she'd put on perfume for him. Thursby-Palmer is gay and married; it was also a video call. But that action showed a transparent desire to be desired that would work well in the Villa. Cely was a "yes girl."

The Archetypes

Yes Girl: a woman who is game for anything that might happen in the Villa; generally seems like she would be doing something like this with her friends if she weren't on the show.

The Glue: an Islander people turn to for advice. Often this person is in a stable couple. (Note: If both people in the couple are glue, they become "Mom and Dad." This term must be bestowed by another person, or the Islander is disqualified from parenthood.)

Brooder: a man who feels deeply and often sexily. Prone to outbursts.

Cheeky Chappy: a boy, usually as or more invested in male friendship as romantic partnership. Cheeky chappies have rarely been in serious relationships before and get a lot of time on *Unseen Bits,* the weekly blooper show.

Woman with Bite: a fiery female Islander who speaks plainly. Coined a "Marmite" personality by Olivia Attwood, a season 3 Islander, after the divisive savory toast spread.

Outsider: a non-Islander Islander; someone who seems like they don't belong on the show, often in a way that makes them appear too good for it.

Really Funny Guy Who Maybe Doesn't Have the Muscles: *see name of this archetype.*

Villain: an Islander who runs afoul of the audience, either because they aren't interested in someone fans think they should be with or because they are perceived as playing the game in a way that keeps viewers from being able to forget that it is a game.

Edge of Fame: someone who is adjacent to celebrity; this can be via a relative or previous partner, or their own appearance in a news cycle.

Head-Turner: an unusually good-looking Islander.

USP (Unique Selling Point): an area of differentiation that immediately allows the audience to identify the Islander by that quality; can range from an unusual job to reading books.

Some desirable qualities are more amorphous: Andy Cadman, an executive producer on the UK and US series, says a good *Love Island* contestant has to be vulnerable, and they have to make mistakes. The Islanders should also be funny, intentionally or not. "It's a totally different show if you have twelve incredibly intelligent people," Spencer-Hayter says. He generously describes his casts as "a cross section of the UK."

A minuscule percentage of truly posh people appear on *Love Island.* The majority of cast members are working- or middle-class, and even the truly rich tend to be new money: the children of footballers, like Michael Owen's daughter Gemma, or soap opera actors, like Danny Dyer's homophonous/eponymous female progeny Dani. A notable exception would be season 3's Camilla Thurlow, a UK bomb disposal expert and humanitarian worker who had also been seen out with Prince Harry. (She and Caroline never discussed their common ex on camera.) "I was obsessed with casting what I believed were aspirational, intelligent people that the viewer would be surprised to see taking part in a show like that," Jain says of Camilla. "Why would a civil servant leave her proper job to come and be on *Love Island*? I continually enjoy surprising the viewers by putting people in there where they are questioning their motivation."

While it may vary in the occupations, personalities, and emotional quotients of its contestants, *Love Island* is a show that strictly adheres to its own beauty standards. Hair is thickened by transplant, extension, or God's grace. Boobs and butts point due north. Lips and brows are zhuzhed by cosmetic dermatology, and errant British teeth are replaced by veneers by way of Turkey or whatever dentist will throw a future Islander a deal for a post.

Casting for *Love Island* means casting for maximum possibility—the more potential couples there are, the more dynamic the season. "You don't want everybody coupled up on day one," Gervais says. "Then they're sitting around on the couch." That means choosing a cast with mostly lowest-common-denominator beauty. The uniformity is often offset by the inclusion of an outsider, or "a non-Islander Islander," as Gervais calls them. The outsider is someone for whom the public yearns to find love, but something about them does not inspire instant connection on a show that began in its early seasons with contestants lining up and choosing a partner by instinct alone without much conversation in front of a group of ass-baring and topless peers. By season's end, the outsider almost always prevails, aided by the quality that sets them apart. This usually isn't a departure from top-shelf aesthetics but a personal value not shared by the larger group, like intellectualism or civic-mindedness.

Cowles told the *Radio Times* in 2019 that "we want to be as representative as possible, but we also want them to be attracted to one another."[1] The brusque statement is pragmatic for a television executive who feeds off the beauty of youth, but it's also intended to spare people from repeated rejection. If creating latitude in coupling increases the odds of a season faring well, it does the same thing for the Islanders: Producers want every cast member to be desired by multiple people so they can then choose who they want and aren't stuck with only one option—or no options.

"No one has said openly in our interviews, 'I love big women,'" Gervais says bluntly. "We've got to set people up for success. You cannot have there be just one singular person who looks different from everybody else in terms of body size." Being inclusive by featuring someone who will eventually be excluded, Gervais says, "defeats the purpose."

"I think the producers are trying to learn, and adapt, and be more inclusive, and be more diverse," *UK* season 4 star Megan Barton-Hanson, a woman with bite, told me in 2021.[2] "It's no good chucking in one bisexual girl, or one bisexual guy, or one girl who's not even plus-sized. Anna Vakili"—an immaculate, voluptuous Islander from season 5 and another woman with bite—"wouldn't even count as plus-sized." This seems solvable; they could, for example, cast more than a few people who are queer and more than one person who represents a different display of hotness. Though former EP Thomas insists that on *Love Island USA*, the size of butts has become more reflective of societal desires than corporate casting mandates for thinness, so far *Love Island* has not significantly shifted the Overton window of acceptable body types among the kinds of people who apply to be on a show where a criterion for entry is being foxy. The most notable physical change on the show is moving the acceptable tightness of pants for men from "castratingly skinny" to "doesn't require the removal of a wedgie every time they stand up."

As part of the interview process, casting teams ask applicants which past Islanders they find attractive. In the UK it's often season 2's Alex Bowen (cheeky chappy); season 9 and *All Stars* 1 and 3 Islander Samie Elishi (woman with bite); *UK* season 7, *Australia* season 5, *Games* season 2, and *All Stars* season 3 repeat *Love Island* offender Lucinda Strafford (yes girl); and six-foot-seven season 5 cast member Ovie Soko (the glue), whom Spencer-Hayter says is named most frequently of all.

Just as the show needs people to react to, the Islanders themselves have to be responsive in a way that's honest, even if it's not always flattering. It's fine for someone to initially have walls up, if that's who they truly are. Some of the most successful Islanders of all time were coy or withholding, from season 5's Amber Gill and her costar Molly-Mae Hague—the biggest Islander of all time by any metric—to *Love Island USA*'s Leah. It can lead to transformational character arcs. Without Islanders demonstrating some form of personal evolution, plotlines can feel stagnant and characters frustrating in their inability to learn. The one thing you cannot be on *Love Island* is dull. You can, however, be radioactively unpleasant.

Season 2's Kady McDermott was a twenty-year-old makeup artist from Stevenage who handled any perceived slight with the grace of a toddler who's just been told they can't eat pie for breakfast. During the season, producers sent Kady and twenty-two-year-old sales executive Olivia Buckland to the Hideaway—a casita filled with cheap sex toys and lingerie that had previously only been used for Islanders to spend the night as a couple, as rewarded by their peers. Now the women were banished to the building under ambiguous circumstances. Though they didn't know it, Olivia and Kady were there so their partners could go on dates with bombshells. "It surprised us in terms of quite how much, uh, *reaction* we got from Kady and Olivia," Gould said of the drama that unfolded. The two women seemed to descend into madness, watching the men through the window while lying on their stomachs. Curtains obscured their upper bodies, leaving only their asses and legs visible to the camera. "You're a cunt!" Kady screamed at her partner Scott Thomas from the Hideaway terrace.

Kady and the twenty-seven-year-old club promoter had a Sid and Nancy vibe that audiences would find refreshingly real, with the kind of sexual charge and threat of violence taken out on inanimate objects that never went quite far enough to make viewers stop rooting for them. They would come in third place after Nathan and Cara and Olivia and twenty-four-year-old scaffolder Alex Bowen.

Scott and Kady's physicality would also convince the public of their connection, as it had with Jon and Hannah and would with many others. The manner of sexual expression didn't matter as much as the veracity of it: When the supposedly frigid Cara did have sex with Nathan, he performed a cartwheel down the runner in between the rows of beds. Viewers were satisfied by Cara and Nathan staying together and holding out until they were both ready to get intimate in front of their peers, and also those viewers, who were now ready to vote for them to win the season.

Alex and Olivia, meanwhile, took advantage of the full *Love Island* experience en route to each other. Olivia had sex with Rykard Jenkins, a twenty-five-year-old personal trainer, in the bed next to Rachel Fenton, whom Rykard was so invested in that he later self-eliminated after she was dumped from the Villa by public vote. Olivia and Rykard were so deliriously horny that they simply needed to hook up that night. It was a sin that was forgivable because the audience deemed the attraction genuine and because fans didn't particularly care about Rachel. "It really does all depend on the kind of strength of feeling amongst the audience in terms of what people's opinions are on it and where they want that story to go," says ITV's head of media relations Justin Jeffreys about why some *Love Island* sex provokes shrugs, while other times rewards or punishments.

With their blonde hair, tattoos, and nose rings, Alex and Olivia seemed to be a matching set who hadn't noticed they were supposed to be paired together when they finally coupled in week three—two days after Alex had sex with Zara when she invited him to the Hideaway. "We never run out of anything to say," Alex said in wonder as he and Olivia lay on the beanbags and covered such engrossing topics as Olivia having another friend called Alex. He and Olivia became the season's runners-up, while Miss GB titleholder Zara had her crown stripped because of their tryst.

It was a credit to the casting team; the Islanders had found the right lids for the archetypal pots, and the final two couples would each get married, have children, and be together a decade later. As the couples became more real, there was a commensurate increase in investment from viewership—it tripled from season 1's average weekly numbers to nearly 1.5 million.

As surely as sex occurs because good-looking single people must sleep together after wearing nearly nothing and flirting all day, media attention followed the swelling ratings: Yet another season 2 couple's encounter would earn *Love Island* its first front-page story. Before Terry Walsh (brooder) and Emma Jane Woodham (yes girl) had open-air sex, Iain set up the scene this way: "It's bedtime and, having newly coupled up with Terry, Emma's got some top secret plans. But she's definitely not going 'undercover.'" As the camera closed in on Emma's bare shoulders, "Toreador Song" from the opera *Carmen* played for viewers at home. The next day, *The Sun* featured *Love Island* on page one, renaming it "Love Vile Land." It was not so vile that the paper didn't publish multiple photos of the act.[3]

Demonstrating their obsession with the show by ripping into its cast members would become the modus operandi for the press and many viewers.

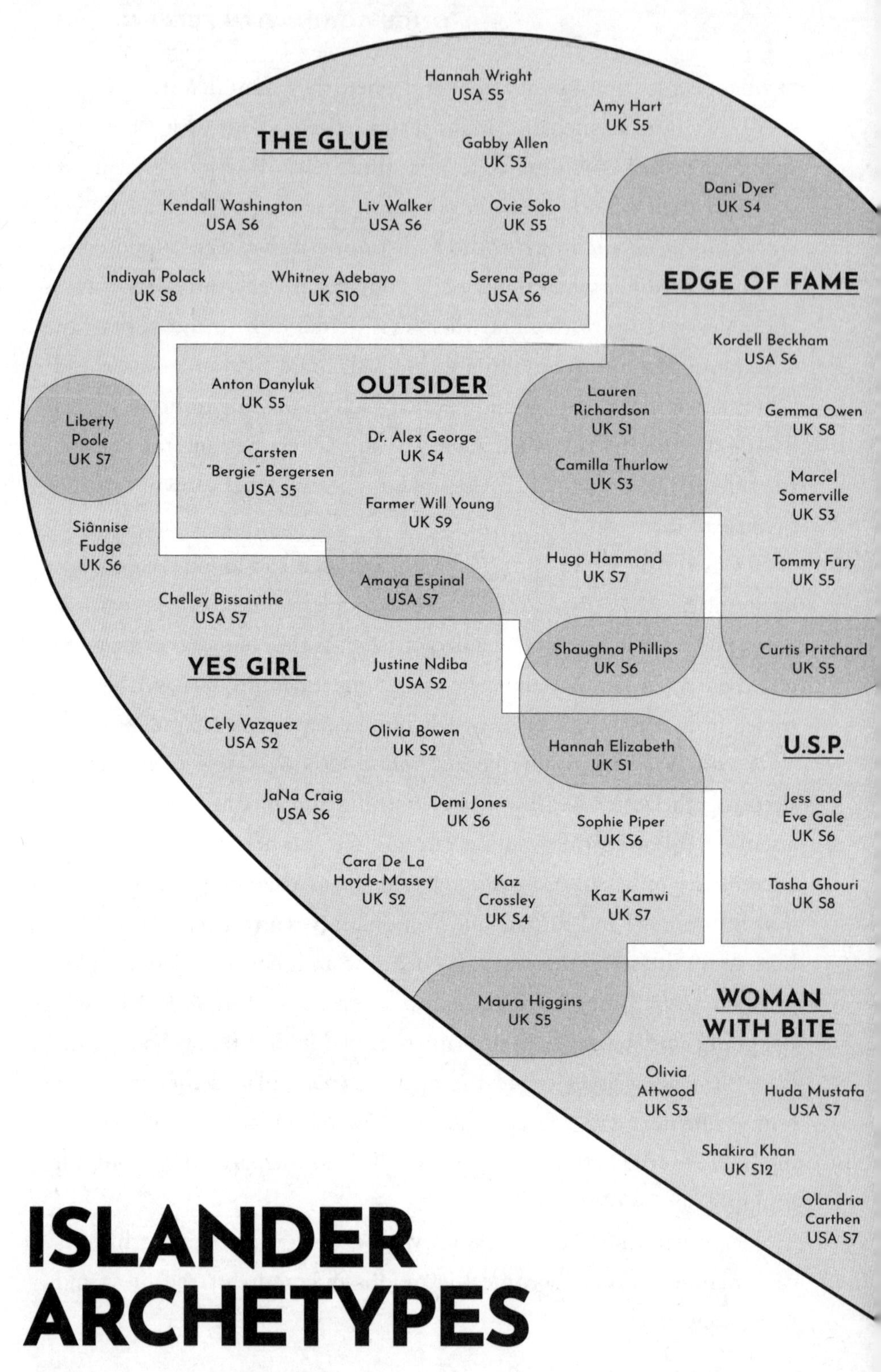

ISLANDER ARCHETYPES

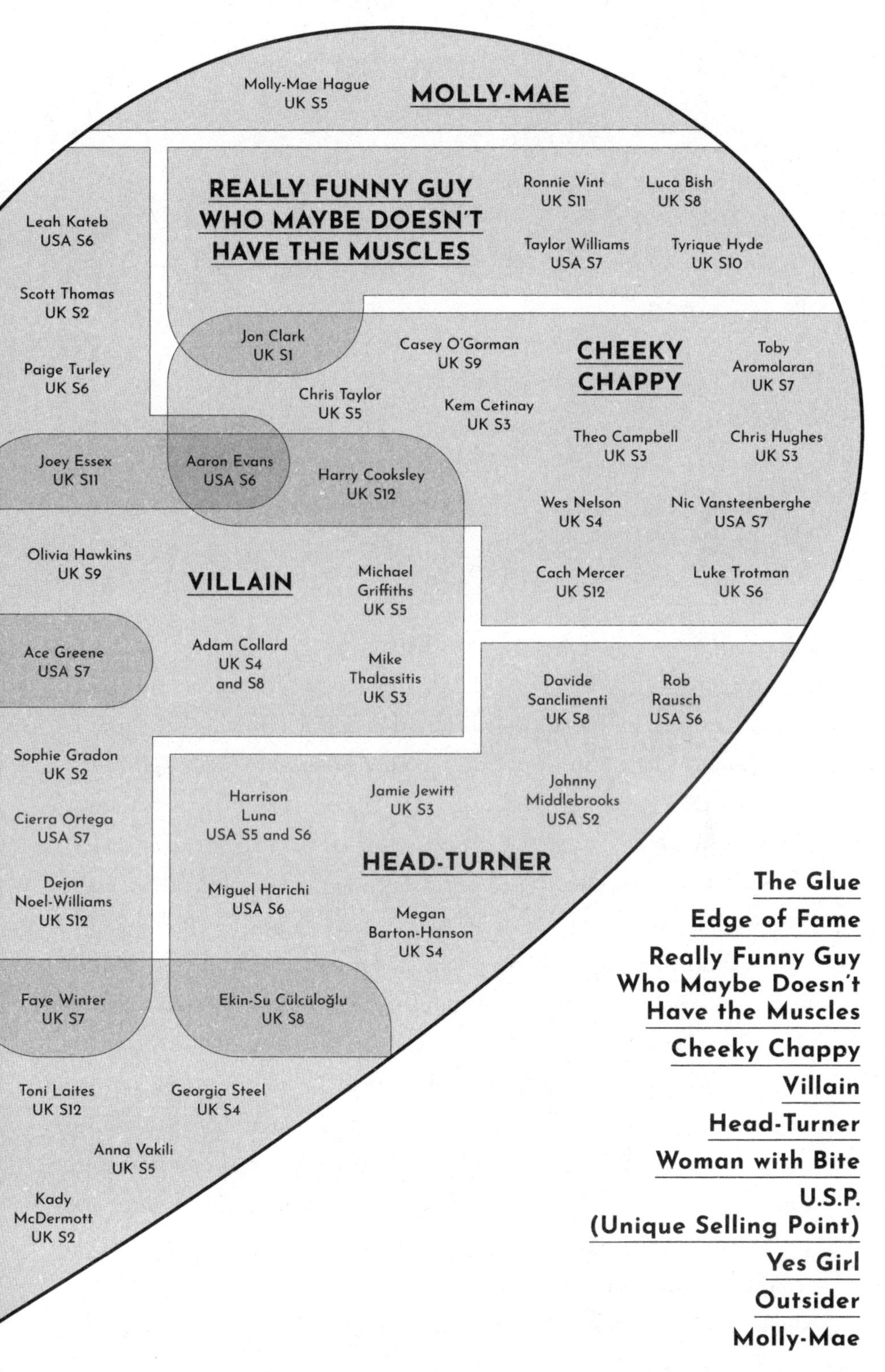
Molly-Mae Hague
UK S5
MOLLY-MAE
REALLY FUNNY GUY WHO MAYBE DOESN'T HAVE THE MUSCLES
Ronnie Vint
UK S11
Luca Bish
UK S8
Taylor Williams
USA S7
Tyrique Hyde
UK S10
Leah Kateb
USA S6
Scott Thomas
UK S2
Paige Turley
UK S6
Jon Clark
UK S1
Casey O'Gorman
UK S9
CHEEKY CHAPPY
Toby Aromolaran
UK S7
Chris Taylor
UK S5
Kem Cetinay
UK S3
Theo Campbell
UK S3
Chris Hughes
UK S3
Joey Essex
UK S11
Aaron Evans
USA S6
Harry Cooksley
UK S12
Wes Nelson
UK S4
Nic Vansteenberghe
USA S7
Olivia Hawkins
UK S9
VILLAIN
Michael Griffiths
UK S5
Cach Mercer
UK S12
Luke Trotman
UK S6
Ace Greene
USA S7
Adam Collard
UK S4
and S8
Mike Thalassitis
UK S3
Davide Sanclimenti
UK S8
Rob Rausch
USA S6
Sophie Gradon
UK S2
Harrison Luna
USA S5 and S6
Jamie Jewitt
UK S3
Johnny Middlebrooks
USA S2
Cierra Ortega
USA S7
HEAD-TURNER
Dejon Noel-Williams
UK S12
Miguel Harichi
USA S6
Megan Barton-Hanson
UK S4
Faye Winter
UK S7
Ekin-Su Cülcüloğlu
UK S8
Toni Laites
UK S12
Georgia Steel
UK S4
Anna Vakili
UK S5
Kady McDermott
UK S2
The Glue
Edge of Fame
Really Funny Guy Who Maybe Doesn't Have the Muscles
Cheeky Chappy
Villain
Head-Turner
Woman with Bite
U.S.P. (Unique Selling Point)
Yes Girl
Outsider
Molly-Mae

4

Game On

SEASON 3 VIEWERSHIP WOULD increase 500 percent from season 1 numbers, and tabloids had started regularly featuring the show. It was clear that fans wanted even more *Love Island*. ITV added *Aftersun*, reintroducing Caroline's live-hosting to a dedicated Sunday panel show. The network also raised the season order by seven regular episodes; production would now have to generate enough material to fill an extra week of daily programming. This meant more games.

In season 1, the challenges had dollar-store budgets and mostly served to make the contestants look foolish, such as mechanical bull riding or a math contest that revealed Jon Clark could barely count (which he freely admitted). There was a field day that featured a three-legged race, notable only for the fact that production spent money on pedometers. The few challenges that provoked real emotion were carried over to the second season: the Twitter challenge, in which the mental meniscus between the Villa and the outside was ruptured as Islanders heard what viewers were posting about them; the lie detector challenge, in which Islanders found out what their partners supposedly secretly thought; and the parenting challenge, which had each couple taking care of the kinds of baby dolls high school health teachers give students to discourage teen pregnancy.

Along with those stalwarts, season 2 introduced more goofy challenges with slightly higher production values, like wrestling in a pool of "gunge"—the nauseating British term for slime—and trying to take each other's socks off. During a new game in which Islanders ranked each other in categories including "most fit" and "most trustworthy," producers hit on something that would be codified into challenges going forward: that the perceptions of their castmates were as important to the Islanders as the viewers' outlook on them. This would become a circular relationship: the internal pecking order had a huge impact on audience opinion, and that affected the Villa hierarchy. The insecurity this caused could prompt a couple to draw closer together, both out of fear of being left behind other cast members who were progressing more quickly and because a partner could be a place of solace to an Islander who was feeling misunderstood. "Once they've established themselves as a couple, they are always looking over their shoulder at the other couples and thinking about how their relationship compares to others," Gould says.

From the outset of season 3, it had been clear to producers that challenges could compensate for the fact that they could not count on casting multiple pairs of organic soulmates every year; love connections might need to be manufactured. The way to speed-run a relationship over less than two months was through the kinds of tests that could create game-show-like versions of insecurities and milestones that happen in the real world.

The headline challenge, in which Islanders saw snippets of current newspaper stories about themselves, was inspired by the idea of friends spreading rumors or talking behind someone's back on the outside. In the Villa, that sort of disloyalty was worsened by the knowledge that it was the entire *country* talking behind their backs, and that they wouldn't get the full context of how their relationship was being received until it was too late to accommodate with any course correction on the show. The Twitter challenge evoked the same feeling with its bitchy online whispers—which, by the time they reached the Islanders' ears, probably would have been forgotten by the person who posted them had they not been added to the text of the show. Gould says, "Our reasoning was that those challenges and that intrusion was meant to replicate your experience as a couple back in the outside world, where friends would have an opinion of who you've coupled up with. Your family would have that opinion. Now, it wouldn't necessarily be the whole of Twitter that have that opinion, but it was meant to kind of replicate, as best we could, those outside pressures."

"Hearts on Fire," also known as the "Heart Rate Challenge," was an experiment in jealousy over your partner being attracted to someone else. It consisted of Islanders giving lap dances while dressed up as sexy tropes—a latex-clad devil, a cowboy. The lap dance recipients' bpms were monitored and announced, leading to accusations: that someone still fancied their ex or wasn't as attracted to their current partner as another Islander. It was an inexact science. Surely sometimes that was true; other times the Islander was just nervous, or being physically picked up and tossed around juiced their pulse. But in a hormone- and anxiety-charged environment, any cause for suspicion felt justified and made for good TV.

Like the deployment of bombshells, challenges can force a complacent relationship to a breaking point or create questions in an otherwise sturdy couple. At the end of every evening, producers sit down with each cast member and ask whom they're most attracted to, whom they're getting along with, whom they don't like. "It might be that two Islanders aren't feeling their partners, they've told us, but they're feeling other people," Spencer-Hayter says. "So we know the next day to put in a kissing game or a dare in a box because we know they want an excuse to break free."

If it seems counterintuitive that producers spend the entire season trying to break couples up when the goal is for people to end up together, producers will tell you that's *Love Island*'s version of survival of the fittest. "Ultimately, our justification to the Islanders was, 'You find yourself in a couple in the Villa, and then your couple will be tested in any which way that we can find,'" Gould says. But when I asked *why* the couples need to be tested, Gould had another, more practical answer: "Because they're winning money"—potentially—"as a couple." The show is designated as a competition series and is monitored by the Ofcom Broadcasting Code in the UK, where a compliance officer makes sure people are being presented "fairly" and that no Islander is advantaged or disadvantaged by the editing or production, but merely by their own behavior. (*Love Island USA* is not monitored in the same way by the Federal Communications Commission, which categorizes such programming as "for entertainment only" "pseudo-contest[s].")

In challenges, Islanders can glean what amounts to evidence about what their partnership would be like in practice. "Kissing games—it's gonna sound really silly, but that's probably the equivalent of you going on social media and seeing they've liked another girl's post," season 6's Molly Smith says. "Or they're on another date with somebody. It's like they've gone on a night out, and you get that little bit of jealousy. Or when a bombshell comes in, that's the equivalent of knowing if they are going to chat to other people or not. So how they do it and how they can get them feelings to come is just very cleverly done; it gives you all that taste of the outside."

Most Islanders interviewed for this book did not feel this way. "I fucking hated all the challenges," season 3's Gabby Allen says. "I'd just get so anxious about it." The twenty-five-year-old fitness instructor was told after leaving the show that she and Marcel Somerville had been the favorites to win before the lie detector challenge, in which they were hooked up to a polygraph and asked the kinds of questions you would only get the answers to by reading their texts or otherwise breaching their trust. Gabby had said she loved Marcel, which the polygraph flagged as untrue. Marcel and Gabby's perfect coupledom was blighted, and they fell out of peak public favor. "Obviously that's shit for us," Gabby says. "But then in hindsight, that's great TV." (The challenge would later be eliminated after the star of the reality show *The Jeremy Kyle Show* died by suicide after failing a lie detector test, which had indicated—to whatever degree of accuracy lie detector tests allegedly provide—that he had cheated on his partner.)

Some Islanders were challenge-proof, such as season 3's Camilla. Because she didn't have any connections, there was nothing to test—they just seemed to wear her down as she endeavored to remain a good sport through a game in which she was never going to score. It was like watching Queen Elizabeth attempt to play pickleball in the heat while holding a handbag and trying to keep her hat on.

Eventually the show had to bend to Camilla and bring in another outsider to match her anti–*Love Island* energy. They dropped Calvin Klein model Jamie Jewitt in as a bombshell, entering in slow motion to the song "Sexy Boy" by Air. "I hear you read a lot," Jamie said when they met. "I do," Camilla conceded and asked him what genre he liked. "Predominantly nonfiction," Jamie said as Camilla's eyelashes fluttered in ecstasy, clearly excited to be in conversation with someone literate. He told her Richard Dawkins was his favorite author. Camilla practically had steam coming off her as she exclaimed the title of her favorite Dawkins book in what would be her loudest decibel level of the season, which was barely over a murmur: "*The God Delusion*!"

"It was such a good day," says Spencer-Hayter, the god who set in motion the reality that created this connection. Camilla and Jamie married in 2021 and have three children.

"We haven't been tested yet" is a constant refrain in the Villa. Islanders know it's one of the boxes a winner has to tick on the way to the finale. People who got together in the first coupling and won after sidestepping any meaningful, producer-induced threats to their relationship can be counted on two fingers: season 2's Nathan Massey and Cara De La Hoyde-Massey, and season 4's Dani Dyer (now Dyer-Bowen) and Jack Fincher. Their tests were more of the internal variety—and very British. Each couple seemed to represent the national discomfort with emotion and fear of exposing themselves as foolish that often presents as retreating or bickering. They also employed self-protective humor—making fun of themselves before someone else could or pushing away someone they were afraid would leave. To pass their tests, these Islanders had to make themselves susceptible to rejection by being honest about how much they cared. It was *Pride and Prejudice* with spray tans.

"Testing" also gives a person in a couple an excuse to go on a date or make out with someone they're not coupled with inside or, God forbid, outside of a challenge. How the couple responds ultimately informs the stability of the Villa. They either develop the tools to navigate their discomfort and self-doubt, or, if they can't stomach seeing their partner kiss or grind on another cast member, it can lead to the formation of another couple and a spurned third party. The possibility of shifting permutations of Islanders is always hovering over the Villa, creating an environment of possibility and unease.

Casa Amor is *Love Island*'s ultimate test: a half-weeklong separation of the Islanders by gender during which a whole new slate of Islanders is available for coupling or dalliances. Inspired by the epic Hideaway freak-out that Kady and Olivia had in season 2 after their partners went on dates with new bombshells, Casa was devised in season 3 to intensify the feelings within couples to the maximum degree. It also answered the network's call for more episodes: "If we're gonna do seven weeks, we need something mid-series that is going to shake everything up, upset the apple cart, and give us the momentum to then get to the end of the series," Gould and the executive producers decided.

Casa Amor takes place at a second Villa, close enough for producers to easily travel between the two locations but out of direct eyeshot. Creating an alternate Villa and cast meant generating an entire concurrent second production, which would necessitate a hundred more crew members joining an already huge team. Producers decided to maximize season 2's Hideaway ploy: Unlike Kady and Olivia, who were close enough to spy on and yell at their partners, during Casa couples would have no communication with each other and limited insight into what was going on at the adjacent Villas or whether their partner's feelings for them had changed.

"Casa Amor came from a notion of, what's the worst thing that can happen in your new relationship?" Cowles says. "Oh, when they go away on a lads' or a girls' trip. That's the worst thing because you don't know what they're up to. And then you'll see an Instagram post and they're talking to another person and that sends you off on an anxiety trip."

Gabby of season 3 remembers the beginning of the first Casa, when they realized that all the men were gone. "Everybody just lost their minds," she says. "You're just like, *What the fuck?* And because ours was the first one, we'd never in a million years thought this was gonna happen."

Eventually, the Casa men were brought in for the women, which made them understand that their partners were also getting a new set of women. Gabby and twenty-six-year-old Monster Energy spokesmodel Olivia Attwood were in couples and too underwhelmed by the selection to consider exploring. Instead, they mooned over the men who had left the Villa. "I can't even remember when the boys came in for our one," Gabby says. "I was so disinterested in the boys that I literally couldn't even tell you any of the names."

This problem would persist across franchises to present day. "The original girls are never happy with the Casa boys around the world," *USA* showrunner Thursby-Palmer says. "Often a lot of the girls will have been unhappy with their [original] guys and their behavior [at the Villa]. Then the boys go to Casa and they're like, 'Oh, I miss him.' You just spent the last week moaning about him!"

Thomas says, "We're just trying to structure Casa so it doesn't end up being, like, the OG girls sit on their hands, and the OG boys treat it like a bachelor party. That's the fucking scenario we try and work against every year."

Love Island had disinhibited the season 3 boys by providing human bait and the illusion of privacy. Not knowing their actions would be funneled to their partners—until they got back to the outside, at least—the season 3 boys began chanting "Do bits!" (effectively, "Hook up!") as soon as they reached Casa Amor. Chris Hughes and Kem Cetinay began a labored metaphor where they compared the women they had been with at the Villa to hummus and olives, and the new offerings to carrots, celery, and breadsticks, which they were now ravenous for.

The producers had successfully heightened Kady's Hideaway tantrum: Despite the absence of an actual relationship, Camilla wept over twenty-six-year-old Essex boy Jonny Mitchell, crying that her feelings for him weren't a game. Olivia had spent weeks of beating back her ick for twenty-four-year-old "model" Chris, which had developed because he was, as she described it to me in 2021, "this boy that still lived at home, never had a job, and we had nothing in common."[1] Now she was dabbing away tears, lamenting that he didn't trust her, and wearing his dirty boxers to bed. Even the Napoleonically confident Kem had a miniature moment of self-doubt about Amber, delivered in song form. In a duet with Chris, he rapped, "Missus still in the other Villa, probably getting noshed off by another guy. He is probably taller than me, probably better-looking." Kem tried to end on a positive note: "But his personality is shit," he wished aloud.

The reveal of what the men did at the other Villa—or what producers could make it *look* like they were doing—began before the women even left Casa, when production slipped a postcard into the Villa. It showed each male Islander in a "compromising" position with one of the Casa bombshells. Some photos seemed to depict bad behavior that hadn't actually occurred, like an image of Marcel in bed with a woman, where they were strictly sleeping. (In subsequent seasons, this would be effectively forbidden by the code of the Villa.) Some were perfectly accurate: Kem had decided to make out with Essex-based stylist Chyna Ellis after convincing himself that Amber was also cracking on. The photo of Kem snogging would make the prediction of his song into a fact.

The postcard bit would reliably inflame women Islanders as well as viewers. During season 4's Casa Amor, producers sent twenty-one-year-old barmaid and audience favorite Dani Dyer a digital postcard of Jack Fincham, a twenty-six-year-old stationery salesman with a penchant for yapping with the girls and the gaudiest veneers that had appeared on the show to that point. The message showed that his ex-girlfriend was waiting for him at the other Villa, which Dani interpreted as the beginning of a reconciliation; actually, Jack was sleeping outside and talking about how much he missed Dani. After the postcard incident, viewers submitted more than twenty-six hundred complaints to Ofcom regarding the "upsetting" nature of the manipulation of Dani. "Everyone went crazy on us," UK creative director Spencer-Hayter says. "They were going, 'How can you do that? No, he's not done anything.' But obviously, it was to show that [the ex was] in there. Half the audience were like, 'She needs to see.' And the other half of the audience were like, 'She can't see.'" Producers decided Dani needed to see.

Dani had had a difficult early season. "You do struggle the first week because you're like, 'I don't get to wake up when I want. I shower at this time.' You become like little *Sims* characters," Dani says of the environment where bedtime is whenever producers turn off the bright lights and wake-up is whenever they flip them back on. This provokes the early-morning sunglass-wearing often clocked by viewers. "You just so quickly adapt to that and forget about the real world—*this* is your world." Within a few weeks, Dani had stopped noticing when couples in a bed three feet away were hooking up. "But it's so crazy how you can literally go from zero to a hundred so quickly," Dani says. "Like, you go from not knowing them to then all of a sudden, you're obsessed with this person."

That obsession—coupled with the knowledge that Jack had cheated on a different previous girlfriend—made Dani distraught when he went to Casa, even before the postcard showed up. "What do I do now?" she thought in between many rounds of tears. "Is this gonna all go wrong?"

Dani started leaving the Villa to follow the producers around, demanding they tell her what was happening with Jack. (Unless they choose to walk away from the show permanently, Islanders can only leave one at a time to smoke or vape—or if they are in pieces, as Dani was.) The crew kept assuring Dani it was fine, but she was inconsolable during the three days of Casa Amor.

Casa ends around the Villa firepit, with each person individually deciding whether to stay with their original couple or switch and recouple with their new partner. Neither Islanders of the opposite sex nor viewers know whether someone is returning alone or with another person until they walk down the stairs. "If he comes in with someone else, I'm not gonna be able to carry this journey on," Dani said. (Typically, if an Islander thinks their partner is going to recouple with someone during Casa, they'll get into their own new couple, lest they be single and at risk for dumping; Dani had not done this.) The end of Casa is a better indicator of Islanders' heart rates than Hearts on Fire; their pulses are clanging so loudly the microphones can pick them up.

That evening, Dani dressed all in black so she would look hot for the funeral of her relationship. When Caroline asked her how she was doing, Dani honestly told her it was the most nervous she'd ever felt. Jack had been in there for half a week—basically a month in *Love Island* time—with his ex-girlfriend. What if they still had chemistry? What if it was stronger than his with Dani, who had gone in resolved to not have sex on TV and, unlike many other Islanders who make that promise, stuck to it? "In my head I was convinced," she says: Jack had gotten back with his ex.

Except he hadn't. Jack and his glow-in-the-dark teeth ran down the stairs and into Dani's arms. "Oh my god, I've just cried for three days over nothing," she thought. *Love Island* was so powerful it didn't even have to present *actual* conflict; by adding space between people who had been together every moment for weeks, they allowed Dani to live out an entirely fictional drama.

It's not easy to be on the other side of Casa, either. The people brought in are typically told they'll be bombshells, then are secreted from rental to rental with chaperones to keep them from being spotted by other cast members. If they stayed in the same hotel, producers learned, cast members would tag their locations on Instagram, see who else was also there, and secretly get to know each other. There was also the press, who by season 3 had begun lurking in the airport near the Villa. If they identified a new Islander, tabloids could start looking into that person and generating stories. Depending on whether producers think they might work in the opening lineup, these bombshells could have been in hiding for weeks before a Casa entrance. During that time, they are not allowed to have access to the outside world, though they are provided with books and a preloaded streaming stick with a few viewing options, including compulsory episodes of *Love Island*. They are also prepped for the dynamics of the show by producers and given a map of relationships to remind them who is together and who's been eliminated.

The bombshells enter the Casa Villa via minibus, meeting with their Casa compatriots/rivals for the first time on the drive. "You don't actually have any loyalties to anyone else," season 6 Casa girl Molly Smith kept telling herself to alleviate the guilt, remembering what producers had told the twenty-five-year-old model. "The boys do, and that's their problem. But those girls coming in, we're just doing what any bombshell would do."

Molly was interested in Callum Jones, a gorgeous twenty-three-year-old scaffolder from Manchester who was coupled up with Shaughna Phillips, a quote-generating twenty-five-year-old who was then working in government as a democratic services officer. They had emerged as a strong pairing from the early season, despite a notable discrepancy in intellectual curiosity. "The more nervous he looked, the more calm I felt," Shaughna said of her waxing confidence as they shifted from her chasing after Callum to Callum trying to keep up with her and her verbal dexterity. By the eve of Casa, Callum and Shaughna had settled into a fairly delightful dynamic and been voted one of the most compatible couples in the Villa.

But from the moment he met her, Callum was infatuated with fellow Mancunian Molly. She, meanwhile, had specifically gone on *Love Island* to meet someone who wasn't from her hometown. Molly lived just down the road from Callum, to the point where driving routes were the subject of their first conversation. The boys warned him Shaughna would be upset, and Callum replied, in the most Callum way possible, "If you think you's doing something right, you're not doing anything wrong."

Nestled behind a wall festooned with a neon "Temptation" sign, Callum told Molly he missed her when she wasn't there and that he was open to leaving Shaughna and recoupling with her despite knowing "I might hurt someone's feelings in the process." In moments that didn't air to maintain suspense, Callum was more candid about the move he planned to make.

The boys and bombshells were shuttled over from Casa Amor together and then divided by sex at the Villa entrance. The Casa women remained in the vehicle. Because Callum and Shaughna were such a popular couple going into Casa—meaning Shaughna was about to be knocked on her ass by what was about to happen—Molly and Callum were informed by producers that he would be the last to enter. Though Callum had told Molly he was choosing her, she wouldn't know for sure until she was retrieved from the van, making the moment even more loaded. This was a man who had seemingly been enamored by Shaughna, and he'd changed his mind about her in just a few days. Molly waited outside the Villa, staring at the clock on the dashboard—the only period in the Villa when she would ever be allowed to know what time it was—and watched the hours pass as the other women exited the car one by one to learn their fate. Finally, it was just her. At 1:00 a.m., Molly was reunited with Callum, who affirmed his decision to recouple with her before they faced what awaited them at the firepit.

"I did have a gut instinct that, from what I'd seen, I didn't think that Shaughna would recouple," Molly says of the episodes she'd watched in seclusion before coming to Casa. "So then the dread of knowing that I'm gonna walk out and she's gonna be stood on her own, I just knew it wasn't gonna be a pleasant experience." The original women's mouths popped open and were covered by acrylic-tipped fingers, and the boys, who had known about the switch, ducked their heads as a sheepish Callum and Molly alighted the stairs. Callum looked nervous, while Shaughna endeavored to project the corresponding calmness. Callum explained that while he hadn't been unhappy with Shaughna, something had been missing with her. He'd found it with Molly in Casa Amor. "Should have never trusted a scaffolder anyway," Shaughna said before throwing Molly a dry "Congrats, hun." She managed to make it away from the pack before melting into tears in the arms of Paige Turley, a twenty-two-year-old Scot. "Why can I never be the girl?" Shaughna asked. "I'm always that other girl . . . I have to put up with this shit, and then they go off and be amazing for someone else."

Though Callum had adhered to one of the rules of the show by following his heart and loins, the public punished the couple, and they were dumped from the Island a few days later. Viewers were annoyed that Molly had supplanted someone so amusing and began swarming online to throw out their judgments. "Callum knows Molly's local Tesco, don't think he'd even know his way to London," one person wrote, referencing Shaughna's more cosmopolitan provenance. "Molly and Callum would work on the outside, him and Shaughna wouldn't. End of."

Molly's brother was designated as her social media proxy while she was in the Villa and told her it had been "difficult" online "because of how loved Shaughna was, and obviously I had kind of gone in and ruined that." By the time Molly got out, the hive had mostly dispersed, and she was able to post her swim shots and workout videos without much pushback. Callum and Molly would go on to date on the outside for three and a half years, but true love does not always engender the love of the audience, or override whom *they* think the person should couple with. Unfortunately for Islanders, coupling for the purpose of winning is an even more unforgivable sin to viewers.

Shockingly, knowing everything they're doing is being televised and that anyone they care about may see footage of any betrayal still has not curtailed Casa's ability to suppress male Islanders' superegos, leaving their ids free to three-way kiss the two Casa girls they'd most like to have a threesome with. Season after season, viewers have watched as boys who behave in unscrupulous ways remain in their original couple, acting like Casa was a dream they've forgotten after waking. But in the world of *Love Island*, crushing scrutiny often follows reckless hedonism—even after they leave the Villa.

The first major post-Villa romantic scandal came from an unlikely source: Gabby and Marcel, season 3's near-winners. She was a teeny blonde yes girl trainer who announced and kept her pledge to not have sex in the Villa. He was an edge of fame former boy bander from the Blazin' Squad. Marcel was also, as he would testify to parliament two years later, the first "fully Black" cast member on the show, though there had been other people of color before. Together, they were the cast glue—the kind of relationship that inspired each of their mothers to express their love for their child's partner the first time they met.

At the beginning of season 3, Marcel was the comic relief, doing silly raps with Kem. He says producers kept suggesting he talk about the moderately successful hip-hop group he'd been in a decade earlier. "Marc, can you go have a conversation with this person and let them know you used to be in the Blazin' Squad?" a producer would ask. Marcel obliged, unaware that it was being turned into a montage of him seeming to brag after Iain said, "How long will it take Marcel to mention Blazin' Squad?"

On day fourteen, Marcel recoupled with bombshell Gabby, who was drawn to Marcel's dichotomy: the storied days of sleeping with hundreds of women who evidently loved Blazin' Squad and the fact that he was clearly the sweetest man in the Villa. Gabby told Marcel about her season-long vow of chastity, and Marcel didn't question it. Islanders began turning to Marcel for advice, and the narrative around him shifted. Iain stopped mocking the band and instead started calling him Dr. Marcel. Despite the polygraph results alleging Gabby didn't really love her partner, the couple was a balm in a season of frenetic male energy between Kem and Chris and both men's tempestuous relationships with their female counterparts. Marcel and Gabby came in fourth during the finale, after those two couples and Camilla and Jamie.

When he got back from the Villa and compared clips of the season to the discourse about him, Marcel said it felt like a feedback loop: People were perceiving him in a certain way and talking about it online, so the show adjusted their framing of him, which further ingrained public opinion. "The show has the power to turn people into whatever they want them to be," Marcel told me in 2021.[2] "Then on the outside of the show with social media, they also have the ability to, in turn, make what the show does with certain people a reality." At the beginning, this was wonderful. "I was called a national treasure, which is great," Marcel says now.

But then Marcel cheated on Gabby during a vacation a few months after the show wrapped. "IT'S OVER" read the headline in *The Sun*. "*Love Island*'s Gabby Allen DUMPS Marcel Somerville after discovering he bedded another woman behind her back while they were on holiday TOGETHER."[3]

"I made a mistake," Marcel says. "You almost feel like the whole world is judging you and judging your character. And you're like, 'How am I even going to come through this?' You feel like literally everything that's said about you is just the worst things possible, even though you know you're not a horrible person; you've not killed someone. But everyone else has villainized you."

Marcel hadn't realized that the fame that lingered after *Love Island* would come with observation and evaluation that felt like a shadow version of being filmed and voted on. It was an odd feature of *Love Island* celebrity. People who gain notoriety in other ways can maintain public interest even when they're not doing the exact thing they're famous for. Actors can walk on red carpets. Singers can make TikToks. Content creators can have feuds. Meghan Markle can have a hospitality show. But the viewers of *Love Island* want to keep consuming Islanders in relation to the couples they're invested in; to them, Marcel's real life had become the storyline continuing in a different medium. And the fans who had voted him into the finale—and those who already felt he didn't deserve to be in it—felt entitled to weigh in with their opinions of his behavior, just as they had on his journey to being a public figure. The parasocial promise of *Love Island* was being violated, though it was a contract Marcel had only thought he was signing for seven weeks.

Marcel doesn't blame *Love Island* for his nuked reputation any more than he blames it for Gabby's heart rate indicating she didn't truly love him after less than two months. Even if the people who make the show have a moral obligation to not actively harm its cast members, making reality TV is generally an amoral pursuit: The responsibility is to produce an interesting season of television, not to make the people on it look good. If the show put Marcel in front of a fickle, demanding public, it can't control how they perceived him afterward based on his own actions. Even during filming, when *Love Island* pokes a cast member just to see what will happen, how can they possibly predict an Islander's reaction will become the meme that overtakes the totality of their life? How can they know who can't withstand becoming a villain?

Marcel lost the season because the lie detector challenge said Gabby was being deceptive. But Marcel says going on the show gave him what feels like a permanent polygraph. Anything you say on *Love Island* will be fact-checked against your actions in the Villa—and anything you do on the outside can become public. Knowing his missteps could be exposed has made Marcel a more cautious person and, he thinks, a better one. "It's just a natural thing that's in your head," Marcel says. While Iain narrated Marcel's season of *Love Island*, the show itself has become his inner Jiminy Cricket.

5 Where's Your Head At?

MARCEL WOULD BE FINE—he had a kid and married a woman who didn't watch *Love Island* and would never talk to the tabloids, even after they divorced. He even returned to the show. But the wake caused by Marcel's infidelity proved something about *Love Island*: It was now big enough to destroy people. Or at least the show was now big enough that the cast members who went on it were conferred its magnitude and treated by viewers as if they were also powerful institutions, not just fallible people who chose to walk through the Villa's heart arches.

Katie Salmon was scouted to be on *Love Island* season 2 when she was twenty. She'd recently bared her breasts at the Cheltenham horse races and made tabloid headlines. Like her friend Jess Hayes, who also participated in the flashing incident, Katie was enlisted for her season's trial run and made it onto the actual show. Before she came in as a bombshell, Katie says she told producers she was bisexual and would prefer to couple up with another woman, which they seemed put off by—it would be a production hiccup. "The UK back in the day were really sticklers for this," says former *USA* executive producer Thomas.

"They're like, 'The whole show will fall apart!' And you're like, 'No. Then instead of putting in a person who wants a woman next time, you put in a person who wants a man.'"

When Katie came in on day thirty-four, thirty-year-old pageant winner and circus performer Sophie Gradon was single following a vote that eliminated Tom Powell, a twenty-four-year-old bartender and fitness instructor with whom Sophie had been coupled since day one. Despite a bold intro where she claimed, "I do what I want," the former Miss Great Britain was a sensitive presence in the Villa. Sophie shyly sang Natalie Imbruglia's "Torn" during the season's Miss Love Island pageant, beaming when her castmates applauded her lovely performance. After Tom was dumped from the Villa—he had never been as popular as sweet Sophie—Scott Thomas told Katie that Sophie, too, was bisexual. When Sophie affirmed that Katie was her type and that information was relayed to its subject, Katie focused on her, to Sophie's evident delight. Katie picked Sophie for a date, on which a producer suggested, "Maybe you should just finish it with a little kiss?" They obliged.

"At the time, me mum was actually battling cancer," Katie says. "So I was already in quite a sensitive, vulnerable state, and she was the only one I confided in about that. And that connection, in that environment, just made it more fun and exciting, like, 'Ooh, what's this? Shall we explore it?'" Their plotline would be historic: the first and only same-sex couple on *Love Island UK* through the publication of this book.

"You're shaking," Sophie said after Katie coupled up with her. Both beamed and held hands, expressing their relief at being together. Sophie explained to the other female Islanders that she'd had a hard time in relationships with men and that dating women had been the first time she'd been able to relax in a partnership. "I have tried it with girls, but I didn't really think this would happen in here," Katie said in the Beach Hut through tears. "So it does make me feel a bit emotional."

Their happiness was brief. In the Twitter challenge, Sophie found that some portion of the viewing public had been chastising her for moving on from Tom too quickly; they evidently wanted her period of mourning to be longer. As viewers' recriminations were internalized by Sophie into self-doubt, she went on a campaign to reconcile her intentions with how they had been interpreted by fans. Within hours, Sophie announced she was going to stay in the Villa but remain single, then meet Tom on the outside, which Katie told fellow Islander Adam Maxted was a "smack in the face." Adam, a twenty-four-year-old personal trainer from Ireland, took Katie's confidence in him as a greenlight to pursue her in a recoupling. He excitedly—and revoltingly—reported to the other Islanders, "Katie's like a dog, but then the owner decided, 'You know what? I don't want you anymore. Free to a good home.' And I'm that guy who's gonna say, 'Hey, I've got a home for you.'"

Bolstered by Adam and the chorus of Islanders outraged on her behalf, Katie questioned how three tweets could change Sophie's mind. As Katie fumed, Sophie dejectedly smoked across the garden, seeming to wonder how a three-day-long courtship had turned into a high-stakes drama in which she was the bad guy.

The Villa became incandescent as Katie reported to the other Islanders that Sophie had just told her, "It's a game, it's a game," which she hadn't—she'd said exploring connections and picking the strongest one was "the name of the game," which it literally was. Then Sophie decided—with some Twitter-challenge-induced self-reflection—that her connection with Katie wasn't as strong as the one she'd developed with Tom. "I'm not being mugged off for my sexuality," Katie said, quivering with indignation and citing the kiss that producers had suggested as evidence that she'd been led on.

Sophie apologized to Katie, but nothing could repair her reputation in the Villa. Once the other Islanders and public have decided a person is fake, every action only seems to add to that effect, in the

Hitchcockian way that someone insisting they aren't crazy makes them *sound* crazy. Even Sophie acknowledging that people thought she was phony seems to validate the allegation. "She's just a nasty bitch," an unseen Islander said in a voice-over as Sophie put her hair up and went to bed. "A spiteful bitch. She only thinks about herself." Kady McDermott said, "I think she thought coupling up with a girl would be a bit different. Katie's a good girl, and everyone's gonna love her, and it would have been an easy win."

The next morning, Katie went to clear the air with Sophie without first telling producers she was planning to, breaking a rule of production. "I didn't want you to feel like everyone was against you," Katie said. After the talk was done, the crew came over and asked them to have the same conversation again but with proper coverage from cameras for the important moment of rapprochement. Katie says Sophie was frustrated by having to reenact something she wanted to move past. "How am I meant to re-express that genuine feeling or genuine words?" Katie remembers Sophie saying before acquiescing and giving her a hug. The camera zoomed in on a face that looked swollen from crying; Sophie was done.

She left the Villa later that day, summoning a beauty queen smile and wearing the Miss Love Island sash she'd won by singing "Torn."

"She already had a lot of worries about how people might look at her out of her close circle," Katie said. "So I think she was just a bit anxious over that whole situation as a whole anyway. She couldn't really deal with the opinions and the negativity."

After Sophie walked, Katie tried to follow. "You can't go home," she says producers told her. "No, you're not doing this. You need to couple up with Adam"—the Islander who'd compared her to an abandoned dog. When Katie told them she didn't like Adam, she says producers told her she should stop focusing on that if she wanted to be in the finale. Like everyone else who goes *Love Island*, Katie did, so she obeyed the directive.

The *Mirror* published an article titled "Love Island Lesbian Couple SPLIT After Just One Night as a Couple as It Becomes Too Much for Sophie."[1] Tom gave an interview to *The Sun* in which he said, "I don't want to hear any bullshit lies."[2] Sophie was condemned by fans for a trio of alleged crimes: They felt she had pretended to like Tom when he had truly cared for her; she coupled with Katie to win the show; and she had broken things off because of audience pushback. Essentially, the audience revolted because they had decided Sophie cared too much about what they thought. They would spend the next several years making those negative opinions very clear to her. Fans criticized Sophie's motives, her loyalty, her hair, her skin. They said they wished she would get cancer. Sophie tweeted and deleted a series of posts claiming the relationship with Katie had been fake and that she'd always intended to stay with Tom.

At the reunion filming, Sophie and Katie went to the women's bathroom to work through their differences in their first conversation without cameras. Katie apologized for riling the mob of Islanders, explaining she had done so out of embarrassment; Sophie said she was sorry for implying that Katie had staged their coupling. "It doesn't need to be like this," they told each other.

"We did share something genuine, and then it was an actual real connection," Katie tells me, starting to cry. "She could see me, really, and I could see her, really."

Caroline approached Katie before taping started. "The only thing I will recommend to you is keep it short, don't say too much, and keep it classy," she told her.

Katie is immensely grateful for the advice. "It helped me not create a bigger narrative or . . . or push anything," Katie says. "And it's only now that I look back and think, she probably also did that to protect Sophie, too, because she probably could see the negative effects it was having on her mental health."

Less than two years later, Sophie gave an interview to Radio Aire where she talked about the potential consequences of being bullied by *Love Island* viewers.[3] "The harsh reality is it can end with that victim taking their own life," she said.

Three months later, Sophie died by suicide. Twenty days after that, her boyfriend took his own life. It was not *Love Island*'s fault any more than any individual factors that make up the constellation of desolation around such a tragic act. An inquest into her death found that Sophie was first diagnosed with depression and low self-esteem in 2013 and that when she died in 2018, she was taking medication for social anxiety disorder.[4] Sophie's choice to appear on *Love Island* had contributed to a strain on these mental health issues, as did what ITV executive Angela Jain called the "febrile atmosphere" of social media, where, she said, "it's so visceral, it's so direct, and it's straight at you—and some of it is frankly disgusting and shouldn't be allowed."[5]

Sophie's mother echoed Jain's words. "I don't want Sophie's death to be in vain," Deborah Gradon told the *Mirror*.[6] "The government needs to do more. If a beautiful, clever girl can be destroyed by public humiliation, then anyone can."

When Kady called to say that Sophie had passed away, Katie had just had a miscarriage and was struggling. "I just didn't think that she would ever do it," Katie says of Sophie, who had seemed so strong. "I felt heartbroken, and I felt like it was partly my fault," she says. "I've carried that with me for a long time. It's only been like the last year that I've kind of took that to God and allowed that to come off me, because it's a burden that I didn't need to carry. But I carried it because that was a traumatic situation to happen to me, to go on a big TV show, to come out on TV to couple up with this girl, and then for her to kill herself. It was hard." Katie wondered if she was responsible. People DMed her to assure her she was.

Sophie was hounded by a public who kept telling her that she was a bad person, and everything she said to dissuade or distract them seemed to further entrench the narrative. Katie, meanwhile, had emerged from

Love Island popular. Beloved. Somewhat famous, especially for someone who'd only been on the show for a week and a half. Katie discovered situational popularity didn't add up to wealth. "I wasn't making any money," she says.

Katie decided, "Right, okay. I'm gonna have to join OnlyFans because then at least I can profit from the followers in some type of way." Katie advertised herself as a former *Love Island* cast member because she knew that would get her profile more clicks and says she made between £10,000 and £25,000 a month before quitting three years ago as of this writing.

"If I never experienced the things that I had, all the pain and tribulations, then I would still be in OnlyFans now, and I would still probably be a nervous wreck to leave the house," Katie says, explaining she is now devoted to God and is no longer attracted to women. "My child would probably grow up and be in a vulnerable situation because of it, and I wouldn't be as strong mentally. I've grown into the person now that would have protected me as a child." Katie says today she wouldn't allow her younger self to go on *Love Island*.

Even after all this—the literal life and death stakes of public punishment, the substance use disorder that Katie subsequently experienced, the press coming to her mother's house after the father of Katie's child passed away, her understanding that part of the deal is companies "profiting off heartbreaking news or traumas"—when *Love Island* approached Katie a few years ago about returning to the series, she pursued it. Maybe this was a way to make everything bad that had already happened worth it. "I'd love the opportunity for the public to really see who I am and how much I've changed my life around," Katie said, to my shock. When Katie told ITV she's Christian and no longer into hookup culture, she says they demurred—that didn't sound like amazing television.

Sophie's death was one of the few pieces of news from the outside world that penetrated the Islanders' bubble in season 3. "It was such a big thing," Cowles said. "For them to be unaware of it would be unfair." (Among the other events that required breaking the Villa's seal was the Brexit vote, which Islanders were allowed to take part in.) In 2021 Megan Barton-Hanson shared with me her experience of learning about Sophie.[7] While cameras were down during lunch, producers came to the cast and told them what had happened.

"Being someone that has on and off suffered with mental health, it did really make my heart sink," Megan said. She became concerned about how she might be perceived on the outside after one of the women from Casa defied production's order and told Megan that a video of her erotic dancing had leaked. Fearing how people would discuss it and knowing what that kind of roiling clamor had done to Sophie, Megan begged producers to let her see her Instagram. They refused. "It was a blessing for me because I didn't have a good time at all with headlines and press and negative opinions and trolling and stuff," Megan said. "For the majority [of that], I was in the Villa, so I missed it all. I was strong enough not to go back after I left the Villa and research everything that had happened. I was quite lucky in the sense that I didn't have to read it all . . . unlike Sophie, who was obviously out and still being trolled and having all this abuse."

Mike Thalassitis was in Mallorca when the cast found out about Sophie. If the moments that would cement the public's view of Sophie were momentous, the ones that would define Mike's image were quotidian. The jaunty twenty-four-year-old footballer entered as a bombshell in the second week and coupled up with Olivia Attwood.

"After bitching about her, somehow Muggy Mike decided to take the girl I like," Chris said during the recoupling ceremony. Chris seemed less worried about Olivia being mugged off than himself being mugged off, but no matter—the name stuck. Mike got dumped by the women after ending up in the bottom with Olivia, but then came back to the Villa a few weeks later after a public vote.

Iain briefly tried to rebrand him, saying, "*Magic* Mike looks even better than he does on the tear-stained photo in my wallet." If the show was trying to move away from labeling him as muggy, Mike was reclaiming the ID. "I'd be a mug to believe that," Mike said of Olivia claiming she was done with Chris, then reiterating, "I'm not a mug," in the Beach Hut after another conversation with her.

It all felt very innocent. Silly, really. It was young adults acting like kids: name-calling, girl-stealing, boy-toying with. There was so much muggy behavior from Islanders that season that Mike's hardly rated. Gabby says the nickname didn't even register as important, like so many other *Love Island* moments that go viral on the outside. "I don't even remember it being a thing when we were in there," she says. "I never called him it. I don't think that's down to anyone in the house; I think it's how the public made that more of a thing." Had Mike not left the Villa and learned that it was, indeed, a thing, he may not have played it up so much upon his return.

Mike was dumped five days after reentering the Villa. He and his agent Dave Read decided it was strategic to continue to embrace the label. By that point, the nickname had already spawned a line of popular Muggy Mike mugs sold at Tesco, from which Mike received no proceeds. But that didn't mean Mike couldn't profit off his experience. Read told Mike, "I've worked in PR for over twenty years. It takes years to come up with things like this. This is just a name. I appreciate it's you, and I don't want to force my opinion on you, but I actually think it's half cool." Read says Mike saw the humor in being "half cool."

"He was self-deprecating," Read says. "He could laugh." With Read encouraging him, Mike started to cash in on being muggy, traveling the country doing paid appearances. "He was enjoying taking the money and enjoying the experiences, [which] is my honest view on that."

Read also says Mike entered a "toxic" relationship after the show, a factor that exacerbated other personal issues, including his mental health struggles.

Mike ended his life on March 16, 2019. When the death was reported in newspapers, some headlines still called him by the nickname he'd been doomed to on *Love Island.* "His name wasn't Muggy Mike," read a tweet from Chris, the person who had accidentally set this chain of events in action. "Please stop brandishing that. His name was Mike Thalassitis, and every inch of my heart goes out to his family & friends. A good guy, taken far, far to[o] soon."

Mike's mother spoke to the *Mirror* and said Mike had hidden from the family his mental health issues and the fact that he'd been prescribed antidepressants. "I wish Michael had confided in us or his friends, but he kept everything bottled up and put on a fake exterior when really he was dying inside," Shirley Thalassitis said.[8]

After Mike's and Sophie's deaths, *Love Island UK* overhauled the Duty of Care, the set of internal standards and procedures that support the well-being of the cast, which had existed since the beginning of the show. It now provided a more extensive pre- and post-Villa briefing on what Islanders could expect from appearing on *Love Island.* Before they are officially cast, finalists undergo an intensive, days-long boot camp. Video interviews with former cast members and sessions with members of the ITV team prepare them for what to expect during and after filming, from their loved ones being approached by the press to how to get comfortable going to the bathroom in an environment with so many people and cameras and so few toilets. They are given sensitivity training that focuses on respect within relationships and inclusive behavior and language around race and disability. After they leave the Villa, Islanders get social media training and advice for how to move forward with financial literacy and reasonable expectations of what might come professionally. The intention is to keep them away from predatory representatives and squandering any windfall. By 2023, social media had gotten so hostile for Islanders that ITV changed the policy to lock their accounts for the duration of the season, rather than appoint a loved one to field abuse on their behalf. During my interviews, I didn't speak to a single latter-season Islander who didn't feel looked after.

The new Duty of Care included comprehensive mental health support during filming, in the form of on-set psychologists. Therapists had always been available, but now Islanders were actively being encouraged to use them. After-season mental health care went from an ad hoc service that cast members had to request to each Islander being given at least eight post-show therapy sessions, plus fourteen months of proactive outreach from producers to determine whether more intervention was needed. These producers continue to check in to the present day.

Read maintains that Mike "loved *Love Island*." He also agrees with implementation of the new protocols that may have prevented Mike from being on the show in the first place. "It's very hard to get on there," Read says. "You need to have skin like a rhinoceros. One of the producers told me that forty percent of people that they want to put in the show will be wiped out by psych." One of his clients was flown out to Cape Town on an eleven-hour plane ride. The welfare team had one last "top-up" mental health conversation with her to make sure they ascertained any "additional information" that would be disqualifying. "She was sent home," Read says. "Now that's not nice to have that phone call from a girl crying down the phone because she's on her way back." But if you don't have the capacity to handle not going on *Love Island*, you certainly don't have what it takes to endure *Love Island*.

The new Duty of Care has, so far, done its job. Like the impact of regulations on seat belts and airbags, most preventable *Love Island* catastrophes since the ones that already happened have been avoided. The least risk-prone Islanders are the ones who already practice the equivalent of safe driving, diligently tending to their mental health and maintaining perspective on the kinds of people who would bother to harass a former reality star because they don't like the way they dated. Season 3's Olivia told me in 2021 that she underwent cognitive behavioral therapy and reminds herself people trolling her are "psychotic. I think anyone that sat at home, writing about me something really nasty, they're not mentally stable people. Imagine your world is so small that you are that emotionally triggered watching a TV show." That allows her to remember, "It's not normal. It's very abnormal, but it's manageable. You just need to manage it."

What also helps to manage it is the immediacy that makes *Love Island* so miraculous in the first place. It stays in that summer, and life goes on, usually.

"I was really lucky," season 6 winner Paige Turley told me in 2021. "For whatever reason, I didn't go in there for two days and the nation hated me. I had a support bubble I could go back to. And you've got to really remember, in the digital world, very quickly people will have an opinion of you. Then very quickly it's over and done with. It's forgotten about. And then there's a new season."[9]

6 Buzzing

WITH THE DUTY OF CARE bolstered and the chatter around the show nearing peak national cultural saturation, the fifth season of *Love Island UK* was a basket ITV could feel comfortable putting all of its eggs in. It followed four straight years of growing viewership, including millions of new US fans who would watch each episode on Hulu a few weeks after it aired in the UK. Six international editions had premiered, and *Love Island USA* and shows in three other countries were about to make their debut.

Half of a £50,000 prize, less taxes, was a pittance compared to potential earnings on the outside. Paid editorial shoots and fees for personal appearances at clubs or openings regularly reached £20,000. Dave Read could call up a fast fashion brand like PrettyLittleThing and say, "We've got clients going to *Love Island* next month. Girl A, she's a size extra small with a thirty-whatever bust, size five shoe." The brands would send boxes of clothes for the Islander to wear. Even if an item didn't have a logo on it, Read says, after the client wore it, the brand would post a still on social media and sell, say, six hundred swimsuits.

(*Love Island*, realizing they were missing out on profiting from their own influence, now has a QR code on-screen that allows viewers to shop each episode.) "Young people are sat at home where it's cold and dark," Read says of UK viewers. "They're watching these people walk around a swimming pool looking glamorous, and they immediately go on their mobile phone, and they've ordered that bikini they've just seen on TV ten seconds ago, and it's landed on their doormat the very next day." Just in time for the next episode of *Love Island*.

The producers were on a high, gleeful from winning the 2018 BAFTA for Best Reality and Constructed Factual show, and they could point to actual romantic success resultant from their program: Season 2's Olivia and Alex Bowen were married, and Cara and Nathan Massey had a child and would be wed before season 5's Casa Amor began. The Duty of Care now had robust therapeutic support for the cast. While all signs pointed to a new level of ascension, the season would exceed expectations.

The opening lineup of season 5 featured twenty-four-year-old Anton Danyluk, a Scottish gym owner whose mother still shaved his ass, though "still" is perhaps not the most surprising part of that sentence. There was a phalanx of scarily hot women who were loyal to each other and feral to anyone who hurt them: twenty-eight-year-old Anna Vakili, a pharmacist whose two-day boyfriend Jordan Hames would be recoined "Mr. Fucking Boyfriend. Fucking fake dickhead!" when he immediately backtracked after making it official; Yewande Biala, a twenty-three-year-old scientist from Dublin who would never return to the lab; and Amber Gill, whose journey would drive the show to perhaps the most satisfying finale in the entire series. (Though not everyone in the Villa would feel so plummy about the conclusion.)

The cast also included twenty-seven-year-old firefighter Michael Griffiths, who would be an important part of Amber's arc. On the first evening of filming, the OGs were joined by bombshell boxer Tommy Fury, the twenty-year-old brother of world heavyweight champion

Tyson Fury and the boy everyone wanted to couple up with in the Villa. Some men would only stick around for a few days, including one who was dispatched from the Island after he accidentally kneed the woman who would become the most famous Islander ever in the groin, then described the action as a "cunt punt."

Amy Hart never said she was applying to the show; before she was cast, she definitively told her friends, "I'm *going* on *Love Island*." On a trip to Jamaica before her plane returned to London, the twenty-five-year-old flight attendant filmed an application video she had storyboarded out, beginning with footage of her being crowned Miss United Kingdom. "International pageant titleholder, still can't get a text back," Amy said, popping out of the covers of a bed with a glass of wine in her hand. "I'm the world's worst drunk texter." When Amy met the executives, she charmed them with an anecdote from the flight cabin in which a passenger had passed out on the jump seat, causing the crew to believe she was dead. "What did you do?" Gould, Cadman, and producer Lauren Hicks asked. Instead of administering aid—what good would that do the deceased?—Amy made up a song called "Dead on the Jump Seat." (The passenger lived.)

When she found out she was going to Mallorca, Amy prepared her body. In lieu of her usually trusty beauty queen starvation plan of eight hundred daily calories of Special K, she needed a diet meant for televised close-ups of asses. "*Love Island* don't say, 'You must look like this,'" Amy says. "That's a personal thing. But if being on telly in a bikini isn't going to make you go to the gym, nothing else ever will." Amy began working out and eating what she believed to be an exorbitant eighteen hundred calories a day in an effort to get her glutes ready for slo-mo.

Amy was sitting in a Mallorcan hotel room when her handler came in and told her she was officially going in. "I had this ball of fire in my belly," Amy says. "I didn't know whether to laugh, cry, be sick, scream." When she entered the Villa, Amy had the oddest experience: She had stepped into her television.

Though she'd spent so much time plotting how she could get to *Love Island,* Amy had never thought about what to do when she actually arrived there. She, for what would be one of a few times in her life, had nothing to say. So on her first day, Amy went to the Beach Hut and heard the disembodied voice of a producer ask how she was doing. The truth: not well. The faceless producer sent the wellness team to check on Amy, who refused to meet with the psychologist. "There was such a big thing about mental health that year," she says, following the off-screen devastations. Producers were doing everything to keep them from happening again. Amy thought, "If I see the psych, they will think that I am not fit to be here, and they will send me home." When another Islander mentioned she'd met with the therapist, and Amy realized speaking to them wouldn't get her kicked off, she started going regularly, eventually attending three sessions a day. "I was loving it," Amy says. As she was embarking on her psychological journey, the audience was focusing on her unusual style of walking upstairs: using one leg to skip four steps, then holding on to the banister and lugging the rest of her body along, as if the leading limb were wooden.

Producers told Amy this lineup was as good as it was going to get, boy-wise, and that if anyone stepped out in the first coupling, they were putting themselves out there, and she should be kind. So when Anton's mom-shaven ass walked forward, Amy coupled with him. "Stay with me," he begged her when other boys would come by to chat. When they weren't together, though, Anton let the girls know he didn't fancy Amy.

But Curtis Pritchard did. Amy started speaking with the twenty-three-year-old champion ballroom and Latin dancer after he entered as a night-one bombshell with Tommy, and Anton's clingy disinterest became clear. "She was the first person I could comfortably have a good conversation with out of all the women," Curtis says. That, coupled with what he describes as "the excitement, lust for sex, the adrenaline of the entire show," made him think, "Fuck, this is really good between us." They immediately became the Villa "Mom and Dad," to Curtis's joy. He was an inveterate people pleaser and overthinker, with the kind of face so transparently expressive that his internal monologue might as well have been written in the subtitles that American viewers put on so they can understand what UK cast members are saying. "To become a world champion [dancer], you have to notice the small things, and they have to be perfect to make the big things perfect," Curtis says of his obsessive attention to detail. He applied the same techniques to *Love Island*. "I've always wanted to try and figure out if whoever it is on the other side of me will allow me to come in for a hug, come in for a kiss, touch their leg," he says. "I'm always very wary of this. I try and read the body language for one, my own protection, and so I'm not being a perv to them and I'm not making them uncomfortable. And two, to just sort of see the whole situation correctly."

But with all of that attention paid to signals, Curtis had ignored a crucial one. When he got to Casa, he realized that rather than falling in love, as he thought he'd been doing, he didn't actually want to date Amy at all; it turned out she was just an attractive woman who had helped him establish his role in the Villa. "Oh, sugar," Curtis thought. "I've put myself in this situation now, and I really have just mixed up the entire excitement—bit horny, all of this and that—with not more than just a friendship, really."

With Amy still in the main Villa and Casa presenting all manner of temptation, Curtis had to figure out how to let her down without vocalizing any of it to either his castmates or producers, which is typically how such quagmires are puzzled out. "What's everyone gonna think?" he wondered. Then he told himself, "Curtis, right, millions of people are watching this. But in reality, who do you actually care who cares about you? My closest friends, my family, and they'll always have my back. So actually, forget about everyone. I've got my support network anyway. [I'll] try and do what's best for me."

After asking twenty-four-year-old model Jourdan Riane if she would recouple and getting rejected, Curtis determined he had to come back from Casa alone and break up with Amy before he could crack on with someone else—Amy and Curtis were the glue in the Villa, and all of the Casa women had been watching the relationship play out. (Spencer-Hayter calls this the "I want to finish with my partner and get with someone else" story, which is one of the most popular with viewers.)

Upon his return, Amy was breathless, and Curtis was visibly apprehensive, speaking even more slowly than his usually drawn-out cadence as he pulled her for a chat. As they sat on a couch as far as possible from the rest of the cast, Amy and Curtis discussed their differing priorities in life while dancing around the foremost point of contention, which was that Curtis was no longer interested in Amy. In what was an ill-conceived attempt to preserve the feelings of someone who would still sleep within feet of him, Curtis did not make a clear break, instead reiterating Amy's beauty and saying their relationship was perfect. Amy was baffled, which made sense; Curtis had cushioned the bad news with an effusiveness that made Amy feel like he wanted to try to keep dating.

Amy tried to convince herself there was a way to salvage things and went over to a group of women for reassurance. "I love him," Amy said, stunned by the betrayal of being "basically cheated on."

"But does he love you?" twenty-one-year-old surfer Lucie Rose Donlan mused.

"Why are you asking her that!" Maura Higgins hissed. "He fucking doesn't."

Meanwhile, Curtis sat recounting the story to the other boys, who told him he'd done what he had to. Amy approached, sufficiently riled up by her friends to consider ending things.

Curtis and Amy walked to the lounge, which would be the site of the breakup of the season, by dint of its multiple coexisting timelines. For Curtis, it was a postmortem on an existing split; for Amy, it was a currently occurring parting—or, possibly, an opportunity to point out all of the ways Curtis had done wrong by her in a manner that convinced him to want her back. This latter approach does not have a high success rate on *Love Island.*

Amy told Curtis that it seemed like he'd been more focused on the group than her—why didn't he bond with Amy by cuddling when they woke up?

"I also want to be the person that gets up and makes everyone a coffee so everyone's ready for the morning," he said.

After Curtis laid out the fact that he'd been lying to himself and her the entire time they'd been together, Amy relayed her incredible misreading of the moment: "I was coming back here to tell you that I loved you."

Following several episodes of Amy crying and Curtis sulking, producers called for a public referendum, allowing viewers to decide whether they wanted to watch things play out or if it was time for a cleanse. That night, the audience was not interested in watching the denouement of Mom and Dad's divorce—Amy and Curtis were one of three couples with the fewest votes. But Amy was incredibly popular within the Villa, and when the bottom couples were thrown to the Islanders for their decision, Amy's goodwill bailed out Curtis. Amy says she had wanted to go in the dumping, but the girls told her, "We've saved you now, so Amy, come on, you've got to pick yourself up. There's gonna be new boys coming in. This is your chance. You've got to try and find someone. You deserve to be happy."

During one of the next day's trio of therapy sessions, Amy miserably predicted that Curtis was going to meet someone new. The therapist said, "But when *you* get with someone else—"

Amy cut her off. "I don't think I'm going to," she said. "There's only three weeks left. I don't think I'm ready." The therapist sat silently while Amy thought through what that meant. "Oh, if I'm not gonna meet anyone else, I should probably just go home," she said. Amy did, becoming one of the small number of Islanders to self-eliminate.

Before Amy exited, Spencer-Hayter made her record one final Beach

Hut interview. She thanked the crew off camera, and then she got to say goodbye to the Villa on her own terms. With Curtis sniffling beside her, Amy gave a noble speech to the teary Islanders gathered around the fire. Even stoic twenty-year-old influencer Molly-Mae was moved, openly sobbing. Amy told the other contestants that she had always felt like an outsider before *Love Island*, and somehow she'd found herself as the "nucleus" of the Villa with Curtis. She thanked the family who had merged around them and told them the last week of emotional torment had been worth it for the friendships she'd made. The speech seemed to profoundly move the Islanders, who couldn't believe Amy was choosing to go home.

"What are you doing?" Michael said in a scene that didn't air, according to Amy. "Just stay." Anna started unpacking Amy's suitcase, telling her she couldn't leave. But Amy said she had to—her mind was made up.

Curtis tried to be supportive: "Look guys, if she wants to go . . ." His affirmation was not well received by the other Islanders.

Amy put on a short red dress, used the stairs normally, for once, and walked away to the applause of her fellow Islanders.

The end of Curtis and Amy was a dramedy that resonated with fans and continued inside the Villa even after she left; Curtis says he spent the next three days crying off camera in the Beach Hut and psych's office. Here he was, stuck with the unforeseen wreckage of his own making. "Fuck," he thought. "I genuinely broke someone's heart, and she's not in a good way."

Amy, for her part, thrived on the outside. She is married with a young son now. She has become a crucial part of *Love Island*'s self-commentary as the co-host of the official *Love Island UK* podcast with season 8 Islander Indiyah Polack and as a frequent panelist on *Aftersun*. She realizes now that if she had been put out of her misery and voted out when she'd hoped to be, it would have just been another *Love Island* dumping. Instead, she'd rewritten her unscripted ending.

Once, Amy says, someone in the TV world told her, "You played a blinder there." ("A blinder" is British for "a massive triumph in a sporting game.")

Amy's response? "I *played* nothing."

As Amy was getting ready to leave the Villa and learning she'd gone viral for her stair climbing, Chris Taylor and his ticker-tape brain were bombshelling in. Chris was a twenty-eight-year-old who worked selling "identity verification solutions," which he explains "was just a lot of lying and chatting to people." He had been cast after a process he describes as "answering stupid questions," peeing in a cup, and flirting with the casting producer for fifteen minutes to demonstrate his exceptional banter.

Chris knew there was a chance of his life turning from mundanity to pop culture deliverance, but also that it was equally possible he'd be asked to leave the Villa after a few days. To his mind, the probability of finding romance was even more remote. "The environment is made to fall in love, but I think it's counterintuitive to that quite aggressively," Chris says. "Even the Villa's fake—it's just some French Olympian's Villa that they retrofit every year. They slap a load of plastic on it and make it look like *Love Island*." He missed the crucial part: Making it look like *Love Island* is part of what makes it *Love Island*.

Chris had not been particularly popular when he was young. More than anything, *Love Island* offered him the chance at validation: Would people accept (and vote for) him now? Though he hoped the answer was yes, he couldn't bear to think about how it was going in the moment. "They obviously don't tell you anything, and to guess would just be psychotic," Chris says. "You can't read the minds of millions of people that are watching the show, and obviously, so many things get interpreted in so many different ways that to even bother trying to assess what's just happened and how people might feel about it is insanity."

Chris straddled the tonal blend of the show with his semi-confrontational flirtatiousness and self-effacing physical humor, which was belied by his studiously tousled hair and a perpetual shirtlessness that exposed copious tattoos and a gym-honed torso. He went after a few women—twenty-one-year-old makeup artist Belle Hassan, who would choose to redeem Anton the outsider, and twenty-year-old estate agent Harley Brash, who noted Chris was the "Villa clown."

"No one's ever asked me to be less funny," he responded. It was like having a second Iain who was telegenic enough to actually be in the Villa.

Chris says that despite the oceans of idle time that seem to exist on *Love Island* as people laze on beanbags, the Islanders were incredibly busy: pulling the next person for a chat, participating in a challenge, maintaining the producer-mandated levels of eating, water intake, sunscreen, and sleep, which were now regimented. Because he was so verbal, Chris was dispatched on an unusually high number of off-site dates, which required the ability to maintain verve in the presence of much more obtrusive cameras. These outings necessitated reshoots to make sure every angle was captured. For a moment's rest, Chris would go have a cigarette alone and bawl, a display of emotion that would have been a surprise to anyone watching. He says he only realized why recently, after listening to a particularly enlightening podcast. "I feel like when you do something like [the show], you have to shed the person you were to become the person you're becoming," Chris says. "That was almost me grieving the person I've left behind, which is a really weird existential crisis whilst having a cigarette in the Villa."

Chris was unable to stop thinking about whether any of the women were sincere long enough to find a true connection and was dumped after fifteen days in the Villa. However, his overactive brain would eventually serve him well on *Aftersun*, where, like Amy, he would build a post–*Love Island* career analyzing other seasons of *Love Island.*

* * *

Maura Higgins's star power was obvious to her castmates before she walked into the Villa; well before their season, Curtis DMed Maura when he was a pro on *Dancing with the Stars Ireland* and she was a local beauty. The twenty-eight-year-old Monster Energy event model came into the Villa on day ten after producers told her she had the personality to be a bombshell. Though Tommy and Molly-Mae were already a tight couple, Maura made her intentions for Tommy clear as soon as she stepped into the Villa, announced he gave her "fanny flutters," and went on a date with him as Molly-Mae watched from the balcony. Molly-Mae was aggravated to her emotional peak, whisper-shouting in annoyance to the other women.

After the date, Maura told Molly-Mae she was freezing, and Molly-Mae reverted to a more typical mode of operation: killing dissension with kindness and co-opting the threat with fashion by offering Maura her jacket—which meant Maura was wearing the white leather moto when she pulled Tommy for a chat in front of Molly-Mae. Maura's brazen interest in Tommy and her lack of intimidation at Molly-Mae's presence activated the normally fluster-proof influencer.

Molly-Mae was understanding on paper if not in practice, in that she recognized that, technically, it was Tommy's decision whom he pursued, and Maura was doing her job. "A bombshell has every right to come in and just do your thing. That's what you're there to do," Maura says. Molly-Mae became much *more* understanding when she realized Tommy was obsessed with her; even during the conversation with Maura where she flirted with him in Molly-Mae's clothing, he'd kept looking over at Molly-Mae with an expression that registered somewhere between longing and extreme anxiety about pissing her off.

After Tommy let down Maura, the two women became close. "We couldn't deny our friendship," Maura says. "We just got on so well, so all of that stuff, it never affected us." Maura moved on to Tom Walker, a twenty-nine-year-old model who was youthfully handsome and immature, which would soon get him in trouble.

In a scene that became indelible, Maura was surprised to learn her fellow Islanders had chosen her for a date with Tom in the Hideaway after they'd known each other for only a few days. "I really didn't wanna go in there with him," Maura says now, reflecting on the situation. "I wasn't at that stage. Like, we had kissed a few times, but it kind of felt very early for that." They weren't even in an official couple yet. While it isn't mandatory to hook up in the Hideaway, the building is strongly associated with the activity, and Maura was unusually sex positive even for an Islander. As he walked to his date, Tom was oozing with entitlement. He told the boys, "It will be interesting to see if she's all mouth or not."

Maura had gone downstairs to grab lingerie to wear to the Hideaway and saw that the men were gasping and clutching each other at the sight of her, thinking she'd overheard what Tom had just said. She had not, and asked Tom to repeat it. For some reason, he did, to which a horrified Maura replied, "Are you fucking joking?" Tom, realizing his gaffe, tried to reframe it as a miscommunication. "You said it, making me feel like a piece of shit," Maura yelled in the dressing room as the other women turned their backs in an effort to do something between disappear from this mortal coil and eavesdrop more effectively. The camera kept zooming in on a mirror, where Molly-Mae hid her face with knit fingers as Tom sputtered, no longer brave enough to slag off Maura now that they were face-to-face. "What? 'Uh, uh'?" she said, mocking his inability to articulate. The shot cut to Molly-Mae's reflection again, shown shaking with silent laughter. "They 'asked you a question'?" Maura said. "Maybe you should have been a gentleman." Cutting Tom to ribbons was what Maura could do with her mouth.

Along with the rest of the show's fandom, *Love Island USA* host Ariana Madix became enraptured with Maura while watching this play out on-screen. "That's my favorite Maura moment, because you know what? That is who she is through and through. She is an Irish queen,"

Ariana says of her friend and *Aftersun* castmate. Maura also enjoys it as a viewer. "Every time it comes up, I still watch it to this day," she says. "You do really forget that the cameras are there, and you don't know what's being shown, what's not. The way it was all edited together was just brilliant."

Episode after episode and riposte after flame-up, Maura generated evidence that she was a Hall of Fame Islander. She was incautious in a way that allowed her to roll with the extemporaneous production style and social milieu; when Tom tried to make her look foolish or she managed to do that herself, Maura never felt ashamed. After she decided she liked Curtis, she voraciously pursued him. Though Chris Taylor was ostensibly a much better match for someone who loved to spar through quips, Maura spent her date with him spying on Curtis, who was telling his own partner that he was interested in Maura.

Once he submitted to her crush, Curtis also relaxed into Maura's improvisatory approach to things. "She brought out a more fun side to me," Curtis says. "I felt like with Amy, I was a married man. With Maura, I felt like I was more my age."

She even got the not-always-quotable Molly-Mae to start riffing. "Maura's going to literally destroy Curtis in the Hideaway," Molly-Mae said when the pair got together and Maura was finally headed to the bungalow with someone who wasn't using her sexuality to make himself look big. (Curtis did briefly workshop a joke referencing the "all mouth" line with the other men before deciding maybe it wasn't the time, though as a bit, he did borrow Chris's kimono, with the caveat that Curtis needed to *fold* the silk, not crease it.) "He's going to come back with a limp," Molly-Mae insisted.

When Maura returned, she issued her verdict: "It was fanny-tastic," she said.

Spending less time in his head—not striving to be the group's parental figure or barista but a guy flirting with one of the funniest Islanders ever—took Curtis to the end. "Maura's vote probably got me to the final," he says, now that he's had time to reflect on it. "She had the whole of *Love Island* behind her. People loved her, so knowing all of this now, like, it wasn't me that got to the final; it was bloody her."

Among a tremendous cast and the fights and bonding sessions that emerged from them colliding, the winners of season 5 were Amber and Greg O'Shea, a twenty-four-year-old rugby player. If Maura brought Curtis to the finale with her, Amber essentially made it to the podium alone, in a storyline that couldn't have played out better if ITV had planned it. "We saw the kind of girl sat with her glasses on, kind of scowling at people at the start, going through this massive journey," Spencer-Hayter says, adding, "We love Amber."

Amber was a beauty therapist whose rare grins felt like the first sunrise after an Arctic winter. She had been coupled up with Michael since day fourteen. At only twenty-one years old, Amber had a difficult time communicating in a way that would lead to an operable adult romance, shutting down when she felt exposed either in conflict or affection with Michael. "He was saying he liked her," Curtis says. "She was giving him nothing in return whatsoever. Absolutely nothing. He was really trying everything." But there was something compelling about the fact that the impediment to their being together was Amber's hesitation to trust her pull to Michael; it looked like a romantic comedy where the main character just needed to realize she'd loved the guy the whole time. Producers didn't need to throw spanners in their works; somewhat like Dani and Jack, it felt like this pair's test was whether Amber would relent to being in a real couple. With time and patience and reassurance, viewers were sure she would open up and quit being what Michael called "chaldish" in his Liverpudlian accent, and he would stop acting like, as Amber put it, "a dick."

What the audience was ignoring as they shipped the ice queen and fireman was that these two were not particularly compatible, constantly winding up in elliptical fights where they blamed each other for their own behavior. "You can smile, you know," Michael told Amber the day before Casa Amor, after they made up from yet another miscommunication-based argument.

"I don't want to smile," she replied, snuggling him and stoking viewers' belief that her words were only a defense mechanism.

At Casa, twenty-two-year-old recruitment consultant Joanna Chimonides was more forthcoming and receptive, as most Casa bombshells are in their quest to make it back to the main Villa. Things were just easier with Joanna. Michael decided to recouple, making him one of the least popular people among Amber's friend group. What happened next would make him one of the least popular people in the UK.

Within days, Joanna was dumped—unsurprisingly, as a Casa Amorian who breaks up a popular couple typically has the lifespan of a Popsicle in the Mallorcan sun. Michael says he told producers that at this point, he wanted to leave, too, which would have scuttled the potential for an all-time great re-recoupling. "The public wanted me and Amber to get back together," Michael says. "[The producers] wanted to give the public what they wanted, but neither of us wanted that to rekindle."

Michael was clearly unhappy but says he was told he couldn't exit until he spoke with various executives and the psych team to make sure he was making the right decision. He stayed in bed and was largely absent from the next few episodes, only emerging to eat breakfast. After meeting with one exec, he realized the timeline for talking to everyone who had to sign off on him leaving would be a week, and likely, a vote would take him out before then.

Michael says he was dazed from sleeping at off-hours and barely interacting with anyone. When producers repeatedly implored him to tell Amber that he might want to try to make it work again, he eventually relented. Michael and Amber had a conversation that was meant to be the beginning of their reunion, except Michael did not say the magic words that would indicate there could still be something between them. He says production asked them to try again. The evening dragged on and on, fruitless chat after fruitless chat. The sun was about to come up, but Michael and Amber weren't opening the door to getting back together, because neither of them wanted to—Amber would later tell YouTuber Murad Merali that she was more embarrassed than distraught when Michael came back with Joanna.[1]

"At a certain point of fatigue, I allowed myself to be manipulated," Michael says. "So my rational decision-making kind of went out the window."

Michael finally told Amber he didn't think she and her current partner Greg would work out, that she was feistier and fierier than him, that he couldn't handle her. In the scene Michael is smiling cheekily, implying that he very much *could* handle her. Soon after the conversation was over, producers told them they could go to sleep.

After watching the scene air, the audience was apoplectic, feeling that Michael was screwing with the woman he'd led on, fucked over, and was now trying to win back for unknown reasons—which were that the producers wanted to satisfy the people who were now furious with the man who'd executed their directive.

"What a storyline that is," the firefighter said to himself that night, as he looked over at Amber and Greg kissing in bed. "You bring in a hero who turns into a villain." (He concedes this was "great TV.") Michael was dumped from the Villa the next day.

The physics of *Love Island* meant *Amber* was now a hero and was edited accordingly. The truth was she and Greg weren't a fit; this was a matter of timing. "Greg and Amber weren't talking for the two days before the final," Curtis says of the moments of tension that were cut from the edit. "They didn't like each other. They were due to break up the day that they left the Villa." (Amber and Greg beat Curtis's projection and stayed together for about a month.)

"I think people felt so passionately about her having a happy ending after what had happened with Michael," the show's comms head Jeffreys says of Amber. "I mean, nothing against Greg, but I think really it was all about, 'She needs to win this now.'"

As for who *actually* should have won season 5, it doesn't really matter—in the subsequent years, Molly-Mae has become the biggest *Love Island* cast member of all time. She and Tommy left the Villa together in 2019, had baby Bambi in 2023, and got engaged the same year. After a brief breakup in 2024 related to Tommy's alcohol abuse following an injury, Molly-Mae and Tommy reconciled, and in early 2026 she announced her second pregnancy. Molly-Mae now has an Amazon docuseries, a £3.8 million mansion in Cheshire, a clothing line called Maebe, a sneaker collaboration with Adidas, the most followers of any other Islander times two, a lasting friendship with former rival Maura, and the confidence to have dissolved her filler.

Molly-Mae, with her impassive caramel face and ash-blonde hair, was the apex Islander in *UK*'s apex season, even though she could never be pushed to the kind of emotional nadir that almost any Islander has to experience as they work toward iconism. Hers were not the most memorable lines. Her biggest plotlines were people failing to come after her man as he endlessly reassured her of his adoration. Her clashes were primarily secondhand, as she expressed her displeasure to third parties.

Molly-Mae's noncombustibility was her draw—she was making slow TV in the middle of a reality circus. While her castmates follied and foibled, Molly-Mae was steady. She was a content creator who came on and pursued finding a partner as thoughtfully as she did making millions of pounds. When she did lightly freak out in the Villa, it was proof of a fallibility that felt perfect. Molly-Mae's dichotomy was her appeal: that she was both aspirational and aspiring at the same time. About casting her, executive producer Lewis Evans says, "I remember calling her up to offer her the bombshell position, and she was like, 'I'm not so sure. I'm going to have to have a think about it.' You could tell she was so forward-minded. But you just knew that she was open to finding love." She was the kind of naturally occurring Islander who producers would have created if they could, providing a model across seasons and countries, for both the casts and the casting teams. "Molly-Mae is the North Star," former *USA* executive producer Thomas says. Molly-Mae represented the kind of *Love Island* success that was theoretically possible but not replicable.

"Molly-Mae knew she was an influencer," Curtis says. "She knew exactly what she wanted to be when she came back out, and she used that to be able to completely relax and have fun in there, and to open her mind up and open herself up to allowing love to happen."

Nearly everyone I spoke with discussed Molly-Mae in something like matter-of-fact deification. Even Caroline was in awe of *Love Island*'s most famous Islander. "Oh my God, that's Molly-Mae," she said when Molly-Mae came on *Aftersun*.

"Okay," her colleague told her. "You're *Caroline Flack*."

Molly-Mae was already Molly-Mae when she went on *Love Island*—the series just happened to be the optimal medium to let people know. She became proof of concept for *Love Island*—the marriage of love and commerce—to the point where "Molly-Mae" is now basically a metonym for the series. "When you're not around, I'm not myself," a besotted Tommy told her right before the finale. It felt like that was also true for the world of the show. When Molly-Mae appeared, Cowles's pitch was realized: *Love Island* had proved itself by producing a celebrity whose fame was forever attached to the series but had broken through to exist outside its context.

7

USA! USA!

ON JULY 28, 2018, *The New Yorker* published a nine-thousand-word article by Ronan Farrow on CBS Chairman and CEO Les Moonves's decades of alleged sexual misconduct and assault. It was the first of a tranche of reports that would lead to his resignation in September. Their contents, which Moonves denied, ranged from allegations of violent and coercive oral sex and Moonves telling an actress, "Come on, you're not some nubile virgin," while he forced himself on her, to Moonves destroying evidence of malfeasance and CBS paying millions of dollars in settlements related to his alleged behavior without admitting to wrongdoing.

A few weeks earlier, Moonves had executed what would turn out to be one of his last acts running CBS: greenlighting *Love Island USA*.

It wouldn't have happened without Billy Bowers. Before *Love Island UK* was licensed by Hulu, Moonves's assistant was given DVDs of season 3 by Sharon Vuong, CBS's senior vice president of alternative programming.

Bowers was rapt by what he saw, including one of the friskiest male friendships of the series. He watched in awe as Kem and Chris shaved their initials into each other's pubes, kissed in challenges, and admired each other's penises, all while maintaining opposite-sex relationships that would get them to the finale. "This is the greatest reality show that's on," Bowers thought to himself.

Moonves trusted his young assistant's opinion on reality television. They would often discuss the network's other unscripted series, including *Big Brother*, which is still hosted by Moonves's wife, Julie Chen Moonves. Some viewers were already complaining *Big Brother* was too much of a time commitment at three weekly episodes; now Bowers would have to sell his boss on a show that would air six nights a week, including the aftershow. Fortuitously, CBS didn't have a dating series at the time. They were in the early years of their proto-Paramount+ streaming app, CBS All Access, and a highly bingeable, follow-along series with dozens of episodes a season looked like a perfect fit to Bowers.

At the beginning of July, Bowers made the same commitment to himself that Kem and Chris also seemed to have entered into as they investigated on camera whether the tips of their flaccid dicks could touch the bottom of a Solo cup. "I'm gonna be the most annoying person on the face of the earth," Bowers vowed.

Every day for a week, Bowers went into Moonves's office and tried to sell him on the show. To help his cause, he made sizzle reels of the most dramatic moments of the season, including the first-ever Casa. He also highlighted the show's popular music and the cultural relevance it implied; season 3 featured the then-chart-topping hits "Sign of the Times" by Harry Styles, "Green Light" by Lorde, and "Despacito" by Luis Fonsi and Daddy Yankee—the more expensive version, featuring Justin Bieber. The rightsholders, who were eager to have their music featured on a hit show, had to clear all of this.

At this point, the first three seasons of *Love Island UK* had begun streaming on Hulu. There was a distinct lack of marketing around its launch—Hulu's PR team had sent out an email announcing new programming in which *Love Island* was named, without further description, between *Jumanji: The Animated Series* and *Mobile Suit Gundam: The Origin*. But there was a word-of-mouth campaign happening around the show as American fans recruited others into their viewing pools.

Before Moonves left for the weekend, Bowers told the CEO he'd put a folder of *Love Island* materials in Moonves's bag and asked him to please (*please!*) read it if he had time. Moonves blew him off.

The next day, an article titled "*Love Island* Takes Hold of Britain" ran on page one of the weekend Arts section of *The New York Times*.[1] The piece noted both that *The Times* of London had called *Love Island* "a vile, sexist, apocalyptically tasteless, immoral, sick, vomitous abomination, made by morons for morons," and of sixteen-to-thirty-four-year-olds watching TV in Britain in that time slot, 40 percent were tuning into the show. Moonves sent Bowers an email:

> *Front page article, "New York Times," about "Love Island." Get the rights now. I mean it.*

Bowers told Vuong, who called the Business and Legal division while Bowers sent screeners to the horrified Standards and Practices department of the famously conservative broadcast network. ("They *sleep together*?" was an initial response.) Bowers, who is now an executive at the production company Blumhouse, did not get a producer credit, but he does want to say one thing: "You're welcome."

The *Love Island USA* creative team assembled. Executive producer Simon Thomas was a wonky genius who had worked on the original celebrity iteration and run the daily-airing *Big Brother Australia*, where he, like Cowles, met his wife working in production. Showrunner Ben Thursby-Palmer was a calmly authoritative Brit with a prodigious understanding of live spectacle. He came to *Love Island* after executive producing *The X Factor*, where he helped create the lineup of One Direction. Sharon Vuong was the visionary executive who had given Bowers the inciting DVDs and championed the show following Moonves's departure. The three had a mission to create a show for the US market that was so addictive that it justified a six-hour-a-week investment from viewers and the proportionate production cost to the network.

By the time Moonves stepped down, Americans had much less delayed access to *Love Island UK*, whose fourth season was airing in the US a few weeks after it ran in the UK. Its appeal for American viewers partially seemed to be a form of cultural tourism. Viewers found respite in watching Essex strivers and roofers from Wolverhampton reach emotional breakthroughs and, sometimes, a shared orgasm.

There was something about a UK dialect that gave US listeners fanny flutters, to use Maura's phrase. "You've heard an English accent," a fictional announcer said in a 2019 *Saturday Night Live* sketch selling *Love Island* to American audiences.[2] "You've heard an Irish accent. Now hear all the little weirdies in between."

American viewers—used to the internet-flattened lexicon of our own television programming—delighted in making sense of the mélange of local dialects through closed-captioning and context. UK Islanders seemed to keep the regionalisms distinct to their own speech—like "minging" (Scottish for stinky) or "cwtch" (Welsh for cuddle and pronounced "cudge"). In season 1, Hannah would rightly be annoyed with Jon for making her feel like "a right tit." While a unique piece of speech on most US dating shows is as rare as a rainy July day in Mallorca, being an American hearing another English-speaker say a common thing a different way has a quaint exoticism, no matter how banal the words are in the King's speech. "Can I pull you for a chat?" became a linguistic shape-shifter—the "aloha" of the Villa. It could mean someone is exploring a new connection or seeking reassurance, or expressing displeasure or a newfound apathy.

Phrases popularized on *Love Island*, sent back to the mainland, then streamed in America included Olivia Attwood's "dicksand," referencing her one-time paramour's ability to entrap her with his penis; "factor 50," the UK equivalent of SPF 50, which means to lay it on thick; and "putting your grafting boots on," or working overtime to get someone to couple up.

It was an element of the show that would be missed in a US version—along with the sex that was cut in deference to the puritanical CBS guidelines about what they could depict. Without the charming Britishisms and the R-rated parts, *Love Island USA* seemed like a wan facsimile. "When we launched in 2019, nobody wanted a USA version of *Love Island*," Thomas says. "And so we had to kind of prove it from the ground up."

Thomas had a clear vision of the show's mission: "It's really ridiculously good-looking people coming together for the summer of their lives to see if they can find love or fun and not hurt each other along the way," he says. "It's about appointment viewing. It's about eventized programming. It's about having a centralized conversation, a water cooler for the generation who never had that. Every episode has to have news, so it's about fear of missing out. That's the difference between *Love Island* and *The Bachelor*."

CBS would have loved to have a staid, no-surprises hit like *The Bachelor*. That show's chaste journey to heterosexual marriage—with a network-approved sexual detour at the Fantasy Suite episode—might have been a better fit for CBS, which as of 2024 had the oldest and largest audience in prime time, with an average age of 67.8. CBS believed it had purchased the premise of *Love Island*—ten or so people would date and compete to be America's favorite couple and a cash prize of $100,000—and that faithfully executing those basic mechanics would come with the success of its British forebear. "We live in a culture of fear around [the fact that] something may not work, so we have to do the simplest, most asinine version," Thomas says.

Doing it the basic way ignored why *Love Island* had really become IP valuable enough for the network to want to buy it and spend a relative fortune on its music licensing rights and wild production schedule. It wasn't just that they were following a formula; it was that the formula allowed the Islanders to go through an amusing and occasionally painful process that made them—and the audience—feel things. Islanders were young and excitable and mostly still had undeveloped prefrontal cortexes; they had the security of simulated solitude and a (perhaps naïve) trust that the faceless people comforting them in the Beach Hut were looking out for their best interests. Yes, the producers were putting them through hell, but they were also keeping them safe. The managed mayhem sustained *Love Island*.

So Thomas, Thursby-Palmer, and the team were left to figure out how to find a satisfying version of the show, for American viewers and broadcast standards. "They were very concerned about under-boob, or over-boob, or side-boob," Thursby-Palmer says of CBS. Bikini bottoms would be full coverage only; thongs were added to a list of contraband items that included alcohol and nonprescription drugs, which were confiscated from Islanders' suitcases on arrival. (Islanders were permitted two drinks a day during filming, furnished by production.) The women on the show tend to swap bikinis, so curvier women were forbidden from borrowing swimsuits that would be smaller on them. Producers would have to step in to police the Islanders' language, because there could be no swearing on CBS. The Islanders could not curse and be bleeped; that did not match *Love Island*'s established tone.

Thomas compared the show to the color green: If the way *Love Island UK* made viewers feel was "green," then he had to make *Love Island USA* be the exact same shade but with an entirely foreign set of base paints, in the form of the nationality and related personality and behavioral sets of the casts. "Americans don't banter the same way," Thomas says. "They don't date the same way. They don't have sex the same way. They don't float the same way." (I'd never noticed.)

The first ingredient of green was the host. They admittedly "didn't know exactly what they were looking for initially," casting director Gervais says. Should they go for someone who was an established presenter? A big name? Could that person be *too* famous and overshadow the dating material? Thursby-Palmer and the network executives went to lunch with Arielle Vandenberg, an actress who had guest starred on the ABC Family sorority sitcom *Greek* and one episode of *How I Met Your Mother* before gaining a following on the short-form video app Vine. "She did not take herself too seriously," Gervais says. "She was always super self-deprecating, and she was a 'yes, and' [girl]. She worked her ass off. She just genuinely wanted to do a great job." No one could say Vandenberg didn't try hard.

CBS's facility with casting reality series was used to great effect on *Big Brother* and *Survivor*. However, those were very pointedly game shows. Bowers says that although *Love Island* is obviously a competition, that's not why or how he tried to get it to American television. "I don't like in *Love Island* when they're trying to win," Bowers says. "I like it when they're there for real authentic purposes, and their emotions really show, and they can get hurt, and they can fall in love, and they can get a crush on somebody else and have that internal struggle." Finding existential pain on the daybeds would not be CBS's predominant concern that first season.

The executive triad and Gervais's team worked with CBS to find middle ground between the network method and the *Love Island* spirit. "I don't think that process was necessarily *Love Island* compatible," Thomas says of casting. "Even though we got some amazing Islanders, it was like, 'Okay, right. Like, we got through it.'" The Islanders approved by CBS were invested in what is referred to on dating shows as "the process"—as in, "trust the process, and you'll fall in love." It came from a fundamental misunderstanding of what they were there to do. They believed that their jobs were to be good Islanders: game and coachable personalities who needed to find someone to tolerate enough to sleep next to until the finale. So they strategized ways to achieve that, which, as Bowers noted, is the exact opposite of what actually makes good Islanders, who are at their best when they are entirely driven by emotion—or so in their heads they get worked up enough to become overridden by emotion. "When they turned up on season one," Thomas says, "we had to reteach them how to participate because they would immediately go, 'What's our connection?'"—a strained thought experiment that is normally encouraged and vocalized on dating shows. "They're playing a game instead of actually *looking* for connections."

"You have a tendency to be more sincere all the time, which is one of the things I adore about America," he continues. "You can sing 'Happy Birthday' in the office and everyone's, like, genuinely into it. Whereas in Australia, I'd rather die. So with an Islander, that is who they are as well."

The earnestness of the Islanders was meant to be offset by the humor of production. But instead of pointing out what was absurd about the show in a way that seemed confident, *USA* projected cautiousness—like they didn't want to screw up a costly show that people loved. The layer of comic broadness on top of the romance also seemed intended to compensate for the fact that the dating itself wasn't particularly compelling. The exquisitely beautiful Vandenberg was tasked with providing comedic relief, which tended to feel forced. The season began with her walking sexily out of the ocean, then "tripping" and crawling toward the camera, picking up wet sand, dropping it on herself, and shouting in a never-to-be-heard-again mid-Atlantic accent, "I'm still ready for love. Here come the Islanders!" Then she had to switch to being in charge, overseeing the dumpings with the solemnity of the rose ceremonies on *The Bachelor*. Unlike the delicious juxtapositions of the UK, it simply felt discordant.

The American brand of sincerity bled into the voice-over. Matthew Hoffman was the show's first narrator. Though the production team continues to extol his virtues, calling him "beloved," he was cast to approximate Iain's tongue-in-cheek barbs. Where Iain was tart, Hoffman was goofy and glib, using the jokey pitch modulations of a fake talk show host to let viewers know that the Islanders' doings were ridiculous. But by the end of the season, his character seemed to have bought into the pageantry of romance in a way Iain never would. "I'm not crying; I'm just covered in rain," he said, holding back what were intended to be humorously fake sobs after what was meant to be a moving conversation.

That fucking rain.

"Every day," Gervais says of the constant downpour and the vacuum of drama it created. "They were sitting around on the couch. They just cuddled." Once they found those connections—and many did on day one—they stayed together, dutifully pursuing their TV relationships.

But eventually, the rain wound up instigating the first moment on the show that was truly *Love Island*. Forced under a covering to escape the endless precipitation was Kyra Green, a twenty-two-year-old musician and openly bisexual woman. Kyra had started out as the most coveted Islander in the Villa but had found herself relegated to soon-to-be-dumped. Weston Richey, a twenty-five-year-old Texan photographer with whom Kyra seemed to be perturbed, pulled her for a chat to try to figure out why she was annoyed with him. She explained to a clearly befuddled man rarely seen without a cowboy hat why she had scolded him in front of the group: Though Kyra had never tried to get together with Weston—and had in fact focused her energy on other men and women the entire time—Weston had once told her he was attracted to her, so she accused him of not being genuine when he coupled up with someone else.

During the brief chat, Kyra says "at the end of the day" six times. It is a transcendently banal conversation in which the text ("at the end of the day, at the end of the day, at the end of the day") underlines a feeling Kyra has that's deeper than any of her romantic connections: the burn of rejection. For what might have been the first time in her adult life, Kyra was not seen as preternaturally desirable compared to her peers. *Love Island* had shifted what had previously been an unshakable self-identification and stumbled into comic profundity.

The scene also embodies what Charli xcx told me, during an interview for *Vanity Fair*, is the reason she watches *Love Island*: "It's fascinating watching humans be mundane but also really entertaining."

That tension—something prosaic or silly culminating in something hilarious and transfixing—achieved what poor Vandenberg and her pratfalls could not. "That was great," Thomas says of that scene. "People would quite happily shit on the first season now, but that's how we knew we had a show."

Summer 2020 was an inauspicious time to film a series with a shuffling cast. During an international pandemic, how could you crack on from six feet apart? In the face of what seemed like an impossible production to mount, the UK team canceled its summer season. "God, how do we do a show about kissing each other?" Thursby-Palmer asked.

Thomas had what he would later consider the greatest idea of his career: *Love Island USA* would take place in The Cromwell hotel in Las Vegas, and the Villa would be built in the rooftop pool club. When they arrived, Thursby-Palmer says, "It was like a movie set. The casinos still smelt like casinos, but everything was empty. The [entrances] were boarded up because they had no doors to put on them, because Vegas never sleeps." The crew of hundreds would live in The Cromwell's empty guest rooms, leaving their rooms to go to work in hazmat suits. Thursby-Palmer took over a two-floor suite that became the command center. When he moved into the room, which hadn't been used since the city had undergone a mandatory shutdown in March, a dead bat fell out of the ceiling onto his head. Thursby-Palmer barely acknowledged it. "What do you mean you just got on with it?" Thomas asked him. "That's all I would think about for the rest of my life." But they had a show to make.

CBS was eager to have a series that could be produced during a time when almost nothing was filming. They were cognizant of the tepid reception to the first season, but also that it had something that could grow as reliably as an erection during the Heart Rate Challenge. The network gave the *Love Island USA* team more freedom to cast outside the CBS framework. At this point, Thomas says, they understood they were "a network that didn't have a natural fit for the show." It was over-indexing with Black viewers, which meant that more Black people were watching the show than other CBS programming, and posting about it on what is colloquially referred to as "Black Twitter." Casting shifted to reflect the viewing demographics, and ITV America's process moved away from the clinical CBS mold and more toward "touchy-feely," Thomas says. In interviewing possible cast members, he says, they sought to understand "who you are as people when you're not trying to prove who you are on television."

Because COVID made in-person casting impossible, the pool of potential Islanders grew hugely, as did the number of people who were willing to go on a not-particularly-successful show. During the pandemic, many twentysomethings were stuck inside working from home or moving back in with parents. Official guidance at the time was to avoid strangers and stay in your quarantine pod, but even the hookups that were happening became more remote: The New York City Department of Health released a manual that recommended wearing a mask during sex, or simply not kissing while you thrusted.

In the final stage of casting, the new Islanders had to isolate for three weeks. While they typically have chaperones available before they go into the Villa, the season 2 cast's only interactions with another human were with the nurse who came by three times a day to test them for COVID. Food was left outside their closed doors. They had no phones but were each given a Roku with Netflix, where they could use the in-app messaging service to send plaintive little updates to their families on shared accounts. They were also allowed to draw in coloring books.

The general seclusion of the pandemic, followed by the intense period of aloneness before entering the Villa, built up a pressure only people who have spent weeks in a Villa where they can't masturbate understood. (Remember, there are cameras in the showers.) "Everyone was little horndogs on my season the second we were released to one another," cast member Cely Vazquez says. "We hadn't seen humans, and then we were allowed to."

Eager to avoid the chaste indoor nestling of season 1, producers had intentionally chosen a location where it would not rain. But filming began in August, when the average high in Las Vegas was 105 degrees. During mock week, where the production setup was worked out with the almost-Islanders whose names would never reach the hallowed web pages of *Us Weekly*, the temperature on the mostly unshaded roof was 110 degrees. While filming the practice initial coupling ceremony, female Islanders' shoes began melting into the plastic turf. When they did the real coupling a few days later, the women stood in the pool to avoid their footwear liquefying and burning their feet.

Not that that solved the problem of the heat itself. "Bitches was passing out left and right," Cely says. "I started seeing white, so they sat us down. Then I look over to my left once I came back to life, and Moira [Tumas] was on the floor, fully passed out." Medics were brought in, and oxygen was administered. These were the first rivulets in a season of visible, torrential sweat.

After multiple faintings, production gave the women an hour inside to cool off. Cely used it to cry. "I fully convinced myself that I was like the DUFF pick," she said, using the acronym for "designated ugly fat friend." The beautiful twenty-four-year-old looked in the mirror as she reapplied her makeup through tears and told herself, "They picked me as a joke. I'm a prank." When Cely went back out to stand in the pool with the other women, she thought, "Damn, I should have got a boob job before this." Her dysmorphia abated somewhat after three of the five men stepped forward for her. She coupled with Johnny Middlebrooks, a twenty-two-year-old student and head-turner of astounding hotness.

Production nightmares continued. A mentally disturbed person started scaling the hotel, and one of the crew members had to go outside and intercept them before they reached the Villa, which would have brought production to a stop. For his trouble, the crew member was deemed unclean and banned from the hotel until he was safely COVID-free. "I didn't need to have *Love Island* dreams because I'm being woken at four o'clock in the morning on a phone call where I'm having *Love Island* reality," Thomas says of the era.

The Islanders were basically unaware of production's issues with bat carcasses and attempted break-ins as they had a summer that felt more real than the weirdness of the pandemic they'd mentally left behind. Being filmed while falling into the *Love Island* lull of "forgetting the camera" was more natural than seeing themselves in Zoom screen squares. The normal rhythm of a *Love Island* season emerged as Islanders became jealous and either drove their partners away or realized the intensity of their devotion. There were love triangles and challenges and bombshells. There was even a Casa Amor, filmed down the road at the Rio. The background images of the Las Vegas Strip and LED billboards seemed like they should have pointed to the falseness in a way that was distracting. Instead, it functioned like Iain and Caroline did in the UK; as an incursion of the outside that showed production could manipulate the interplay between the manufactured and the reality in a way that let Islanders and viewers relax into feeling things.

Cely and twenty-seven-year-old billing coordinator/go-go dancer Justine Ndiba became the Villa's best friends, supporting each other in the weeks before Justine and Caleb Corprew's victory. Cely was anointed production's queen of the yes girls, conducting sweetly annoying jokes like banging on a pot to wake everyone up one morning before the lights flipped on and weeping her way to forgiveness after Johnny hooked up with someone else at Casa.

Cely and Johnny were the runners-up of the season, which typically confers a level of public acceptance of the pairing. But when they emerged on the outside, the difference in reaction to them among the small but focused fandom was stark. It would lead to a nasty breakup centered on The Cheesecake Factory.

After their season, Cely received more sponsorship opportunities than Johnny, though he was cast on MTV's competition series *The Challenge*, which she says prompted him to give a speech at a Christmas gathering to mark the honor. "They only call the most elite humans," Cely remembers him telling her family. (Cely had also been contacted by *The Challenge* team.) Because of her brand deals—she had gotten $10,000 for a post—Cely began paying for more of their shared life, including the cost of an entire vacation to Hawaii. But when they went to The Cheesecake Factory after arriving, Johnny committed a sin more egregious than cheating at Casa Amor: He wanted to split the bill for her $13 nachos. (Johnny denies this.) Cely was done. She was crying over the breakup when a lone fan spotted her. "Oh my god!" they said. "Cely!"

Cely had achieved a level of fame equivalent to caring about the cost of an appetizer-sized portion of tortilla chips at a chain restaurant. As the year's breakout star and runner-up, Cely was making the kind of money UK Islanders had been three seasons earlier—even minor season 5 players were getting twice that now. *Love Island USA* was still playing catch-up.

8

The Flack

THE BEST TV HOSTS represent the core quality of their show. Alex Trebek was knowledge incarnate. Jeff Probst is grinding, greasy strategy. Andy Cohen is gossip.

Caroline Flack embodied the quest for romantic love. If she never managed to find the genuine article in her personal life, on *Love Island* Caroline earned the adoration of the audience. She'd achieved it by demonstrating her care for the Islanders, permeating what could have just been a paycheck job with curiosity and empathy.

"Caroline, for me, is the blueprint," says *Love Island USA* host Ariana Madix.

"Caroline fucking loved it," Spencer-Hayter says of *Love Island*. "I'd send her the story notes every morning—she wanted them every single day."

"She was so invested in the people on that show," Caroline's colleague told me in 2021.[1] "She lived it with them. I'd go to her dressing room, and she'd be crying because she was so invested. She was so inspirational for all those people, and they loved her. She became like their auntie—their favorite, fucking cool, sexy auntie."

Caroline was human glitter, messy but sparkling. When Islanders came on *Aftersun*, Caroline could be found before the show singing in her dressing room with a karaoke machine, exuberantly enough to be heard from the hallway. Amy Hart remembers Caroline's rendition of "A Whole New World" from *Aladdin*, in which she took on both vocal parts.

Caroline was not just supportive of the cast—she marveled at them. "When I suddenly see them come out of the greenroom, it's like meeting the most famous person in the world," she told her colleague. "She loved the contestants," Caroline's mother, Christine, affirmed. When Christine questioned their actions or motives, Caroline backed them. "Mum, they're all there for a reason," she'd say.[2]

Caroline formed true friendships with some of the Islanders, based on trust, respect, and a camaraderie that came from also knowing the intimate pressures of public life. "I had an incredibly close relationship with Caroline," Olivia Attwood told me. After her relationship with Chris Hughes ended, Caroline warned Olivia, "Look, people are gonna say shit about you online. They're probably going to take Chris's side over you because the public is generally kinder to men than they are to women. You know who you are—you just have to ride the wave. Don't take that water on board. You need to just enjoy this, because people who are hating are not worth your time."

Caroline would not be able to follow her own advice. "This girl is half woman, half phone," her colleague said. "I mean, there is no way she's not going to look at it, because it's human nature."

There was a sharp delineation between Caroline the presenter, who could settle even the tensest moments with her warm command, and the Caroline who was pestled to dust by the press: for dating the younger Harry Styles, for growing up working-class, for ending her 2018 engagement after three months. "The viewers also saw Caroline's endless terrible choices in boyfriends and things falling apart," her colleague said. Yet "she could be [living] in an absolute nightmare, then she turned up for work and everything was fine."

Caroline also had private mental health issues that included untreated bipolar disorder. In 2021 Channel 4 released a documentary about her, with her family's participation. In it Christine shares that Caroline attempted suicide at age sixteen. "Nobody knew about that," her colleague said. "Not us, her friends, nobody."

"She'd have her highs and lows, and you always worry about that," Christine told me of her daughter in an interview for *Vanity Fair*. "I don't think Carrie had that brain that [went], 'Oh, if I take this pill, I'll feel better. Get me through the day.' It was, 'Oh, I'm going to take lots of pills, and then I won't feel like it anymore.' It was just 'cut out all feelings.' And it does. If only we could say [to her] that it does pass, and everything does pass."

As detailed in the Disney+ docuseries *Caroline Flack: Search for the Truth*, on December 12, 2019, Caroline's boyfriend, professional tennis player Lewis Burton, called emergency services, saying the five-foot-four host was coming after him physically.[3] After a night of drinking separately, Flack had seen messages on Burton's phone from another woman and hit Burton on the head. When the Metropolitan Police showed up, the bed was drenched in blood, and Caroline was intoxicated, half naked, and in the middle of a mental health episode. It wasn't Burton's blood; after he made the call, Caroline picked up a broken piece of glass and cut her arms to the muscle. A small mark on Burton's head was deemed not to require medical care, but Caroline was sent to the hospital for twelve hours, where she was told she'd need reconstructive plastic surgery.

Because he'd been asleep at the time, the six-foot-four Burton wasn't sure what she'd smacked him with—a lamp? A fan?—but Caroline repeatedly took responsibility for the incident and maintained she'd hit him with her cell. Burton, who has not spoken publicly about Caroline since a 2020 Instagram post, relayed many times that he did not wish to pursue charges, and the Crown Prosecution Service agreed. But then a Met detective inspector who wasn't present on the scene filed an appeal, citing the significance of Burton's injuries and Caroline's lack of accountability. Neither fact was accurate. CPS relented, agreeing to move forward with the domestic abuse case.

"I never hurt anyone in my life," a sobbing Caroline says in a video she recorded on her phone in the middle of the ordeal. "The only person I ever hurt was myself."

The public would not wait to hear from Caroline before rendering their verdict. Burton sent a shocking photo of the ruined bed to a friend, who subsequently sold it to *The Sun*, according to the documentary. The paper published it on the front page, and it was broadly assumed that because Caroline was the aggressor, the blood was Burton's.[4] In *Caroline Flack: Search for the Truth*, Caroline's older sister Lizzie says even she initially believed the tabloids' macabre framing of the case, including the police testimony that Caroline's assault on Burton made the room look like a "horror movie." Caroline's mental health decline made her recede, which was encouraged by her representatives. Her silence seemed like an admission.

Caroline was supposed to start filming *Love Island*'s first winter season, which would begin production in Cape Town in a few weeks. Within forty-eight hours of the arrest, it was clear that wasn't going to happen. Caroline wasn't doing well, and *Love Island* couldn't have someone who might be going to trial for domestic assault hosting their dating show. The decision was framed as a temporary one that Caroline made, but it was ITV's choice. Laura Whitmore, who is married to Iain Stirling and was close with Caroline, took the job at the last minute and stepped in to host season 6. Though ITV said they would continue to monitor the situation and see if Caroline could come back, she made it clear to her friends and family that she felt like she'd been fired.

Caroline was panicked about *Love Island* going on without her and conflicted about how to engage with the program as it continued.

"*Love Island* was a massive thing for Caroline," her friend says in the doc. "Laura"—younger, taller, coupled—"taking over brought up every single insecurity." Caroline initially barred her friends from viewing the program, then had them watch it with her, becoming fixated on the audience size. "You take somebody who has that fragility and those issues," Caroline's colleague told me. "You can see all the triggers, and it was almost like a horrible, perfect-imperfect storm of events."

Caroline's emotional state degraded as the season aired and the case pushed forward. On Valentine's Day, *The Sun* published a holiday card with a drawing of Caroline that said, "I'll fucking lamp you," referring to the alleged weapon.[5] That night Caroline took so many pills she couldn't communicate. When her friends called the paramedics, she refused to go with them. "We were more scared of her going to hospital because of what the press would do than getting her life saved," Caroline's friend says in the doc. Caroline also forbid them from telling her mother what had happened.

A week before the finale of season 6 and two weeks before her trial was set to begin, Caroline's twin sister, Jody, came to the apartment where Caroline had been hiding from the press. The door was locked, and her dog Ruby was barking. When the super opened the door and let Jody in, she found Caroline. She tried to revive her, but as Christine says, "She couldn't do anything." Caroline died by suicide on February 15, 2020. She was forty years old.

At the behest of Cowles and the network, the Islanders of *UK* season 6 were gathered into a room and sat down by the production's psychologist. "I need to talk to you about something very serious that's happened on the outside world," the therapist said. It would have had to be very serious indeed for production to temporarily shut down. "There's the live final next week, and there are going to be people who might shout things out," the psych told them. "So I'm just having to tell you now so you guys don't get caught offside." She said there had been a tragedy.

As soon as she said the word "Caroline," cast member Jess Gale says, "I feel like everyone already knew." The Islanders looked at each other with the sudden understanding that the unthinkable had become real.

"It was such a horrific time," Spencer-Hayter says. They canceled filming for the rest of the day, as well as the airing of that evening's episode. The cast heard from producers that the end of the series might be scrapped entirely.

As the news spread, a stunned grief reverberated across the UK and US. "It was only a matter of time before the media and a prolonged social media dogpile—hers lasted for MONTHS—pushed someone completely over the edge," actor and presenter Jameela Jamil posted. Boy George, Kelly Osbourne, and James Blake offered tributes, and Islanders expressed their sorrow, including Amber, Amy, and a "heart-broken" Molly-Mae.

"Today my friend wandered into heaven," wrote Iain before referencing the Villa entrance of the woman he always introduced as "The Flack." "I bet it was in slow motion and sassy as fuck."

A few years later, Prince Harry eulogized Caroline in *Spare*, saying how funny and sweet she was and ruing that the press mistreatment that came from her dating him wasn't worth it. "Goodbye and good luck," he wrote.[6]

Days before her death, Caroline had drafted an Instagram post that she never sent, which her family released after her passing in the local newspaper where Christine had worked for thirty years. "Within 24 hours my whole world and future was swept from under my feet, and all the walls that I had taken so long to build around me collapsed," Caroline wrote. "I am suddenly on a different kind of stage, and everyone is watching it happen . . . I've lost my job. My home. My ability to speak. And the truth has been taken out of my hands and used as entertainment."

Her words attempted to explain the cost of fame, and how the kind of attention that once seemed desirable had been perverted into a public obsession to frame her as something vile. Caroline had articulated what it felt like to be heeled—turned from a real person to an antagonist in their own life, in a portrayal that was being controlled by others.

Love Island did not kill Caroline. As it had with Mike and Sophie, the celebrity she achieved from it contributed to the decline of her mental health. At the inquest for Caroline's suicide, the coroner ruled, "For some, it seems she had a charmed life, but the more famous she got, the more mentally distressed she became. Her trauma was played out in the national press, and that was incredibly distressing for her."[7]

Many notes on the police documents about the events of December 12 and what followed flagged that Caroline was a public figure and that there would likely be "significant media interest" in her. These notes suggest internal pressure to pursue a domestic violence case, despite Burton's stance and the lack of evidence for a charge that severe. Nazir Afzal, a former prosecutor for the Crown Prosecution Service who was not directly involved in the case, had publicly commended the decision to pursue charges at the time. He recanted those remarks in 2025 after reviewing the case files Christine collected over the five years since her daughter's death. "My take on it is that Caroline would still be with us if certain decisions weren't taken back in that month or two," Afzal tells Christine in the documentary.

A week before Caroline passed, she texted Spencer-Hayter to wish him a happy birthday. "It's not the same without you," he wrote back.

It couldn't be. Caroline had set a standard for hosting that elevated a dating series to something humanistic. *Love Island* now had to compensate for the loss of that depth without letting the life-and-death stakes of being human interfere with a show that was supposed to be fun. Season 6 endeavored to find freedom within that restraint, and it still had its moments—it gave the audience Callum, Molly, and Shaughna, and the more straightforward love stories of winners Paige and Finley Tapp, and Luke Trotman and Siânnise Fudge. It also lost more than 20 percent of viewers from season 5. They would have to find a new way to create what fans now took for granted.

9 Knackered

MIKE SPENCER-HAYTER WAS PISSED. "THIS ISN'T FRIEND ISLAND," he yelled at the cast of *UK* season 7, who were, frankly, barely acting as if it were Friend Island. "THIS IS *LOVE ISLAND*. YOU ARE NOT HERE FOR A FREE HOLIDAY. YOU ARE HERE TO MAKE A TV SHOW. NONE OF YOU ARE GETTING TO KNOW EACH OTHER. YOU NEED TO MAKE AN EFFORT. IF NOT, WE'LL GET YOU ALL OUT. WE'LL GET ANOTHER CASTING."

It was the first UK season after Caroline had died and the first after COVID restrictions lifted, and the mood was just off in the Villa. They were a few days into filming, and the Islanders seemed to be in suspended animation. They were lounging laconically. Waiting for better options. Not cracking on. As Thomas says, "There's two kinds of casts in *Love Island*. There's the cast who gets up in the morning like, 'Holy fuck, we're gonna get going.' Then there's the kind of cast that you have to get up in the morning and go, 'Go and talk to somebody.'"

This season was the latter. As a host, the lovely and professional Laura still seemed to be getting used to the more impromptu elements of the job, like the chatty back-and-forth and smooth transitions required to keep *Aftersun* buoyant but also close to trenchant, as former Islanders and the loved ones of people in the Villa critiqued the moves people were making and debated the viability of the attachments forming. Laura was also solidifying her role as something beyond "not Caroline." In her first year, some of the Islanders—and many of the viewers—didn't know who she was at the beginning of the season. By season 7, Laura kept things moving. If it felt effortful compared to previous iterations, a record-high hundred thousand people had applied to be on the season, and viewership had ticked back up to more than four million average weekly viewers.

The season 7 Islanders seemed to believe that after the show they would automatically become as rich and famous as their recent predecessors, and that it was better to play a safe game where they didn't do anything that could cause them to lose reputational points with the audience. This would not work. Thankfully, Spencer-Hayter was there to poke the season 7 cast with his pitchfork to make the television show he'd promised viewers.

When the creative director told the Islanders to get their asses up and work, Faye Winter, then a twenty-six-year-old property manager and now a philanthropist and horse girl, says the attitude among the group changed. "Okay. Like, shit," she remembers thinking. "So sorry, Dad, we'll do better."

And they did. A few days later, a game was sprung onto the group that producers thought could spark something—anything!—between Islanders that hadn't yet ignited on its own. In it couples had to match each other's answers to questions like "What's your partner's favorite sex position?" or "Which Islander would your partner couple up with if it wasn't you?" The challenge had a dual purpose. The first was to encourage slow-developing pairs to bond before the challenge by sharing personal information to prep for the game. The second was the activity was meant to be light and titillating.

The result was instead a new kind of classic, fan dispute–prompting *Love Island* quandary. The scene would make explicit the expectations female Islanders felt about how they needed to look in the Villa and on the outside and how they were judged for attempting to live up to the standards—standards they would also be punished for not meeting. Hugo Hammond, a twenty-four-year-old gym teacher who functioned as the season's outsider, responded to a question about his biggest turn-offs with the word "fake." He doubled down by answering a different question the same way, saying his ideal mate would be a "leggy blonde, not fake."

Faye, whom Hugo had previously approached as a possible connection but wasn't coupled with, saw the comment as being directed at her—she was blonde and leggy, and as she had revealed minutes earlier in the game, she had filler, Botox, and, courtesy of her parents, "a boob job for my eighteenth birthday." She took double umbrage at the comment, interpreting Hugo's first statement to mean not only was he saying her cosmetic work was bad, but that he was extending his assessment of her "fakeness" to her honor. "Ironically, [this] has left several Islanders looking genuinely furious," Iain said as the women—who nearly all admitted to having work done—became incensed. The boys explained to Hugo what seemed obvious to most others: These women had gotten cosmetic intervention because they didn't feel good about themselves, and now Hugo was saying their new incarnations were also wrong.

Hugo was dismayed to learn his words had harmed; he thought a game was just a game. He weepily apologized to Faye and to Sharon Gaffka, a twenty-five-year-old civil servant who also had a breast augmentation. The women pushed back, claiming that because he'd cracked on with Faye and was now disrespecting her, maybe *Hugo* was the fake one. After many more tears and sorries from Hugo, they all hugged it out in a perfect encapsulation of the hills and valleys of conflict and resolution an Islander must travel over a fifty-plus-episode season. An argument about plastic surgery and integrity: *This* was *Love Island.* It also offered another fresh avenue of drama to pursue in an era when Islanders might be focused on proceeding with caution romantically: the group dynamic and how it reflected the large audience's higher expectation for correct behavior, and the growing online space in which they could discuss such things. The boors of season 1 would never have apologized for implying they didn't like injectables or implants. The season was locked in on a new path.

Toby Aromolaran needed little prodding to make the most of his *Love Island* journey. The year before Toby entered the Villa, the twenty-one-year-old had graduated from college during the pandemic and was a semiprofessional footballer. This meant they paid him to play but not enough to live on; that was covered by his 10:00 p.m. to 8:00 a.m. night shift at an Amazon warehouse.

"I was just like, 'This summer is the worst summer ever,'" Toby says. "'I need to change my summer—next summer's gonna be the best summer ever.' And what's the best summer you can really have? It's *Love Island.*"

When he got to the Villa in 2021, Toby was the cheekiest of chappies, happy to share how many women he'd slept with and that he'd once had sex in a parking lot. "I wasn't even worried about no exes coming out of the *Mirror* because I had none," he says. Toby had not only "never fallen into a relationship"—though he did want one that met his "high standards"—he didn't understand why others seemed to have such issues with theirs. "I was like, 'Relationships are easy. If something don't go right, then just leave them. Find someone else.' I used to think leaving a relationship was honestly the easiest thing on Earth."

Toby's entrance into the Villa was the pinnacle of his existence. "They build you up so mad that you're buzzing," he says. "They'll be like, 'What would you do when you talk to the girls? How would you feel if you found your first relationship? What would you do on the nights in the Villa? What would you do in the games?' The way they're talking to you, you're thinking, 'Oh my god, get me in there now. I'm ready to go.'" When Toby's enthusiasm flagged as he waited hours and hours to walk into the Villa, producers whipped him back up. "Oh, the girls are really good," they told Toby. "They're tight."

They weren't lying. Toby flitted from tight woman to tight woman like a pollen-drunk bee, coupling with twenty-six-year-old fashion blogger and Villa darling Kaz Kamwi, then scratchy-voiced twenty-five-year-old yes girl Chloe Burrows, whom he twice mugged off before switching to twenty-seven-year-old tattoo artist Abi Rawlings, whom he swapped for twenty-two-year-old Mary Bedford at Casa before realizing, no, he actually wanted to be with Chloe.

Toby was doing what he was supposed to: exploring connections, honoring his impulses, being himself. He has heard other Islanders accuse producers of instructing them to do things—to go after one person or have a conversation for the sake of pushing a story—but that was never his experience. "I feel like the producers have always just been so natural," he says. "They've just been like, 'Toby, what are you feeling like?'" And then he'd follow his desires without any pressure or expectation.

The problem with this freedom, however, was there were women on the other end of his actions who had their own feelings about his behavior. "I'd never been in a situation where I'm chatting to a girl, and then if I wanted to chat to another girl, I would have to do that in front of the first girl," Toby says. Plus, he'd always been under the impression that connection was not possible without reciprocation, the way a light bulb can't turn on if both sides of the current aren't flowing. Ergo, in Toby's mind, if he wasn't into a woman, she *couldn't* be into him.

Toby was disabused of this misunderstanding when he saw the emotional fallout his actions caused. *Love Island* had done with Toby what OpenAI has not yet been able to do with ChatGPT: created sentience.

"In real life, you can get away with not really self-reflecting, because you can do your actions and no one really knows," Toby says. "But in the *Love Island* TV world, you have to sit with them and, for your own conscience, be happy with what you've done; or, if you're not happy with it and regret it, then you have to learn from them at least."

The first time Toby was up for a public vote, he was among the least popular, which left him balky. "I'm just being myself, and I'm at the bottom," he thought. "How can being myself be bad?" Producers and the on-set therapist told him not to try to "fix it" by ceasing to go with his own instincts, unpopular as they were with viewers. They told Toby that the way he would get in trouble—not "in the bottom once" trouble but the life-ruining trouble he'd seen befall previous Islanders—was if he acted in a way that was meant to please others, which (a) wouldn't and (b) would leave him sitting across from someone he didn't actually want to be with, whom he now understood had their own rich interior life that didn't necessarily mirror his. Toby could hurt someone, or public opinion could turn in a way that would hurt him.

"I'm not good with empathy," Toby told me, demonstrating his nascent self-awareness. During the time at the Villa, though, Toby learned enough that he was able to have his first serious relationship. He had tired himself out enough that he could concentrate on Chloe, who reciprocated his feelings; they would have such a vigorous hookup in the Villa that they broke the bed. But sweetness developed alongside the lust; in what counted to him as a show of maturity, Toby made Chloe a "cringe-y" breakfast picnic to demonstrate he deserved to be freed from the doghouse he'd built for himself. "You've gone all soft since you come back from Casa Amor," Chloe said, hugging him.

Maturing (as much as one can in two months) allowed Toby to experience love, and that growth was rewarded with votes. The public chose Toby and Chloe as the Villa's funniest couple and the season's runners-up. The pair dated for a year after filming.

If Toby came in hot and clueless, Faye was cold and gimlet-eyed. "Straightaway, I was gonna be the character that was going to be the bitch," Faye says. She walked into the Villa with a closed-off dominance that she broadcast physically in everything from her work-wear-inspired evening looks to her don't-kiss-me matte lips. One of the most memorable images of the season was Faye filing her nails on the terrace as all the other women neared Blanket Jackson–levels of danger on the balcony, craning off it at precarious angles to get a peek at a new bombshell. "I don't mind that at all because I didn't ever really want my soft side being shown," Faye says of her portrayal. "I was like, 'I don't know these people. I'm not gonna let them in. You can't hurt me if I don't give you all of me.'"

Part of her initial coiling was that Faye was not attracted to any of the men, something she complained to producers about early in the season. Faye told them the most important criteria in a mate were that he was "tall, dark, and handsome," and to clarify exactly where she landed on the height issue, she said he needed to be "taller than her." Toby, with his vulpine teeth and incredible abs, almost worked, but Faye deemed him too short—the outfits she'd picked for the show didn't work without heels.

Financial consultant Teddy Soares ticked all of those boxes. But to Faye, the twenty-six-year-old was initially not the one. She says he was "tactile" in his flirtation, which Faye (but not the audience) read as "sleazy," and that he was very calm, which she correctly assessed was ill-suited to her temper. As she said in her intro video, she wanted a man "who can literally rip me a new arsehole." Teddy was more the type to ask Faye about *why* she felt she needed someone to be unkind to her. But, Faye thought, "Maybe I've been looking in the wrong place for what I need. Maybe these producers knew what I needed more than *I* know." Faye saw what *Love Island* had done for others and told herself to go with it. Viewers loved the interplay of opposition—Faye was the storm, and Teddy was the mountain who could withstand the tempest.

Faye started being vulnerable with Teddy and more forthcoming with the women; as Faye had with most people, she had inured herself to closeness with them through humor. During one of the morning check-ins that the Islanders typically hold to discuss the previous night's sexual exploits, Faye told the girls she had to take off her bracelets so the hand job she gave Teddy wouldn't jingle. (Most seasons have a secret code for sex; season 7's hand stuff was called an "NVQ1," in reference to the levels of National Vocational Qualification people in the UK can receive for trade certifications.) Faye had been worried coming into the Villa that the kind of women who would go on *Love Island*—models, influencers, and, obviously, expectant reality stars—would not like her. As she thawed, Faye became even more liked within the Villa and, attendantly, outside of it. It was a plot anybody could root for.

Though the Islanders had woken up, the season still felt tentative. Some of the most delectably provocative challenges were excised in what seemed to be an unspoken part of the Duty of Care. The headline and Twitter challenges both disappeared after season 5, when the potential for a cataclysmic event was both obvious because it had already happened and more possible as the fan base grew larger and more frenzied. Some previous games captured the spirit without bringing in the specter of public humiliation, like season 2's "Mugged Off," in which Islanders heard mostly unkind quotes from their castmates and had to pick who each was about by throwing a cup of tea in their face, after which the muggy person revealed themself. But even that type of confrontation was studiously avoided in season 7.

That year, challenges became goofier and more geared toward entertainment value. This was partly to lift the mood on a Caroline-less season during an ongoing pandemic, but it was also an indicator that the show's novelty had waned. "I felt the challenges were more artificial than they had been and that they felt like they had less connection to the stories," says Tom Gould, who is now director of entertainment and formats. "They shouldn't just be a bit of fun . . . They need to have an environment or context within which some of the relationship dynamics that you are seeing in the Villa can be poked and prodded at. And then there needs to be fallout."

None of this seemed intentionally present in most of the season's games, which strove to be dumb in a delightful way but were mostly dumb in a way that made you want to fast-forward to *Love Island*'s more salient content. "Playing the Field" featured the men presented like football players, trying to shield the women (in cheerleader costumes, obviously) from getting squirted with ketchup and mustard, then kissing until a bell was rung. In "Cat-titude" the men dressed like mice, and the women went through a feline-themed obstacle course in which they crawled through a pet flap and got into a big bowl of milk, then performed the classic cat activity of doing a pole dance on a giant scratching post. Even the matching challenge at the beginning had only appeared to spark conflict accidentally—*Newlywed Game*–style contests typically get a rise out of established partners feeling misunderstood by each other, not inspire the type of gendered discourse Hugo's gaffe did.

The exception to these anodyne games would be the most momentous challenge introduction since Casa Amor: the first "Movie Night." The mood going into Movie Night was ebullient. "What fun!" the Islanders seemed to tentatively think when they got the text informing them it was happening. They would finally get to watch the show they were on. It could be a balm after Casa, which had shredded Faye's nerves to bits. Production had sent one of their famous misleading postcards over, featuring a photo of Teddy making out with someone. The image was clearly taken at night, while the women had done their Casa game during the day. Because challenges are typically filmed simultaneously at the two Villas, Faye made the reasonable assumption that Teddy was kissing outside of a challenge. Unless the directive is something like "snog the Islander not in your couple who you're most attracted to," kissing during a challenge is basically a clinical intimacy, like a Pap smear. Kissing *outside* of a challenge is usually considered a barely sub-death-penalty offense.

It was all a producorial sleight of hand: Rather than seducing other women, Teddy had actually been so loyal to Faye that he slept outside. Faye had done the same until she received the postcard, at which point she unraveled while trying to seem entirely jaded. "Honestly, I'm fine," Faye told Kaz. "I was expecting it, so don't worry about me," she insisted, which could have been engraved on her tombstone. Though the postcard episode did show Faye crying over her friends' upset, it did not include the footage of Faye weeping over what she assumed was a betrayal from her own partner. "It just cut to me being angry," she says.

Which, to be fair, is the point Faye preferred to be aired instead of her being outwardly vulnerable. As Faye lay on the ground in despair off camera, senior producer Coco Jackson did her part to goad Faye into doing something more proactive than being sad and supine. "If he's doing that over in the other Villa, Faye, don't you think you should at least give these lads a chance to get to know them?" Faye says Jackson asked.

Faye got up and said, "Do you know what? Yeah. Fuck it. Why not? I'm not gonna let him know he's fucking hurt me." ("She was doing her job," Faye says of Jackson, whom she calls "such a love.")

Faye revenge-recoupled with another Islander, only to find out that Teddy had come back from Casa single. After realizing she'd been rampaging for naught, Faye ceded her rage, snuggling into Teddy's chest like a little girl, and sobbing after he said, "You're not the only one who let your guard down, Faye."

A few days later, Movie Night premiered.

From the producers' standpoint, the whole point of Movie Night had been to expose Liam Reardon, a twenty-one-year-old Welsh bricklayer with the personality of his work material. When he returned from

Casa alone, he did not disclose to darling twenty-four-year-old fashion buyer Millie Court the full extent of his Casa escapades, which included sharing a bed with another woman, snogging recreationally, and making out with more than one woman at the same time. Liam and Millie resumed their relationship as if nothing had happened. Producers were not going to let Liam's elision rob them of what could be the biggest drama of a season waiting for it.

Though Spencer-Hayter says the audience feedback was that they wanted to protect sweet Millie from the information, he couldn't let that happen because "selfishly, as a producer, it's going to play out outside"—as in, when Millie eventually did find out about Liam's indiscretions the second she left the Villa and got her phone back, the resulting fight would happen privately and be relayed ex post facto by the parties via some non–*Love Island* outlet and be dissected by fans off-season. Because Millie was so popular, voters would presumably stick by her until then, dragging Liam along to the finale as ballast. "It almost felt like she might go on to win the show on false pretenses if she doesn't know," Spencer-Hayter says. "So we were just like, 'Let's air it and call it Movie Night.'"

Movie Night allowed the couples to watch footage of each other and see exactly what happened behind their backs. Millie bore the news that Liam had partaken in a three-way kiss with typical grace, chewing her fake nails and saying, "It wasn't nice to see." Liam's defense was that Millie hadn't specifically asked him if he'd kissed two other people at once, the kind of sex act that only happens in the Villa and at eighth grade parties in finished basements.

Caught up in this extravaganza of truth-telling was Teddy, who was shown in a clip admitting he found another Islander attractive. Faye made a very Faye face—massive lips pinching together, eyes widening to express fake shock. After initially reacting only to the fact that Teddy hadn't mentioned the moment and had told her he hadn't had a connection with anyone, she started aping his kindly self-presentation.

"Mr. Nice Guy," she said in a mocking voice, laughing mirthlessly. "Uncle Ted. Get your sandals on and fuck off."

As the rest of the Movie Night clips played, Faye began to feel stupid for allowing Teddy to hold even her tentative trust. The version of herself who had started on day one and had anticipated such treachery was now indignant over her present self's vulnerability. She yelled at twenty-four-year-old water engineer and foot fetishist Jake Cornish for encouraging the other men to hook up in what seemed like a dual play to live vicariously through their transgressions and lock down his win with Liberty Poole, a twenty-one-year-old marketing student from Birmingham. "Jake's in here like, 'You're my big sister,'" Faye said. "And he's basically telling the guys to throw their fucking Twix down an alleyway."

After Movie Night ended, Faye stalked around the kitchen, ranting about Teddy's lack of transparency to the other Islanders, who were silently trying to evacuate the scene. When Teddy came over to try to ameliorate the situation through a reasonable conversation, Millie and Abi snuck away, and Faye's pitch became a scream, her finger brandished at Teddy like a dagger she was happy to stab him with.

Across the garden, Liam did not seem appropriately appreciative that, somehow, he was not getting the most stick from the film festival of misbehavior. Using his best powers of deduction, Liam observed that Faye's delivery meant she wanted everyone to hear her business. It was true—Faye was freaking the fuck out and happy to let the whole Villa know. "You look like a two-faced prick!" Faye yelled.

"You're an idiot," Teddy muttered as he walked off.

"Yes, I am," Faye said, her volume escalating throughout the sentence, "for fucking believing your shit!"

It seemed like by externalizing her anger, Faye might be able to validate the feelings of hurt that were real to her, but which came off as completely disproportionate to Teddy's actions to anyone watching at home. After comporting himself nearly flawlessly throughout the whole thing, Teddy eventually called Faye a "twat." Amid the ballistics coming from Faye, it went largely unnoticed.

A spokesperson for the broadcast regulator Ofcom says that after the episode, they received 24,911 complaints, the most ever for an episode of *Love Island.* Of those, the spokesperson says, more than "twenty-four thousand centered around Faye's behavior towards Teddy, with some complainants citing emotional and verbal abuse and bullying behavior." The remaining complaints were "about the manipulation of contestants by producers and concerns about the mental health of the contestants."

Teddy was ennobled by the audience for taking Faye back after her outbursts—the Movie Night aftermath went through multiple movements, which Iain introduced like rounds in a boxing match—and redeeming her through his absolution. The audience followed; if Teddy could move past it, the UK could, too. The couple got third place in the finale, after runners-up Chloe and Toby, and Millie and Liam, who had ridden Millie's fan support to win the season after the depths of Casa and Movie Night.

"I was very aware and constantly reminded that if Teddy hadn't forgiven me, everyone would've hated me," Faye says. "I would've been the villain of all villains, so I was expected to be very grateful for him at all times."

According to Jeffreys, this was true. "People seemed to be more supportive of him than they were her," he says. "If two Islanders have had an argument, then you'd have a real outpouring on social media of people saying, 'You need to kick this person out of the Villa.' So you'd be staying quite close to production, then, saying, 'Is there any remorse or anything like that that we can draw people's attention to?' Day by day we were saying, 'Has she apologized as yet?' And she did end up apologizing."

Faye accepts responsibility for her behavior. She subsequently underwent years of therapy and says she now realizes she felt sensitivity was a weakness and wrath a strength. "Nope, no one's gonna see me upset," she had told herself before lashing out at Teddy. "They're just gonna see the person I want them to see, which is somebody that doesn't cry, isn't hurt." Unfortunately, Faye says, "What everyone saw was me just being a massive bitch."

"I would never, ever blame ITV," Faye says. "They gave me an amazing platform and let me do amazing things, and I'm forever grateful they really allowed me to go on my own journey and do self-discovery." Faye also says she would never have sought mental health counseling without that incident. "But," she says, "they also didn't want to take any accountability for the way they treated me." Faye starts to cry, which she no longer feels the need to hide. "They were happy for me to take the fall," she says.

Even if you don't leave a villain, it can be hard to exist in the muted tones of the outside world once you've lived under the neon lights of the Villa. "There is no feeling on Earth that I have felt after that" that could compare to his *Love Island* entrance, Toby says. "It might be a good thing, a bad thing. In a weird type of way, it's kind of brought down a lot of feelings in life. It's a bit hard to really enjoy and be excited for things because that was—will always be—the most exciting thing in your life that you've done." It's still fodder for therapy sessions with the psych whom Toby had initially declined to see on set but came to need on the outside. No one who wasn't there could possibly understand.

If Faye was conflicted about the character she played on *Love Island*, Ekin-Su Cülcüloğlu was happy to be typecast. When the casting team reached out to her for *UK* season 8, they asked if she was "ready to cause chaos." Ekin-Su responded in the affirmative: "I bring the drama everywhere I go!"

Ekin was a twenty-seven-year-old actress who had starred on the Turkish soap opera *Kuzey Yıldızı İlk Aşk*. To say she was comfortable engaging in on-camera romance and conflict would be like describing Captain Ahab as "interested in whales." Ekin was exactly what producers needed to renew interest in a show that had been on for seven years and was several seasons past its cultural and viewership peak.

Ekin entered the Villa on day three as one of the first female bombshells. "A part of me wanted to be part of the original lineup, but then I realized the power of that bombshell entrance," Ekin says. "As a Leo, I love to steal the show, and it allowed me to go in and really shake things up."

"Ekin-fucking-Su," twenty-three-year-old fishmonger Luca Bish said in the Beach Hut after meeting her. "She's gonna cause trouble!" He fell backward in rapture and delivered *Love Island*'s version of a prayer to Ekin: "Oh my Jesus, God."

"I'm sorry, I'm not here to find seasonal girlfriends. I'm here to find the love of my life," Ekin informed the female Islanders before stealing Villa hunk Davide Sanclimenti, who had arrived two days earlier and introduced himself by announcing, "They call me either the Italian stallion or the Greek god." While other Islanders would say things like "I'm a ten out of ten" in a half-kidding and clearly boastful way, the twenty-seven-year-old hookah supplier delivered this information in the matter-of-fact tone one uses to inform a grocery store–bound spouse that they're out of eggs and peanut butter. When Davide walked into the Villa at the end of the first night, after everyone had already coupled up, he shouted in his thick Frosinone accent, clearly at the urging of the producers, "Did anyone order an Italian snake?" (He meant "snack," but seeming to allude to having an enormous dick also worked.)

In Davide, Ekin would find what Iain described as "her greatest role: flirty single who finds Italian man's joke[s] hilarious." They initially bonded over their mutual self-regard. "I'm very confident in myself," Ekin told Davide while making the exact face you'd conjure if someone told you to imagine a seductive smile. "I feel like a lot of girls think you maybe love yourself, but I feel like deep down, you're sweet."

"That is the first thing that people can see from outside," Davide said. "They see I'm good-looking."

Ekin-Su told him she was excited to work out together— "I want to see if you're all talk or action," she said while making a thrusting motion with her arms.

Davide observed, "Everyone is excited for our workout."

He was correct. The entire Villa diligently talked about how much they *didn't* care while they ogled Davide lifting Ekin into chin-ups like she was a medium-sized dumbbell. For the deservedly conceited Davide, having eyes on him was like being a lizard under a heat lamp, a necessary reality as he went about his business. For Ekin, other people's attention was a spotlight shining on her starring performance as Ekin-Su. But even with their all-eyes-on-them workout and charged conversations, she didn't feel she was getting enough warmth from Davide.

On day nine, twenty-eight-year-old Scottish investment analyst Jay Younger came into the Villa. He turned Ekin's head, prompting what appeared to be a first-time feeling for Davide: jealousy. Obviously, Ekin loved that. During an evening in which Ekin kept studiously mispronouncing Davide (DAH-vee-DAY) as "Dah-VEE-day," she summoned Jay to the terrace for a private conversation that would become Villa-wide, and then nationwide, news. Ekin started her encounter with Jay by having him follow her and then dropping to her knees in a condom-tight cocktail dress, lowering herself below the sight line of the handrail and crawling to the balcony in front of him. Jay asked about Davide, as if he wanted to double-check Ekin knew she was with him and not the Villa *bell'uomo*. They made out under a sign that read "Stunning Scenes" while the rest of the Islanders speculated that they were doing this exact thing in the exact location they were doing it. Davide snacked and relayed how pissed off he was that Ekin seemed to be open to Jay, who was handsome but not someone

Davide seemed to consider a peer in male beauty. After concluding their session, Ekin slithered back across the terrace, flipped her hair over her shoulder, looked back at Jay, and wiggled her ass. She needn't have worried if Jay was paying attention: His face was as red as the early-season Islanders before producers started forcing them to wear sunscreen. He literally started panting.

The incident whipped the rest of the Villa into the kind of fervor only Ekin could induce. Under interrogation from the Islanders, Jay twice denied, at Ekin's instruction, that they "lipsed." Ekin followed the stonewalling plan for a few seconds, demanding Davide make her food and claiming she'd been standing by the front door. Then she summoned shocked nineteen-year-old dressage rider Gemma Owen and twenty-four-year-old Welsh paramedic Paige Thorne to the firepit to tell them what had just happened.

Davide walked over to confront Ekin about the short-lived secret—if something people were mostly aware was happening as it occurred can be considered a "secret."

"I want to know where the fuck are you, firstly," Davide said. Ekin could see the scene needed a table flip.

"Oh, all of a sudden you care!" she said. "I wanted this side from you days ago."

"I cannot fake feelings," Davide said calmly, at least relative to Ekin's tone. "After three days, I'm not going to show you the affection, the loving Davide, and the romantic Davide. If you want someone that show you this, go find fake love."

Ekin thundered away, infuriated at what she considered his unreasonable response.

"'Oh, Davide,'" Davide said to the sniggering boys, imitating Ekin. "'What I want from you is give me what I expecting of you.'" His initial annoyance at her fermented into anger as the boys told him about what had happened with Jay. For his part, Jay's night had really taken a turn. He'd gone from being the romantic lead in a sexy, clandestine drama to being the supporting character whose plot is acting as the messenger for information that would drive the main love story.

Davide was finally activated, getting ready to deliver what would end up being the most quoted moment of the season. "They're gonna give you an Oscarrrr!" Davide yelled, rolling the R languorously. "Fake person!"

"Go on, do you want to show off even more in front of the boys, Mr. Perfect Bully?" Ekin said as she stalked toward him, appearing to relish every clomp of her heels.

"Now I don't give a shit about you!" Davide said from under glasses that seemed to have cocked themselves crooked from his agitation. It would be his lone moment of physical imperfection on the season. "You are a liar!" Davide shouted. "Actress!" ("Liarrrr! Act-RRREESS!")

Jay thought the middle of this battle might be a good time to go talk to Ekin. "I think just stay out of it, I reckon," castmate Andrew Le Page advised.

Goading the dispassionately vain Davide into active combat was Ekin getting him to speak her love language: He cared about her enough to be dramatic. This set the scene for the type of reunion viewers were craving, and *Love Island* had so far been unable to deliver, despite their best efforts with Michael and Amber. After two weeks of attempting other relationships, Ekin stood in front of the Villa at the recoupling ceremony and asked Davide for another chance. A public self-humbling was Ekin's advertisement for what the boys named the "new Ekin-Su" and Ekin called "not the crazy bitch Ekin-Su."

Davide commiserated about Ekin with Jay and twenty-eight-year-old real estate agent Charlie Radnedge, the two other large, gym-centric men Ekin had been talking with. The trio imagined the next man producers would send in for the actress: six feet, three inches; benches 180; eats a dozen eggs every morning. It was the kind of joke that was only funny to Davide now that he'd won out.

Ekin is not the kind of person who changes—she is fundamentally herself at all times, which is what fans responded to. But she cared about Davide enough to alter her behavior, from something intended to provoke to something she was doing for someone else. Davide was pleased by Ekin turning her frequently referenced "fiery side" down to a smolder and her (often culinary) offerings: making him breakfast while he worked out and competing in a pancake-making contest with a bombshell who was going after him. They figured out a way to maintain the contention that had fueled their early attraction but made it sustainable. "They love an argument," Andrew said during one, as Ekin and Davide smirked. "And then they're cooking in seconds in the kitchen."

They would go on to win the season and date outside the Villa, filming a rare post–*Love Island* ITV spin-off where they took a road trip to Turkey and to Davide's hometown in Italy.

"You look at someone like Ekin and Davide, and their relationship was so hot-headed and quite volatile," Jeffreys says. "God, in some years, people might not have liked that—if they'd been in a different series, it might not have gone down in the same way. But at that moment in time, it really caught the public, and people really did get behind them."

Ekin would be the last star Islander *Love Island* would mint for a long time.

10

Bergielicious

AS *UK* WAS ENTERING its slump years, *USA* was beginning its rise. Sharon Vuong had moved from CBS to NBCUniversal and brought the show to Peacock for season 4. The platform, which also released Bravo programming, seemed better prepared to host *Love Island*—its primary audience was about twenty-five years younger than the average CBS viewer, and there are different decency standards for over-the-air content versus streaming. "Once you name the channel, you understand why that happened," says Mike Beale, head of international non-scripted division ITV Creative, explaining why the first few seasons failed to catch fire. "Look, it was a really brave move. [CBS] wanted a young audience, but they were struggling tonally with the sensibility—especially the early series of the UK version, which were a little bit racier." Peacock had more lax standards of propriety that gave the show the space to be more unfiltered; Islanders could now curse, dry-hump on camera, and wear swimsuits that were as small as they wished. Underboob was legal now.

Iain was hired as narrator, which he did in addition to his UK duties.

Arielle had been replaced by *Modern Family* star and *Love Island* superfan Sarah Hyland, who was able to better handle the show's rhythms, which it was finally settling into. As versions of *Love Island* were proliferating around the globe, a growth pattern emerged: The first season had small ratings, the second became a minor cultural touchstone but was not going to make a life-changing amount of money for most of its Islanders, and the third exploded. Now that it had found its true home, *Love Island USA* was effectively in the "season 2" position in what was actually season 5.

Carsten "Bergie" Bergersen would be a harbinger of the show's inchoate relevance. He was the ultimate non-Islander Islander that the US team had long been searching for, their version of *UK* season 3's Camilla, the outsider bomb-removal expert who toiled through most of her season before finding one of the happier endings to emerge from the series.

Bergie applied to *Love Island* out of necessity. The twenty-three-year-old was going to college in North Dakota and seemed to be running out of options in the bank of local singles. In a town of fewer than twelve thousand people, Bergie was only getting one match a month from the hundred-mile radius he had set on Tinder. After a shift at the local Dairy Queen, he came home and turned on Netflix, which had licensed *Love Island USA*. In its second run, the show had finally found an audience, and it included the DQ manager.

Incited by the difference between the people making out in Fiji and the loneliness he felt that night, Bergie googled "How do you get on *Love Island*?" If this sounds like a less probable path to love than changing his Tinder radius to 150 miles, don't worry: Bergie hedged his bets and also applied to *The Bachelorette* and *Too Hot to Handle*.

Four months later, Bergie got a call from a *Love Island* casting producer, who asked him to make an audition tape. Thirty minutes after he submitted it, the producer called back and said she'd like Bergie to meet with the execs of the show; Vuong was entranced.

"You just won't find men who looked like that—because he was very handsome—and working at a Dairy Queen, and kind, and so open," casting director Gervais says.

The interview confirmed that Bergie was special. "I went and rewatched when we met him for the first time, and I cried again," Gervais says. "He read his journal to us, and it was a freaking love letter he was writing to his future wife." This level of yearning had been completely absent from *Love Island* to this point. In the UK, cast members—at least in the beginning and certainly during their auditions—used humor to fortify themselves from that kind of horrifying exposure. On *Love Island USA*, primacy was placed on projecting what a good time an Islander would have if they got into the Villa. Bergie couldn't have taken the normal routes if he wanted to. Consequently, "Everybody fell in love with him," Gervais says.

Everybody at ITV America, that is. The Villa would take longer to warm to Bergie.

On the first day of filming, there was a surprise elimination in which the Islanders made an in-the-moment decision about who was the least compatible. They picked Bergie and Anna Kurdys, a twenty-three-year-old from Boca Raton. The vote was technically correct; the pair had, objectively, no chance of or interest in being a couple. Anna had a kind of upscale Florida confidence, while Bergie was the sort of person who sweatily unspooled his spotty dating history to the other Islanders. He had had sex with two women and kissed five but never slept in a bed for a full night with anyone. As he delivered this confusing tangle of information in a breathless staccato, his cheeks reddened. It evoked the scene in *The 40-Year-Old Virgin* where Steve Carell's character says women's breasts feel like bags of sand.

As part of the vote, Bergie and Anna had to choose which of them would leave. Bergie self-eliminated, only to be told moments later that he was being rewarded for his valor and sent back in. (No matter what couple the cast selected and which person had decided to go home, this fake-out would have been executed, and the exiled Islander would have returned. "To get rid of someone that soon just would feel kind of harsh," Thursby-Palmer says. Not to mention, this would have been a total waste of a dumping. On the first day, viewers "don't really know them well enough to care that they've gone," he says. It was meant to put Islanders on alert—anything could happen at any time.)

After one day, Bergie was ready to accept that his departure was providence; he wasn't meant to be in the Villa. The women didn't want him, and he assumed the audience wouldn't, either. "Oh my gosh, I just spent the whole first day embarrassing myself left and right," Bergie said. "I can't hold a conversation with anybody."

"You got this," Thursby-Palmer told him. "We picked you." Back in Bergie went.

The next three weeks were awful. Bergie was used to approaching women whose interest he was already assured of because he knew them through others, or because they had a common experience, like a shared class or extracurricular activity. In the Villa, it felt like the only thing to talk about with possible partners was whether there was potential between them. The subtext of dating becoming the text itself made Bergie too self-conscious to act normally.

As America became charmed by Bergie's flushed authenticity, the women of season 5 decided the best thing to do was mold him into a different person. They got together to instruct Bergie on how to seduce, a patronizing exercise that, of course, went terribly. The whole time, Bergie was thinking, "I'm embarrassed right now that these girls are teaching me how to flirt, thinking I don't know how to." When Bergie tried to make moves after the lesson, the girls deciding he was hopeless became an omen, and he began fumbling, chattering through silences, and saying, "Yeah, yup, yeah," over women while they talked. It was like an endless, televised version of posing for a portrait and wondering, "What should I do with my hands? Where do they normally go?" Then you wind up in some photo with your fingers crossed under your chin or your arms akimbo in some arrangement your body has never been in before. Bergie didn't know what to do with any part of himself.

The awkwardness ascended to high-end lowbrow comedy thanks to the newly added voice-over from Iain. "Nurse Jasmine and Detective Anna are giving Bergie some relationship coaching," Iain said of the flirting lesson from twenty-four-year-old ICU trauma nurse Jasmine Sklavanitis and criminal justice student Anna—the one Bergie had spared to sacrifice himself on night one. "So if all goes well, he'll be able to read someone their rights while performing a prostate exam."

"Those were some of the most stressful, uncomfortable moments I've ever probably gone through in my life," Bergie says. "Just a lot of spiraling. 'How are we looking on TV? I probably look like the biggest idiot you know right now, because I don't know what I'm doing.'" It was the most genuine reaction anyone could have to being on television for the first time—an outward, unmasked deluge of disquiet about being watched and not knowing how he was being received.

"If anybody was always looking out for me, it was Ben," Bergie says about Thursby-Palmer's support among production. He also started seeing the on-set therapist at least once a day, and she tried to assuage his anxiety. "Not everyone is going to find their person here," she told him. "There are going to be seventeen girls. What are the odds out of those seventeen girls that are wanting to be influencers that one is going to be your wife? So don't put pressure on that. Think about all the other boys and twenty-year-old males and thirty-year-old males that struggle talking to women. You're a role model for a lot of them out there."

For a different kind of person—the sort who was hoping to look cool on television—this might not have been the feedback they wanted to hear. Bergie understood he represented a huge cohort of young men who fumble through courtship, or forgo it entirely to avoid inevitable discomfort, or find communities who blame women for their feelings of inadequacy. A 2023 study found that only half of Gen Z men dated at all as teenagers. Bergie was bringing forth the blundering romantic experiences that were much more relatable to the average viewer than what Islanders with triple-digit body counts were going through in the Villa.

Bergie developed a friendship with Hannah Wright, a lovely twenty-four-year-old teacher who was the only US Islander the team can recall making it onto the main cast from mock week. While the other women were prescriptive to the point of condescension, Hannah accepted Bergie. "She treated me how I *was*," Bergie said, "while other people were like, 'You've got to be *this*.'" Meanwhile, the men made Bergie a scapegoat in intra-Villa conflicts because of his unwillingness to blindly advocate for their positions during Bergie's conversations with female Islanders. It led to even more agita for him. But the therapist hinted that Bergie's lowly status within the group did not reflect the impact he was having on viewers. "I think people are really liking your character," she told him. "So just keep being you. You're fine—you're liked on the outside."

But things in the Villa continued to get worse for poor Bergie. The boys ganged up, all five of them assigning bro-ish blame to him for the relationship issues of twenty-eight-year-old wrestler Victor Gonzalez, a machismic Khal Drogo–lite type. Bergie left the pile-on devastated and went to the cloistered balcony space Soul Ties to bawl. An elimination was coming up, and Bergie felt sure that despite what the therapist was telling him, he was the most despised man in America. Consigned to his destiny once again, Bergie comforted himself by eating as many gratis cookies as he could from the *Love Island* kitchen and packing his toothbrush, ready to leave for the second time.

When the vote revealed that Bergie was among the most popular people in the Villa, the Islanders' attitude toward him shifted. "Once they saw America liked me, they began to try to hang out with me a little bit more," Bergie says. He knows it was tactical; he assumes Islanders who had watched any of the show were thinking, "Okay, if I want to stay in the Villa, I need to be around this person more to get more screen time and be essential in the story."

One of these people was Marco Donatelli, a twenty-two-year-old chiropractic student who, despite being coupled with Bergie's best Villa friend Hannah, had never been particularly warm to Bergie. This antipathy was expressed in less than subtle ways, such as calling Bergie a douchebag during the men's berating session. "After that vote, I felt like he was clinging on a little bit," Bergie says.

Not that Bergie was above strategy. "I was the only one to watch all seasons beforehand," he says. "And I also realized Hannah and Marco were the most popular people in there. I would work with them and strategize who we were sending home and who we were going to keep." Bergie says that while his goal had been to find love, he understood that was contingent on playing the game well enough to stay on.

Bergie grasped onto the hope that he might finally find someone in Casa Amor. After speaking with six of the seven women, he went to the therapist and told her it was over; he accepted that the odds had been borne out and his soulmate wasn't there. She told him he shouldn't be sad because he'd done his best, and Bergie confirmed he was self-eliminating—after he had a final chat with Taylor Smith, the only woman he hadn't talked to.

Taylor was a twenty-four-year-old hotel manager from Orange County who appeared as a uniformly reserved person over the course of her time on *Love Island*, revealing little but her impeccable abs and composure. Though she said she was open to getting to know him during Casa, Bergie wasn't sure of her motives. Maybe, Bergie thought, Taylor just wanted to couple up with him now that it was clear he was one of the most-liked guys on the show.

The day they finally started speaking, Bergie looked like he'd taken off a fifty-pound backpack. He excitedly told Taylor about baking a chocolate Swiss cake roll from scratch for the first time, to which Taylor responded with a moaning "Oh, fuck!" Bergie had impressed someone. "You've really surprised me," Taylor told him. "You feel like a safe space." That she went on *Love Island* looking for safety might be why Taylor wound up being a fit for Bergie.

The pair chatted for seven hours, breaking only for a Hideaway make-out session involving Bergie wearing furry handcuffs, his arms over his head and his legs flopped open into a full spatchcock position. For viewers, the kiss elicited mortification and pride in equal measure, but what other kind of on-camera hookup could Bergie have?

A week and a half of idiosyncratic ardor later, Bergie and Taylor were on a date. As they filmed and refilmed a walk down a dock one, three, five times, Bergie began smiling. Every time they reshot it, Taylor found a new element to appreciate. "It's so pretty," she said during the fourth trip down the same wooden path. While Bergie was fretting about the potential for future fuckups and dwelling on the past ones he could never undo, Taylor was appreciating the present. By the fifth runway walk, he'd decided to cease perseverating on the matter and ask her to be his girlfriend. He read to her from one of the sixty-one letters he'd written to her before he knew who she would be. "Why haven't I given up?" Bergie said. "I really hope you're out there looking for a guy like me . . . I want to eat ice cream on the floor when we could so easily eat it at a table . . . I want to dance with you before going to bed."

Taylor began crying. "Are you serious?" she asked when he made the request to be official. "Yes!" Taylor would be Bergie's girlfriend. They shared a kiss that was, remarkably, kind of hot, which Bergie ended so he could share with Taylor how nervous he'd been the whole evening.

Now that he knew the public accepted him—and Taylor did, too—Bergie was able to stop focusing on what he calls "the three layers" of observation he felt in the Villa: castmates, producers, and the outside world watching him. He could act like himself, whom he calls "nerdy Bergie," and not as the sexy stranger the girls were trying to shape him into. And now that he was in a couple, a willing fandom was ready to vote him into the finale. During the Heart Rate Challenge, Bergie stripped off a pair of tearaway denim cutoffs, revealing a pair of American flag swim briefs, and yelled, "I throw my ass in your face!" The man who had been the unwilling joke of the Villa was now its comedic and emotional center. Bergie was buoyant through the end of the season, where he was so sufficiently redeemed that he had the honor of rejecting the advances of another female Islander.

Bergie's transformation from skittish bystander to fan favorite reflects as much about the viewing public who were coming to *Love Island USA* as it did about the outsider himself. He achieved what the therapist had said he would for himself and other nervous young men: demonstrating how to socialize through anxiety. On-screen, before coupling with Taylor, Bergie's impulse in conversations was to affirm that he was listening, which presented as yammering over the other person or saying something he didn't mean because he was panicking about how the conversation was going. As Bergie struggled through his feelings about being perceived and survived indignities on the way to a relationship, he became a better communicator. The Villa taught him the value of reflection, of holding his words for the right time. And he continues using the format of the show on the outside. During recoupling ceremonies, Islanders must stand around the firepit and articulate to their partner—again, in front of their peers, producers, and the public—the qualities they value in them. It functions as a gratitude exercise that many Islanders say caused them to like their partner more because they were consciously attaching positive words to their feelings. Bergie and Taylor still do it to this day.

Bergie had waited years to find the woman to whom he had penned those letters during the cold nights after his Dairy Queen shifts. He found her in Taylor. They celebrated the second anniversary of that date in August 2025. "I love the way you communicate with me," they tell each other in their private couplings, thousands of miles away from the Villa. "I love the way you trust me."

Bergie grew so much that he expanded what *Love Island USA* could be. Internally, the team referred to the season as "Bergie Island."

"We are always looking for new versions of Bergie," casting director Gervais says wistfully. Thomas says it was bigger than that.

The next year, people started asking him, "Why did it work in season six after you were so shit at making television before?"

Thomas says Bergie was an answer: They now understood how to change *Love Island* without breaking it.

11

The Villaverse

MALTA IS A TINY, 122-square-mile island in the Mediterranean with a population of about 560,000. The country has a unique broadcast system, where rather than selling a show to a network, any individual with the means can rent out a time slot, which they then fill with content and advertisements that they also provide. In 2022 Ben Camille, an entrepreneur and the host of *X Factor Malta*, approached ITV about licensing *Love Island.* To produce it, Camille bought forty cameras and hired the team behind a daily radio show, with the host of the program acting as showrunner. It worked, though ITV executive Huub van Ballegooy notes, "I'm not saying that in season one we aired an episode every night." While he was in the country trying to encourage nightly broadcasts, van Ballegooy kept running into people who were vocal fans or connected to the series in some way. "Oh, my niece is on the show," his cab driver told him. By the season finale, it was a national phenomenon: Sixty percent of people living in Malta were watching *Love Island.*

When someone wants to join the twenty-three countries that have franchised *Love Island*, they speak with ITV's Mike Beale and van Ballegooy, who travels around the world selling the show's format for the company. Parties interested in licensing the series range from network execs like Sharon Vuong to wealthy people living in countries where having a reality show is a status symbol. "Greece has a very competitive market, which is basically owned by private billionaires that want to outshine each other," van Ballegooy says. "So if one commissions a show, the other one wants to commission one, too. It becomes prestige, though not necessarily a moneymaking vehicle." Van Ballegooy compares it to the ultrarich buying soccer teams. When we spoke, van Ballegooy was negotiating a *Love Island* commission with a country in Asia, where a well-known producer of cooking shows wanted to buy rights to the series because his daughter had become addicted during an internship in Montreal. The producer called ITV and said, "My daughters tell me that I have to program *Love Island*."

Thomas says of van Ballegooy, "His stories are like Mad Libs. Country? Let's say Tajikistan. Job? Oil mogul who owns the network. And then insert, like, lover/mistress/wife wants to buy *Love Island*. They buy the show, but it's not financed like we do with ad money. It's just their play money. And then it all kind of goes one way or another, and then suddenly he's being driven out into the forest and being threatened with a gun."

When they deal with more standard network arrangements, there are inevitably questions about the production. Often, those commissioning the show want to know what will happen on, say, episode 6 of the forty-two-episode season they might produce—impossible for a show where a willingness to throw out a plan to follow an unexpected move by Islanders is one of the chief reasons why it became a worldwide phenomenon. Beale and van Ballegooy have to tell potential clients, "I don't know. Oh, by the way, I want to spend your entire marketing budget on this show and about half your entire production budget." The pair also prepare buyers for the fact that it takes three seasons for a franchise to understand itself and for fans to grow used to the tremendous time commitment.

Each commissioner is given a show bible, consisting of hundreds of pages of the written rules of *Love Island,* put together to give other countries a guide for replicating the mood, look, and standards of the current version in the UK. The Duty of Care, meant to ensure the welfare of the Islanders, is paramount. Van Ballegooy says, "It's not just a show like, 'Oh, let's put twenty hot people in the house and see what happens'"—anymore, at least.

A universal safety mechanism for the production itself is that producers check in with cast members about the evolution of their feelings so the show isn't caught off guard by someone pivotal being dumped by the other Islanders. They also use that information to make sure eliminations aren't confusing to viewers. "There's never any weird curveballs where you're like, 'Oh god, why have they gone?'" Spencer-Hayter says of producers setting up pre-dumping beats by getting Islanders to verbalize on camera what they're thinking about doing. Given that Islanders' feelings can completely change in just a few hours based on any factor—a challenge answer that kicks off a skirmish, a tearful confession of regret or the ick—the mandatory updates are nearly constant.

Another touchpoint is sex. How much can be shared is dependent on the broadcasting rules of each individual country airing the program and the appetites of the network or streamer. At this point, the general sensibility across the franchises is that sex is implied, rather than explicit. ITV can suggest the fluttering of sheets, or a pan to a bra on the floor, or brief close-ups of feet in what can only be described as "military position," with toes clenching in the ecstasy occurring a few feet north. Cowles compares it to "the old-fashioned movies, where there was a champagne cork" popping. Like the show's other credos—"People are drinking, but they're never drunk," and "People are arguing, but they never fight"—ITV says, "*Love Island* is sexy, but it's never sex." As Hannah, one of the first people to have visible intercourse on *Love Island*, says, "They would never put that on now. Never. Can you imagine?"

In season 3, *Love Island UK* stopped showing hookups so baldly. Ratings went up, and the average age of the viewer went down. Beale says, "The young audience almost don't want to see that. It's like, 'Oh yeah, that happens—we know, we don't need to see it. Just give us the gossip.'"

Though there is a common understanding of the general concept of *Love Island*—sexy singles searching for connections in a summer of love—different franchises have different predilections within the remit. Spain and Portugal are reserved in what language they use because both are extremely Catholic. Many non-UK countries in Western Europe refuse to produce challenges involving food. Holland, for example, was invaded during World War II, and there are still people alive today who lived through the resulting famine. "If you're not an occupied country and it's not in your direct DNA, then you are much more easygoing with wasting of food," van Ballegooy says of Islanders expectorating pork into each other's mouths in a relay race, to name one such grotesquerie.

The countries with the highest production budgets are UK, Germany, France, Australia, and USA. Even among what ITV calls the "top tier," America induces envy over resources. "The way it's shot is so beautiful," Spencer-Hayter says longingly. "I mean, the money. I'd love to know the cost per episode." Thomas says a season of *USA* is now twice as expensive to produce as it was in season 1.

In 2017 Beale and van Ballegooy hosted the first *Love Island* Exchange, a summit for both peers and potential licensees interested in creating a real-time television series. Having people like Thursby-Palmer and Spencer-Hayter there to talk through the minutia of production reassures would-be franchisers that it is possible to make this seemingly impossible show and helps them comply with *Love Island*'s rigorous criteria for excellence in the art of semi-live television production and young adult corralling.

As the Exchange grew over the years, each franchise represented a totally separate *Love Island* fandom. With the exceptions of *Love Island UK* airing in the US and Australia and *Australia* in the US and UK, there was almost no overlap in viewership—which meant there were tremendously popular Islanders who were completely unknown outside of their home countries. This presented a new opportunity. A growing American fan base was hungry for even more *Love Island* and were being deprived of the best Islanders of France, Belgium, and Malta. By 2023 it was time to execute Thomas's ultimate goal of building a repertory cast of stars: *Love Island Games.*

"We made a conscious decision when selling *Love Island Games* that this was going to be a universe," Thomas says. "We wanted to have an environment where you could come in and out of the story." The first five seasons of *Love Island USA* were about making a show that served an entirely distinct—and much more diverse—audience than *Love Island UK. Games* had a different purpose, which spoke to the audience's role as longtime stakeholders. It would be a way to integrate former *USA* Islanders and global talent, and they could, at last, poach fans of the original British series. It was a gamble that was made possible because ITV America now had a permanent Villa at a resort that production had taken over for season 5. They could roll right into the new production without the costly shutdown and ramp-up usually required of a season.

Love Island Games would keep a kernel of the romantic aspect of *Love Island* through the recoupling ceremonies that girded the show, and nighttime hookups that were inevitable with so many beautiful people sleeping in the same quarters. But the games were the main point. These were much more demanding than regular *Love Island* challenges; those normally didn't entail anything more exerting than tongue-kissing or getting sprayed with a hose.

The general conceit was that couples would team up to win games, eliminating Islanders along the way until one couple triumphed—though, as always, the rules would change depending on what would make for the most interesting TV. If teams lost challenges, they were up for dumping, while the winning duo, called "the power couple," had authority to upend the existing order: to add another team to the bottom, mix up the pairings, save Islanders, or otherwise disadvantage their enemies and protect their friends. It was also the first season of *Love Island* with no public votes because it was filmed in advance and aired several months later, in November.

Within the show, there are classic *Love Island* challenges to provoke insecurity—in *Games* season 1, Islanders played the familiar "Snog, Marry, Pie," a version of "Fuck, Marry, Kill," in which someone throws a pie in the face of someone they would ostensibly "murder" rather than sleep with. Other challenges included bitchy questions about what people thought of their castmates, creating conflicts that would have usually just encouraged resentment on the dating show, but which in this new context led to open warfare.

There were a number of gross-out games, like the "baby birding" challenge where Islanders spit fake beer into each other's mouths, trying to move the most liquid. Other challenges left the Islanders soaked in water or unidentifiable goo, which they would have to sit around in for hours afterward. It was a gynecological nightmare; the women almost always wore tight, synthetic costumes, making every game a potential prelude to a yeast infection.

Most of the Islanders I spoke to were not aware that *Games* would be as demanding as it was, both from a physical and a mental perspective. The show's gameplay and tactical social maneuvering mirrored *The Challenge*, in which eliminations were based on a mix of athleticism and navigation of the social element. Those things had always mattered on *Love Island*, but the Islanders who succeeded on the strength of those qualities did so because it seemed to be their natural inclination, not because they were actively attempting to win the show.

The new spin-off also hired Maya Jama, who had taken over hosting duties from Laura on *Love Island UK* the year before *Games* debuted. If Caroline was the Islanders' fairy godmother and Laura a kindly, higher status colleague, Maya was big sister. The twenty-eight-year-old of Somali and Swedish descent was the first person of color to host *Love Island USA*, *UK*, or any of their spin-offs. Maya's relationship with the rapper Stormzy and a wardrobe that Jessica Rabbit wouldn't be able to pull off contributed to a kind of coolness that wasn't always present in the kitsch of the Villa.

Maya had presenting experience across sports, red carpets, game shows, and competition series. She also had the craic—pronounced the same way as the first word of *Love Island*'s operating principle, cracking on—an Irish term that filled a lexical gap in British English for a supernatural spark. On a 2024 episode of *Aftersun*, the panel discussed the logistics of how a Welsh contestant could have had sex with 120 women, given the low population of the country. "Might have shagged a cousin, who knows," Maya theorized, displaying the type of cheekiness that won over viewers.

Maya's humor belies the fact that she treats her role with total seriousness. As Caroline did, Maya wants Spencer-Hayter to tell her everything that's happened in the Villa every day. "Hang on a sec," she'll say when a person goes from being inside someone one night to blindsiding her the next. "That's so mad. What? No, but how did it get to that point?" Her investment gives her the data to scrutinize Islanders' choices with panelists on *Aftersun* with the evangelical finesse of Stephen A. Smith debating draft picks on *SportsCenter*.

When asked to elucidate the difference between Maya and her forerunner Laura, Toby, who was coming back for *Games*, affirmed the special place he had in his heart for Laura as his first ever host, then noted in the politic way nearly everyone I spoke with did, "Maya's more down with the kids—like, she can understand the lingo and stuff like that. Maya gives that whole spice."

While Maya provided glamour on a show that would feature a lot of skinned knees and helmet wearing, the success of Bergie's *Love Island* tenure altered how the team would cast going forward.

"You're not looking for another Bergie; you're looking for another three standard deviations from the norm," Thomas says of the shift in mindset. Leaning into outsiders left room for them to cast people like *UK* season 7's Liberty, who was smart but daffy, and not particularly athletic—a completely normal Islander who was both yes girl and glue, but not someone who seemed primed for a series that required feats of strength. It also opened the door for Callum Hole, a twenty-five-year-old Welshman who was ripped but not obvious as a person who would thrive in a strategy game. (On his season of *Love Island Australia*, Callum had explained how he thought dairy evolved. "It starts with a cow and becomes milk. Then it probably becomes yogurt," he recited. "Then it probably turns into ice cream. Then it probably turns into cheese or something.")

"We were afraid about the *UK* Islanders being so famous that it was going to fuck up the dynamic," Thomas says. "English people are so funny and clever, and their banter is so good. But the Americans are so brash and out there and full tilt that the English people felt like they needed to step up," Thomas says. "And so suddenly you've got this cast that is vying for the attention, not from us, but from each other."

"*UK* people just carry themselves differently, I think," Cely says of her time on the season. "I respect it, but it was even weirder in *Games* because you're in this bubble, and everything is heightened. So if people really walk like their shit doesn't stink, it just creates such a different dynamic, and it makes it even more intense."

Bringing in people who lived internationally had downsides—the first being that there was little chance of a lasting couple coming out of the show. Producers were still hopeful it could happen, the way it had many times on *The Challenge*. "This is still *Love Island*—there's still a *Love Island* aspect to it," producers kept reminding the contestants. A few people obliged, though the pairings would evaporate outside the Villa. The focus of the show was the games, not the love.

The overtness of the contest fostered a new dynamic in the Villa couplings. Islanders had to think about not just whom they fancied but who was good at competitions, whom other Islanders would like, and who understood how to improvise within a plan of action. They were also allowed to openly muse about whether they could get the prize money with their current partner. Producers would have ordinarily forbidden cast members from these types of discussions on *Love Island*—and if for whatever reason it did slip through, it would be the type of crass positioning that would have almost certainly gotten an Islander dumped by the public. Now, with the new dynamic in place, and without a vote to hold cast members in check, permissible behavior was more mutable, and the new precedents were set. On *Games*, it became a benefit for Islanders to show their work in a way that would be disqualifying on the regular series.

The season was significant for other reasons, too. Though women had discussed their attraction to each other on *Love Island USA*, *Games* featured the first same-sex coupling on the show. Bombshell and *USA* season 1 cast member Kyra Green homed in on the lascivious Megan Barton-Hanson. "I'm very openly sexual," she immediately told Kyra, who was glad to hear it.

"Megan is one of the best contestants we've ever had," Thomas says. "She is the reason I was able to move the show more sex positive." Initially, there was the old fear that if a woman coupled up with another woman, it would mess up the even gender numbers and create production headaches, or it would "other" the woman so boys would no longer pursue them.

There was no trouble with the first point: Almost everyone wanted Megan. After coupling with her, Kyra was disappointed to learn Megan had propositioned the beauteous but laconic Eyal Booker, who was the first man she hooked up with on season 4 of *UK* before she dumped him by saying, "You're not exactly Jim Carrey. I can't have fun with myself." (Eyal defended himself by saying he didn't have the opportunity to be funny because all Megan wanted to do was have sex with him.) On a usual season of the show, this might have revealed itself on Movie Night, but there was no time for that—Maura Higgins came on to guest host and pressed Eyal to admit that he'd pied Megan off when she'd secretly tried to kiss him. Kyra seemed amazed by the news but handled it with more aplomb than she had managed in season 1 when she made her "At the end of the day" speech during her first televised rebuffing. Unfortunately, the plot cut off: Megan had to leave because of issues around pelvic inflammatory disease, scuttling both her carnal rampage of the Villa and Kyra's hopes to reconcile.

"I think Kyra was so happy that she could be all her authentic self," Thursby-Palmer says. "As a gay man, very happily married to my husband, we're really proud, and we take that storytelling really responsibly as well. We don't want to just be like, 'Oh, let's show two girls kissing.' You've got one girl that is very happy in her skin and knows who she is and sees herself as bisexual and the other girl that's like, 'Oh God, is this a thing? Do I actually like her?' I went through that myself, coming out."

After Megan went home, Kyra pioneered another *Love Island* first: making out with all the girls in the Heart Rate Challenge. Viewers were much less worked up about the same-sex doings than the producers had been—the main reaction seemed to be people wanting to know where they could buy Kyra's bondage bodysuit. *Games* had raised the stakes about what constituted something shocking on *Love Island*.

The goal of *Games* varies from contestant to contestant. In the first season, Curtis spent the energy he normally put into people-pleasing into calculating. Unfortunately, he was coupled with *Love Island Sweden* season 3's Lisa Celander, a sturdy Scandinavian aesthetician whom he had identified as an asset in physical challenges but who seemed to be incapable of any goal-setting beyond pursuing Curtis. After a few episodes of talking the twenty-eight-year-old down during the day and making out with her at night, Curtis seemed exhausted from trying to middleman Lisa's coexistence with the group. She was, understandably, having a hard time getting along with people she was in explicit competition with. She was also on a show that required an enjoyable-to-watch group dynamic, to which she was not contributing much. Lisa's inability to have fun with anyone but Curtis was fucking up his plan. "It could be the game of making friends with people," Curtis explained slowly to Lisa as she complained that her standing in the Villa should be entirely based on challenge performances and not impacted by her personality. Lisa kept arguing with him, so he switched tacks and attempted to flirt her into a better mood, which worked.

"I really tried," Curtis tells me of his judicious communication. "Sometimes when you'll see me thinking, I try and put myself into their perspective to just try and see what they're feeling." Curtis could not make it to the vantage point in Lisa's mind where she would see that they needed strong connections with other couples to succeed on this version of *Love Island*. Instead, Lisa went for a bridge-torching option, approaching *USA* season 5 cast member Imani Wheeler, a twenty-two-year-old YouTuber, and calling her two-faced. When Imani discussed it with Lisa to try to move forward, Lisa told Imani she took things too seriously and that they weren't going to be friends. Curtis ran up to Imani to say *he* didn't think she was two-faced, but it wasn't enough; Imani won the challenge and had the power to make Curtis and Lisa vulnerable for dumping. Curtis bent the knee, lauded the decision, and congratulated her for her win. Lisa complained that it was unfair, which, unsurprisingly, was unhelpful. They were eliminated.

While Kyra and Megan were breaking the heteronormative structure of the show, and Curtis was failing to overcome Lisa's utter incomprehension of gameplay, Cely was just there for a good time.

Cely was the kind of Islander who spent her season giggling and flirting. She expected *Games* to be the same way and began cozying up to Toby and spending time with her best friend from season 2, Justine Ndiba. "I thought I was on vacation—I just wanted to, like, make out a little bit, sprint a couple times," Cely says. Then Justine ran up to her and told her people were talking about alliances. "We're on *Love Island Games*, bro," Cely responded. "What do you mean 'alliances'?"

"Everyone was so serious and intense and dog-eat-dog," Cely says. "And then there's just me cackling in the corner, and they're like, 'Who the fuck is this bitch?' People kind of hated me on that season."

Love Island USA season 4 cast member Deb Chubb came in on episode 14 of the nineteen-episode season and was, as expected by producers, awed by the *UK* Islanders. "I was fangirling so hard because I loved Toby, I loved Liberty, I loved Curtis," the twenty-seven-year-old aspiring actress says. "And then when I, like, became friends with them, I was like, 'This is so cool.'"

Like Cely, Deb had imagined something a little cuter when she was invited on *Love Island Games*. She was shocked by the ferocity of the experience. Unlike typical *Love Island*, the bombshells were not able to watch past episodes, so Deb had no clue about the miasma of bad vibes she was walking into. Deb's first challenge was the "Mega Dual." Couples were chained together for a three-way tug-of-war, which wound up not being aired because everyone was so depleted that it ended in a tie, with the contestants huddled in downward-facing fetal positions to protect their ground while expending the least amount of energy possible. "I have never been in so much pain in my life," Deb says. "There were toenails falling off; people were twisting their ankles."

Producers were not having much fun, either. Production had begun on *Games* two weeks after *USA* season 5 wrapped; for budgetary reasons and so that they could finish filming the three-week shoot before monsoon season began. There were no days off. "Death," Thomas says by way of describing the schedule. "Do not make television this way. Absolute pain."

Deb was partnered with Callum, whom she'd watched on *Love Island Australia*. "I'll never get along with this man," she thought of the man who thought cheese was ice cream's second act. "Like, he is so dumb." It turned out Callum was a smart guy who leaned into his doofy appearance for his advantage. "There was a lot of strategy," she says of the other players. "Callum played it the best, where he was just like, 'I'm just, like, running around doing whatever. I'll vote you out, but I'm gonna own up to it.' Whereas other people shocked everybody, going against their friends."

Deb says it was hard to have a good time on *Games* because of the competitiveness. "I remember the next morning after a huge dumping, it was literally silent in the Villa," Deb says. "Everybody was so mad at each other, and me and Callum were just so afraid to talk. I was like, 'This is gonna come across so boring.'" She was incorrect.

After their eliminations, the cast-out Islanders were sent to stay across the property until filming wrapped. From the other side of the resort, they watched footage of the season and worked themselves up about the perceived failings of their castmates. In a twist cribbed from *Survivor*'s Final Tribal Council, the dumped Islanders would eventually come back to the Villa to vote on which two couples they wanted to go to the finale.

Kyra would later tell Cely that as they were waiting for their time to return, the Islanders had questioned her about Cely's "real" personality. "I don't trust anyone who's that nice" was the general tone of the inquiries. They also stewed over the fact that Cely had treated *Games* as if it were ordinary *Love Island*, leaving them to scheme and look bad. The vote from the dumped Islanders would reflect their anger about Cely yes girling all over the Villa while their toenails were falling off, recoupling with Eyal and kissing him after Toby was dumped. Justine and Jack, who were Cely and Eyal's closest friends—and, as Justine explained to Cely, their allies—were immune from elimination, so whatever energy that might have been directed at the front-runners who had played a ruthless game was transferred onto Cely. As a member of the jury, Toby stood in front of his ex of several days and went off.

"One thing I hate in this world are actors," Toby said, doing a slow clap for Cely and Eyal's "performance." "Fuck you guys," he told them, claiming the tape he'd seen after he'd been eliminated had made Cely's deceit obvious. The pair was dumped, leaving two real, romantic (for the time being) couples: Justine and Jack, and Johnny—who continued to deny that he hadn't paid for Cely's nachos—and beauteous German nonentity Aurelia Lamprecht. The pairs banged each other up in a series of challenges that culminated in dragging enormously heavy bags with dollar figures written on them around a boxing ring to try to collect the most money. It looked exhausting; when Maya blew the final whistle, all four collapsed to the mat, gasping. After medics revived Jack, who had started to pass out after hyperventilating, he and Justine were awarded the $100,000 prize.

The lag between filming and airing would be a wretched time for Cely, who was used to not only getting signposts throughout the season about whether the public liked her but emerging from the Villa to immediately receive firm answers. On *Games*, she had no idea how the edit would play out or whether anyone watching would respond well to her; her castmates certainly hadn't, and Toby was telling her there was footage so damning it had justified his explosion.

To cope with the dread of what she believed she would see, Cely spent every day between filming and airing getting drunk. "I completely spiraled after *Love Island Games*," Cely says. "So that entire two months before we got to watch the show back, I fully convinced myself that I was about to see a version of myself that I never knew existed. And I think mixing alcohol with all of the anxiety that I was feeling,

I convinced myself that I was a terrible person." During these weeks, Cely fretted to Justine, listing all the things that might have turned people against her. Justine, her "sister for life," kept saying, "Cely, I don't know how many times I have to fucking tell you: You didn't do anything."

When the season aired, Cely thought, "Are you shitting me? I actually *didn't* do anything." The audience was as perplexed as she was about everyone turning on her. As a result of the experience, she became sober. Cely never wanted anything to impair her relationship to reality again.

It was another moment of growth for Toby; unfortunately, this time on Cely's back. His outburst at her is the only moment he regrets in what would turn out to—so far—be four seasons of *Love Island.*

As all variations of the show are, *Games* seemed primed to be a grower. The impact of the first season was fairly modest and made possible because of the economical production schedule. But there were promising signs: Sixty percent of social media engagement was coming from overseas for a show that was only available to watch in America. "The piracy on *Love Island Games* was insane," Thomas says. So many people were illegally streaming it that they couldn't take all the links down. Peacock doesn't share internal data like that with audiences, or even the show's producers. However, Thomas says other major streamers use piracy as a metric for success because it drives subscriptions.

Producers decided that season 2 of *Games* would be live. The thought behind doing so would be, as Thomas says, to "leverage that passion internationally to make the conversation global, because that's how you flip the algorithm." If the world wanted to watch, *Love Island Games* would make TV for the world.

12

Get the Show On, Get Paid

AS TEAM USA WAS conquering Earth, the UK was doubling down on the motherland. "We're for a UK audience, so that's what we're trying to aim for," Cowles says, speaking to the American writer who was writing an entire book centered on his British show.

"To be honest, we are *the UK*," Spencer-Hayter says with typical zealotry. "We are the hub. We are the number one *Love Island* brand in the world. We have some fantastic countries like America and loads of incredible versions of the show, but everything factually stemmed from the UK version." *USA* had borrowed *their* host, and unlike the American viewers and their devotion to *Love Island UK*, the British public was not watching *Love Island USA*.

ITV executive Stavri says the UK audience had been requesting a version of *Love Island UK* composed of returning cast members. Their answer was *Love Island: All Stars*. "It enabled fans of the show to reconnect with iconic Islanders and give them a second chance at finding love," Stavri says.

All Stars would change the format of the show from casting strangers and watching their feelings develop to putting known entities (and more seasoned television personalities) together and exploiting external relationships. The interest in seeing established caste systems crossing over from different eras would allow *Love Island UK* to keep doing two seasons of the show a year without fatiguing the audience by giving it the same formula. "It gave us a nice point of difference from the summer series," Stavri says. Now they had a dating show in the northern hemisphere and a winter sister show that was half unscripted soap opera and half dollhouse producers could move figures around in.

Nearly a year before *All Stars* filmed in Cape Town, the team called their season 1 queen Hannah Elizabeth to inquire about her interest. Though she had reservations about leaving her four-year-old son, "there was no way I was not gonna do it," Hannah says. When she watched subsequent seasons, she'd seen hundreds of Islanders come onto what had originally been her show; in addition to being the first person cast, she was the first female Islander to walk into the Villa. "That's *my* gaff," she thought as new cast members entered, using a slang term for *home*. Hannah was ready to relive the *Love Island* experience, though this time without starring in an infrared sex scene.

Faye was also approached, but the team's psychologists said she was too high-risk because she'd been briefly diagnosed with depression after season 7. To Faye, it felt like she was being penalized for getting help. When she saw the cast list, she felt better about not going on. "I was thinking it was gonna be Maura Higgins and Chris Hughes and big names like Ovie," she says. Viewers did, too. Producers *had* approached Maura and Ovie, the best of Islanders, but they'd turned it down. (As far as anyone at ITV can remember, no official offer was made to Chris, who wound up going on *Celebrity Big Brother*. It was a fortuitous decision: Chris would wind up meeting and dating his castmate, the ubiquitous reality TV personality and performer JoJo Siwa.)

Toby, like fellow *Games* and *All Stars* season 1 castmate Liberty, was back on *Love Island*. He was coming off a quick elimination and a final scene that he was ashamed of on *Games*; *All Stars* could provide a comeback, he thought. Despite the fit Toby had thrown on camera, Mitch Taylor still managed to be less popular than him coming into the Villa. On season 10, the twenty-six-year-old gas engineer had acquitted himself in a manner that rightfully earned him the nickname "Messy Mitch," a reputation he shored up in the tabloids right before going on *All Stars* by attending a party where an influencer reported that Mitch had said, "We are the most famous people in here," and thrown money at an unhoused person. In a response video, Mitch said the latter was an attempt to perform a "kind gesture."

As always, the goal was to get the right blend of personalities. The pool for casting was vastly smaller—a little more than three hundred personalities to choose from, versus the tens of thousands of annual applicants, plus the even larger group of good-looking eighteen-to-thirty-year-old Brits who could be recruited. Producers were in touch with most former Islanders to keep tabs on their general health and doings, so they roughly knew who of the potential *All Stars* was unattached. In addition to the obvious big names and known exes, the team sought more minor Islanders whom viewers had lingering affection for and ones with the potential to shine but hadn't particularly in their seasons because of timing or circumstance. Anton Danyluk of mom-ass-shaving fame, the quick-talking Chris Taylor, season 9 head-turner Tom Clare, and identical twins Eve and Jess Gale would return, as would sort-of exes from the outside Georgia Harrison (season 3) and Casey O'Gorman (season 9), who ended things because Georgia called him from a wellness retreat and told him she'd communed with his dead grandfather while meditating.

As the UK team compiled a roster, producers created a chart of entanglements and exes as complicated as Charlie's conspiracy board from *It's Always Sunny in Philadelphia*. Prior hookups were empirical proof of attraction and made for a sturdier hypothesis for who might couple than the self-reporting from regular seasons—or at least, they might identify some pain points that production might pick at to make things kick off. But it created the tiresome question that would continue to loom over *All Stars*: If an Islander knew they liked someone on the outside and were in touch with them, why weren't they already together?

The answer was that there is nothing else to do on *Love Island* but play *Love Island*. And this particular iteration of *Love Island* would not include the disruptive temptations of Casa Amor, which would have been logistically difficult in a five-week season and required booking (and paying for, at a significantly higher rate than regular seasons) at least ten additional returning Islanders—who, if we're honest, were not going to be the A team if they were willing to show up and possibly get canned after a three-episode appearance. Producers hoped the isolation would cause something in the cast to revert to the pre-famous-ish people they'd been, to open them up to love the way they had during their first run.

Again and again in interviews, former Islanders expressed nostalgia about the weeks they had been in the Villa, away from their phones and social media. Rather than scrolling through dull or awkward moments, they were forced to talk in the way you can only when you're bored on a group trip with no internet. Hopefully, revisiting that idyllic, cell-free space would counter the reality that virtually all of these Islanders pursued careers in "being a personality" after their first appearances on the show.

Jess was discouraged by how the casting dynamics played out. "On *Love Island*, everyone has different jobs: plumbers, engineers, builders. Then suddenly on *All Stars*, it's reality TV guys." (Jess was not an antidote to the problem. Before going on season 6 of *Love Island*, the twenty-year-old was studying psychology, and her sister, Eve, was pursuing a degree in geography and planned to work for a humanitarian organization. Now they are professional twins with nearly identical influencing careers.)

There was a lot of encouragement from producers to hash out previous flirtations, which led Islanders like Toby and season 4 Islander Georgia Steel to crack on. Not everyone responded to the provocations. "It's a lot more PG," Hannah says. "I'm not gonna say set up, but it's a lot more like, 'So what are you planning to do? Maybe you should go and speak to them and tell them how you feel.' Where mine was a free-for-all. Like, I ran around with me boobs out."

Hannah failed to find a match in the stilted environment, instead spending her time eating chicken nuggets and chips with fellow single Liberty. Hannah was dumped and went back to Liverpool on day sixteen, taking a plane ride that would be one of her favorite parts of the experience. "Me and Mitch flew home together," she says. "I had a white Skims maxi dress on. We got so pissed on the plane, and I had red wine all over me, and all these old people were looking at us. We were like, 'Look, we've basically been locked up. Leave us alone.'"

Molly Smith is one of the cast members best suited to thrive in the morass of *Love Island.* She had been recruited for season 6 through her modeling agency and was cognizant of the professional opportunities that could come from the show. She was also aware of the personal upside: She and Callum Jones had dated from the middle of their season until just a few months before *All Stars*.

There was a lot of speculation among fans about whether Callum and Molly would once again fall in love on *Love Island.* She almost didn't go on *All Stars* because the breakup was too fresh for her to be ready for a new relationship. Molly also didn't know whether Callum would be invited back, though she assumed it was a possibility.

Molly came on as a night-one bombshell, which seemed to boggle Callum. "You all right?" Molly asked Callum.

"*You* all right?" Callum replied. He rebounded from his initial bafflement and chose to couple with Molly out of familiarity or a misguided chivalry. She took the gesture as an opening to reconciliation and recoupled with him to see if the relationship could "progress and blossom" if they talked through their issues. Callum, meanwhile, seemed happy to be on *Love Island* to find a person who thought he didn't need to change a thing. They had a series of frustrating conversations: Molly regaling the group with the story of the first time she told Callum she loved him and he laughed in her face; Callum saying he was open to other women and wondering why Molly thought he needed to be "tested" before she put effort in; Molly explaining that she was not willing to put herself out there with someone she'd thought she would marry if Callum was equally open to cracking on with her as someone he'd just met. Callum's limited engagement brought back the ugly feeling Molly had during their relationship: that Callum was taking her for granted. He couldn't understand Molly's unhappiness; if she didn't like how he was in a relationship, why was she trying to get back with him? After a week of this drain-circling, Molly became so upset that producers sent her to bed early and let her hide in the Beach Hut for half a day with a sleeve of Oreos.

Despite Callum being totally unsuitable for Molly, viewers started madly shipping them, encouraged by the Heart Rate Challenge. Vacuum-sealed into a latex bikini and boots, Molly bit Callum's ear. "It makes me feel sick thinking about it," she says of how nervous she was before coming out for the challenge. She had begged the producers to let her have both of her daily drinks at the same time. The request was denied, though Molly would later learn the boys had been given the two at once. Callum's heart rate was raised the most by Molly, and Molly's by Callum.

On day eleven, Molly recoupled with Tom, a shy twenty-four-year-old footballer who seemed to pine for her, even if he had a hard time expressing that (or most other things) verbally. The audience, however, clung to the notion of Molly and Callum. On Family Day, when loved ones tell each Islander what they and the public think of the cast member's performance, Molly was shocked to learn that people were still rooting for the exes to get back together. "I think it's because everyone just kind of wants it to kind of come back to this fairy tale," she told Callum during what would be one of their final conversations that season. "I'm happy that you found Tom," Callum said. "He makes you a lot happier." It was the nicest and smartest thing he'd say to Molly all season.

After that closure, Molly went to the terrace with Tom and told him she really, really liked him and that she saw something serious coming out of this.

"You are what I've been wanting," he said sweetly.

The pair would win *All Stars* and continue to date on the outside. The connection that had incubated in the Villa would survive transplantation: a year and a half later, Molly and Tom got engaged. "I didn't think it would happen in there, I'll be completely honest with you," Molly says. "I was hopeful, but I just thought, 'There's no way you can do it twice.' You see so many people who go on and they don't meet someone, so I thought, 'What's the chances in me getting to actually gel with someone again?'"

In our conversation, as on the show, Molly was unusually sincere for a *UK* Islander; when she listed reasons why the time since the show had been the best of her life, she pointed to Tom accompanying her on international modeling jobs she was sent on. The post-Villa experience had retroactively made meaning of all the televised pain and humiliation that had led to it. And the plan had worked: As their fellow All Stars kvetched and rehashed and feuded, two non-illustrious Islanders were now genuinely in love—and, at least collectively, the couple was now wealthy and famous. As every season of *Love Island* seems to be in reaction to the last, this would not be the model for the winners of *All Stars* 2.

13

Diving In

THE FIRST CASTING ANNOUNCEMENT for *Love Island USA* season 6 was a big one: Ariana Madix would host the show. Ariana had been a guest on the previous season for mostly synergistic reasons: She was a cast member on *Vanderpump Rules*, which aired on Bravo, another of NBCU's platforms. Ariana was given the full-time gig just a few months after Scandoval, the 2023 public ordeal which erupted from the news that Tom Sandoval, Ariana's costar and boyfriend of nine years, had been sleeping with another *VPR* castmate. Ariana discovered this betrayal through an explicit video that Sandoval, in a show of poor judgment both typical and inexplicable, had saved on his phone. Scandoval became a massive cultural pageant because of the timeline: Sandoval's infidelity was revealed while season 10 was airing; during filming, he had been secretly conducting the affair. Viewers were insatiable, collecting evidence from social media and cast interviews so they could overlay the foreshadowing of the reveal with the real-time fallout. When fans watched season 11, which documented the reverberations of the crisis, they had the satisfaction of knowing that the Ariana they saw being forced to live with her cheating ex as they worked out the sale of their shared home was going to be hosting *Love Island* soon.

Season 10 of *Vanderpump Rules* would become a lodestar to Thomas in its ability to provoke 360-degree engagement in viewers. "The show occurs off the show," Thomas says, meaning the conversations that could happen among fans became as important as the season itself—which then of course increased viewership for the series as new fans rushed to take part in the gestalt. In the case of *Love Island*, there was an added layer: The audience was invited to influence what happened on-screen; the discourse was flowing in both directions. "And then you watch the show looking for the things that are occurring off the show," Thomas says. "And then the show comes back and tells you the rest of the story. Fucking great. That is the goal now for me."

Scandoval was crushing for Ariana. It also (thank God) severed her commitment to Sandoval and made *VPR*'s massive fandom protective of her—during Scandoval, average weekly viewership reached 11.4 million. Ariana had been a mid-level ensemble member; now she was a solo star. After she decided not to return to *VPR*, the show was entirely recast.

Ariana's journey was a backward *Love Island* story: Her romantic saga happened on the outside and brought her to the Villa to act as the patron saint of people who find love on television. During the prelude to her and Sandoval's breakup, there was a serendipitous moment on-screen that served as both an advertisement for *Love Island* and audition tape for Ariana. "You don't sit there and watch episodes of *Love Island* with me," she told Sandoval, explaining a source of their disconnect. "Well, no, I don't have time to watch fifty goddamn episodes of *Love Island*!" he replied. A year later, Ariana's job was live-viewing the show that her boyfriend used as pretense to cheat on her.

Danielle Gervais says they booked Ariana because they knew "she

[was] coming in as a real fan." Like Caroline before her, Gervais says, "You feel like Ariana cares about [the Islanders]. She's not sitting in her hotel room getting a facial; she's watching all of this go down. She comes in invested, which is huge. It's crucial."

Being compared to Caroline is "the highest compliment," Ariana says. "I loved watching her host because she had a connection with [the Islanders]." Ariana's own bond with the cast is informed by her singular position as the sole host of *USA* or *UK* who was on a reality show that focused on her love life. "I'm actually the only cast member who simultaneously is with them, and on the show, and also online at the same time," Ariana says of the Islanders. "I am enmeshed in it, and that's why I was brought on. And I don't want to change that in order to just become a more detached host."

"Detached host" in this context seems to mean "someone with more professional hosting experience"—Ariana's presenting résumé was sparse. Never mind. She could learn on the clock.

Ariana was emblematic of the cast that season: both slightly off and perfect for the job. "I remember coming out of the screenings of the bio packages," Thomas says, "and I was like, 'There's something odd about this group.' If I had to guess—and it's probably not fair on them—they were ugly-ducklings-to-beautiful-swan types." Casting producers returned to Florida Atlantic University, an academically undistinguished college with a 73 percent acceptance rate that had yielded the previous season's male winner, Marco Donatelli, and recruited twenty-two-year-old Australian Liv Walker. "Not the rudest way," Liv says, "but I had no high expectations and nothing really to lose—it was not a massive show at the time." She thought about trying to get on *Love Island Australia*, which was more popular and established, but the casting processes were totally separate. Why not go on this series that barely anyone would watch and see if anything happened? As Liv remembers executive producer Courtney Rosenthal telling her, "*Love Island* can give you three things: love, friendship, and personal growth. And if you can get two out of the three of those, then you're winning at life." Liv got two, as well as a fourth thing Rosenthal hadn't mentioned because at the time it wasn't feasible: enough money from *Love Island*–related sponsorships and appearances that she would be able to start shopping for a house.

When Liv came in as the first bombshell on day two, she joined Kendall Washington, a good-natured cipher who always looked like he was posing for an employee ID photo. The twenty-six-year-old sales manager from San Diego would become the women's confidant and coin the repulsive term "nausty," a derivative of "nasty" spoken in an Austin Powers accent and used to indicate something was sexual. Others in the lineup included twenty-seven-year-old British yacht crewman Aaron Evans and twenty-two-year-old graduate student Kaylor Martin, who would almost instantly become the season's first real couple.

JaNa Craig was the season 6 yes girl, with comic-book cleavage and a breathless optimism for true love. Like Bergie, the twenty-seven-year-old day trader tended to inadvertently stomp over conversations, smothering them with affirmation in her sexy baby voice. She was inveterately root-for-able.

JaNa bonded with Serena Page, a twenty-four-year-old media planner and one of the most well-comported Islanders to appear on *Love Island*. They would quickly enmesh with Leah Kateb, the High Priestess of the Villa.

"Leah is the same person she is on the show as she is in real life," Thomas says. During her casting interview, Leah sat on her floor surrounded by plush toys and talked about her dating history—she had once bought an ex a Louis Vuitton stash box to store his blunts in. Though Leah never confirmed this verbally, Gervais believed that she—who, like the Kardashians, lived in Calabasas—had dated Ye, then known as Kanye West. "Sometimes I go, 'Why did you make this choice?'" Thomas says of Leah going on *Love Island*. "Leah never watched an episode of the show before, has never watched a show after, is independently wealthy. Why did she come? I do not know. I'm glad she did." Viewers were, too.

From day one, Leah focused on Rob Rausch, a snake catcher who almost exclusively wore overalls sans shirt. He had a breezy charisma that bumped up nicely against Leah's more tightly wound appeal. Rob's torso was covered in tattoos depicting his beloved reptiles and spiders, which he would catch in the Villa and show off to the many women who became captivated by him. In our interview, Rob tells me—while shirtless, in a bucket hat, and eating a banana—that during his psychological evaluation, he was asked to describe himself before the therapist went over the results of the five-hundred-or-so-question multiple choice personality test he'd taken. "I'm caring," he told her. "My toxic traits are I can't open up; I'm a bit avoidant; I'm a creative thinker, an introverted extrovert." The therapist told him he was also self-aware and ended the session. Rob had done her job for her; he was approved.

Rob had been cast on season 5 as part of the original lineup but could simply not film his introductory video in a way that worked. Thursby-Palmer kept pulling him aside to coach him. "We know you're amazing," he told Rob. "We know you're funny. But you're doing terrible." Rob was aware he was coming across weirdly, but there was nothing he could do to get comfortable in front of the cameras. Rob says the sense he got from producers was that they felt like if he couldn't even make it through his intro, he was not going to be good on an entire season of the show. Rob was instead put in the Casa lineup, where he caught a toad and displayed it to a woman as part of his mating ritual. Despite being encouraged to go for someone single, Rob went after future *Games* star Imani, whom he was warned would never recouple. She did not.

A year later, only two weeks before season 6 would begin filming, Rob was out looking for milk snakes when he saw a turtle walking in the middle of the road. Rob pulled over, and as he held the creature he had just saved in his hands, he got a call from Rosenthal. She wanted him in Fiji, she said. Rob says if she had called him at a different moment, he would have told her no. Luckily, the turtle had put him in an amazing mood. "He could take it or leave it, any of this," Thomas says, encapsulating Rob's appeal—along with the fact that, he says, "Everyone says when they meet him that he is the most attractive person they've ever met in their lives."

"Anyone who knows anything about snakes knows a thing or two about women," Rob said in the stiff intro he managed to record for season 6. "If it's agitated, you should probably take a step back. If *she's* agitated, you should shut the fuck up."

That season, producers decided to start with a challenge that would give the Islanders some information to go off for the initial coupling. Ariana supplied superlatives to the cast, who then kissed the people they thought most fit the label. Rob picked Leah as the Islander who was the biggest red flag, which she loved; they made out, and she elected to couple with him. Leah told Ariana she had chosen Rob because the suit jacket he was wearing "was just giving very sexy Wall Street banker." Rob, who would never be seen wearing that outfit (or basically any top with sleeves) again, lives in a trailer in Alabama.

"I think they might have literally sought you out for me," Leah told Rob during their first conversation, in between giggles. "Well, let's see if you have what I want," Rob said. "I mean, looks-wise, you're doing great, but I don't know anything about you."

"The more you talk, I think the more I like you," Leah responded. "And the more I talk, you're like, 'This bitch is nuts.'" This interplay—Leah pursuing him like a sexy Iranian American Pepé Le Pew, and Rob acknowledging her hotness while being radically honest about his doubts about their compatibility—would endure.

Leah had a manicured beauty that was no less perfect than the usual Villa standards but pointed at a different true north—long witchy waves, a nose job she was open about, bitsy tattoos sprinkled over her body, huge eyes that tracked around searchingly when she tried to comprehend normie behavior or her own feelings. It all worked well enough for Rob until Andrea Carmona came in. Though he could have chemistry with anyone—and Leah was not just anyone—viewers now saw what it looked like when the normally nonchalant Rob was awestruck.

Rob flirted with the bombshell in Soul Ties by performing his signature move: catching a bug and putting it on the twenty-five-year-old singer-songwriter's arm. This led to the infamous pool dive and Leah's crashout. Serena was supportive via her utter derision for Rob, telling Leah she couldn't sleep next to him and that Serena would spend the night outside with her. Leah was fully bereft as Rob continued to bob under the deck.

When he became too cold, Rob got out of the pool and went with a producer to chain-smoke and sob more. He'd only been on season 5 for a few days; he hadn't realized what it would be like to be in the Villa for so long, or that he'd never be alone to process his feelings about the decisions he had to make to stay on *Love Island*. "It was terrible," Rob says of his breakdown. "I hope that never happens again. I actually now have anxiety, and I think it's because of that."

Leah didn't know any of that when she went off about him to the girls the next evening in the changing room. "Everyone should be scared because I've been behaving myself so fucking well, and look what it got me," Leah yelled while the women agreed that Rob was terrible and had led Leah on. "*You* can cradle him while he cries in the corner," she said in reference to Andrea, who was with Rob out of earshot. "After I saw him crying like a bitch on the floor yesterday, I literally got the ick." Liv gave "exaaactly" nods, drying her hair with a Dyson Airwrap as Leah revised history, claiming her revulsion—not her hurt or Serena's insistence Leah not further degrade herself at the altar of Rob—was the reason she slept outside. Leah finished with a "Fuck you, bitch," which she'd also mouthed to Rob as he walked Andrea to the scene of his crime: Soul Ties, *again*.

Rob's inward-turning emotional distress and Leah's more expulsive expression of it was played as melodrama by producers who trusted the straight presentation would read as a sitcom to viewers. They were right: It was the first scene of *Love Island USA* that started a bona fide moment, largely at Rob's expense.

What happened as Rob hid in the pool broke Thomas's ethos for the show: Don't hurt anybody. But like Leah, Thomas didn't know the state of Rob's mental health. He just knew he was creating appointment television—and this moment was sticky. Viewership quadrupled over the next three weeks.

Rob would go from divisive to unpopular with fans, who voted him out on day thirty. The pool moment was broadly interpreted as manipulative—viewers thought Rob was trying to get out of a difficult conversation with Leah and that he had only pretended to have the collapse he was actually experiencing to engender sympathy.

When Rob left the Villa, producers told him two things: *Love Island USA* was the number one show in America, and Donald Trump had been shot. Then they gave him his phone back. "I had a bunch of hate," Rob says of the fan reaction. "And then I had a bunch of . . . it wasn't love, because it was like, 'Yeah, no, he is actually a terrible person, but he's so hot.' At least there's that." (Other viewers found Rob refreshingly weird and amusing—and also hot.) His DMs were full of offers for sponsorship; the height of these opportunities was an offer to star in a Super Bowl commercial for Poppi soda. Rob made enough money to buy a second home.

But the effect was depersonalizing. "I was like a completely different [man]," Rob says—one he didn't like or respect. Though he says he's blessed to have had the opportunity, "I hated it. I am so unhappy when I'm on a brand trip with a bunch of people, and they're like, 'Let's do shots.' I'm like, 'Get me the fuck out of here.'" Rob returned to Alabama to spend time with snakes and work on his grandfather's farm, where he would largely stay until a revelatory performance on *The Traitors* season 4.

Leah being labeled as what she interpreted as unfuckable (though Rob's words didn't actually suggest that) was clearly something she never would have wanted to happen. Neither would the moment where she reacted to a mental health episode by calling Rob a bitch, nor getting dumped for a woman who wore her hair in a ponytail with two tiny braids hanging down the sides of her face. But had none of that occurred, and Rob had fulfilled Leah's wish to stay in the couple, she never would have met Miguel Harichi, a twenty-seven-year-old model from London.

Leah went into the Villa with fewer than fifteen thousand followers and now has more than five million. She actually changed the American Duty of Care. Producers specifically tell cast members, "You might not be Leah," Gervais says. She became chief creative officer of the niche fragrance line Skylar and was on *Forbes*'s 2026 30 Under 30 list for her social media reach. But more than any business accolade, Leah has found success doing the thing that every influencer wants to but almost none manages. Her product is herself, and her currency is sitting around with Miguel, cooking, and spending time with her many, many animals. Her job is being Leah.

Aaron had been on TV before *Love Island*. He'd won the first season of *The Traitors UK*, which, unlike its American version, features ordinary people. (*The Traitors* was also developed by Sharon Vuong, an Anglophile with an incredible insight for which British properties would translate in America.) Airing on the BBC, *The Traitors* is a much gentler show than *Love Island USA*—it feels like a contest set at a summer camp in comparison. Like a children's game, the players get upset if they're accused of being the bad guy when they're not—in this case, pegged as one of the titular traitors. Aaron says while filming, he only interacted with production through the welfare team, rather than the field producers he would work with at the Villa. "If we ever felt uncomfortable or if they could see that we felt uncomfortable, they would stop the show straightaway," he says. "They very much were there for us."

When Aaron filled out his psychological evaluation questionnaire for *Love Island*, he says he got bored and started randomly answering the "true or false" section. (Aaron has ADHD.) The psychologist who went over Aaron's results with him and asked if he was "sure" about his random answers for some red-flag questions, which he then changed. Aaron mentioned to her something the psych for *The Traitors* had told him during the evaluation for that series. "He'd actually advised me not to go on the show," Aaron told her. "He said that I wouldn't be able to deal with it mentally. I would take things to heart too much, and I would get too upset." He also mentioned he'd had his first panic attack while filming *The Traitors*. The psychologist apparently didn't find enough red flags to stop him from being cast. Aaron remains doubtful about that conclusion: "I don't know whether or not she should have let me go on it," he says.

There were problems for Aaron even before he got into the Villa. He was in his hotel room for more than twenty hours a day, leading to extreme loneliness, and the suitcase with his homeopathic ADHD medication got lost in transit. He started smoking cigarettes because it would allow him to leave his room and give him fifteen minutes of conversation with a chaperone in addition to his allotted outdoor time. Before he was cast, Aaron had disclosed to producers that he had been sober for six months because he realized he'd get intoxicated to deal with stress. At the hotel, Aaron started drinking again. During the several hours a day he was allowed out of his room, he'd go to the pool and get strangers to buy him cocktails. It would preview both his ability to charm and his difficulty in making good decisions for himself.

Aaron's scattered boyishness was broadcast from his introduction. "I don't want to sit down," he said to camera, grinning. "I kind of want to just stand up. I kind of want to look around. Am I allowed to look around?" Aaron stood in the fluorescent box he was filming in. "I'm looking around. You guys need to Hoover down here, by the way. Just saying!" He said he was moving to the US if he found a girl with blonde hair and blue eyes who could be his best friend that he had sex with.

Kaylor had all three qualities, along with a set of Miss Piggy eyelashes and a very strong Pittsburgh accent. She did not own the golden retriever Aaron had hoped his partner might have, but he basically filled that role anyway. They kept up a giddy, endless jabber, nattering about what kinds of beans they liked and discussing who fancied whom the most as Aaron straddled her. "I love speaking with Aaron!" Kaylor exclaimed. "I could talk to him all day, spend all the time with him."

But then in walked Liv, who was also blonde-haired and blue-eyed. Aaron flirted with her, though the chat was not as effortless as with Kaylor. Meanwhile, Kaylor was inconsolable and cried for the first of what would wind up being more than seventy-eight times, according to the chart Aaron started keeping.

Liv was not impressed with Aaron's lifestyle. When he wasn't working as a crew member on a yacht, he lived in a home with his mother, whose down payment had been paid for with his *Traitors* winnings. Despite his initial attraction, Liv's apparent derision insulted Aaron, and he told a senior producer he called "Auntie" that he was going to move on. Auntie encouraged him to keep talking to Liv. Aaron reiterated his disinterest to a field producer with whom he'd become friendly. Aaron says the field producer told him he couldn't be sure he didn't like Liv until he kissed her. Aaron interpreted this as an attempt to cause drama between him and Kaylor, who would have happily carried on snuggling on the daybeds and chatting about legumes—and not contributing to the plot.

In a scene that didn't air, Aaron told Liv not to choose him to couple up with; he was sticking with Kaylor. "I do not want to be with you," he told her bluntly, walking off and ending the discussion. "I think that fucked the storyline for the producers," Aaron says now. The field producer came up to Aaron after he spoke with Liv. "What the fuck are you doing?" he asked, according to Aaron. "When you have these conversations, you speak to a producer beforehand, and you tell them what's gonna happen." The next day, Aaron says, Auntie was walking up the stairs. "At this time, I was happy-go-lucky, pretty full of beans," he says. (More beans!) He called out, "Love you!" Aaron says, "She didn't even look at me, and she was like, 'It's not reciprocated.' It was the first ever time where I realized, 'Oh, actually, you're not really like Auntie vibes. You are a producer. If something doesn't go your way, you get pissed off.'"

Meanwhile, Kaylor's attention shifted with the arrival of Connor Newsum, a day-two bombshell who locked in on her. Connor asked Kaylor if she wanted to talk, and a rapport-free conversation ensued. "I had, like, no sleep," Connor says. "I was running on pure adrenaline, and it was like, 'Okay, I gotta pull her for a chat. We're gonna go do this conversation in Soul Ties.' And there was just, like, THE CAMERAS. I could just feel them, and I could see them pivoting. It was probably one of the few times in the Villa where I was just so painfully aware that I was on a TV show and that there were people at home watching." Connor's abject handsomeness and amiability earned him a second chance.

Kaylor and the twenty-eight-year-old publicist would return to Soul Ties that night for a less self-conscious interaction—despite the fact that Leah, Serena, and JaNa had slunk over to secretly watch them in an unprecedented triple-terrace crawl. "Don't fuck this up," JaNa said as Leah and Serena's gasping giggles threatened to blow their mission. This was one of the triad's first official acts as PPG, named after the animated superhero trio The Powerpuff Girls. It was a canny branding move for the group that would be at the center of the entire season, propping each other up and reacting with an appropriately vicious level of disgust whenever any men dared to hurt one of them.

In Soul Ties, Connor and Kaylor kissed, which she told Aaron happened with a producer's urging. (ITV refutes this: "Islanders are never pressured or encouraged to kiss or otherwise engage in any sexual behavior that they're uncomfortable with.") Kaylor did not appear uncomfortable during the makeout that aired, but afterward she began sobbing in panic when she thought about telling Aaron the news. Producers suggested she wait to do so.

Thomas says this is a major part of producing. "You will speed up or slow down the content depending on what you need," he says. For example, a producer may have told Kaylor "to sleep on it" to let tension build, though that would be a more common note in the UK. (Thursby-Palmer says telling someone to sleep on it may be helpful to them so they don't escalate the conflict to a point that is destructive—they do need continuing plotlines for the show to work—or because there are too many stories happening and they can't all be captured at once.) In America, producers usually speed up the pace by encouraging conversations between third parties: in this case, Connor and the rest of the men, who were supposed to learn about the kiss and inform Aaron. However, Aaron already knew because Kaylor had told him, first in an unmic'd whisper and then again in a calm discussion, ruining what could have been an interesting confrontation between the boys. Aaron felt like because he hadn't listened to producers, *then* hadn't given them the big reaction they were hoping for after the Connor-Kaylor kiss, they had started disliking him. "They wanted me to fail," he believes.

If that is indeed what they wanted—and production assures me it isn't—Aaron obliged. At Casa he was taken with Daniela Ortiz-Rivera, a twenty-two-year-old student who shared with him a childhood trauma regarding her mother. The story, which only aired in part, moved Aaron to tell her, "I already feel like I love you so much." Aaron says he told the field producer he wanted to sleep outside and that the producer told him there wasn't anywhere to do so, which should have been obvious to Aaron wasn't the case. "I'm a very easily influenced person," Aaron says by way of explanation.

Aaron claims producers offered them extra alcohol that night, and he got drunk because he'd only been allowed two small drinks a day and had a low tolerance. Thomas concedes it's possible to sneak drinks but says producers would never deliberately give Islanders more than the allotted amount of alcohol, and if they realized someone was drunk, they would immediately be taken off camera. ITV denies that anyone has ever been given excess alcohol, saying, "*Love Island USA* has been committed to its longstanding drink policy/limit since season one. This policy has never been paused or lifted at any point in any season."

Aaron's threshold for intoxication was also low because he lost almost twenty pounds over six weeks in the Villa. He is vegan for ethical reasons and says he was given the same meal every day: avocado toast for breakfast and tofu and a baguette for lunch and dinner. A crew member noticed Aaron was dropping weight and started bringing him pistachios and dried mangoes, which he says is the only thing he ate for his last two weeks in the Villa. ITV says, "Dietary limitations and restrictions are always respected throughout filming." When asked specifically about Aaron's weight loss, they said, "Production of course monitors both the physical and mental well-being of the Islanders at all times."

That night, Aaron slept in bed with Daniela—and, he says, tipsily thinking she was Kaylor, put his hand on her hip bone inside her underwear. Whenever there is visible sexual contact, producers ask Islanders how they're doing and if they gave consent. Daniela confirmed that she had.

The next day, when he was not drunk, Aaron told Daniela, "How were the minor cuddles last night? I think you're a difficult person to not cuddle . . . It was difficult last night, not kissing and shit." Daniela was charmed; they made out on the beanbags, which concluded with Aaron telling her, "Right now I can't stand up for about two minutes," and asking if they could go in the shower, one of his sexual peccadillos.

The scene had come after a conversation with the field producer, during which Aaron was asked why he wasn't kissing Daniela. "Kaylor's down there in Casa Amor having the Casa Amor experience, and she's getting involved in it," the producer said. It was basically a singing telegram version of the old Casa postcard from *Love Island UK*. "You look like an idiot," Aaron says the producer told him, implying Kaylor was hooking up with other people.

Thomas, who was not in the field during season 6, elucidates a technical difference in how the cast internalizes the messages of this kind of producing with the specific words producers use. "You wouldn't say, 'That person is . . .' or 'I heard . . .' You would say, 'You don't know what they're up to. If you wanna have faith in them, good, that's a really great place to be. But if you have feelings for someone else here, if you've met someone here, you actually don't know what that other person is doing. I hope they're being right for you, but maybe they're not. You don't know. You only get one chance at being here on this show. You have to do the thing that's right for you in the moment. So whatever that is, you should do that.'" In addition to crossing what Thomas considers a red line, deceiving the Islanders takes away ITV's continued ability to produce those contestants. "This is producer in the field 101," he says. For example: "If someone said something to me in confidence and I go and tell another Islander, it will be fucking *EastEnders*"—the British soap starring Dani Dyer's father, on which any hidden misdeed is a Chekhov's gun that will eventually be fired. "Never in the history of that universe has anyone ever gotten away with anything," Thomas says.

Regardless of the circumstances that got him there, Aaron says after the kiss, he lay in bed for three hours, feeling "like the biggest piece of shit. It almost felt like I was just retaliating to what she was doing"—actually, what Kaylor was *not* doing—"which I didn't think was healthy at all."

All of this was revealed at an apocalyptic Movie Night. "Look at him just eating the popcorn, Kaylor," Leah said after a clip was run of Aaron teaching Daniela the same handshake he'd taught Kaylor. "Typical Aaron," Liv said. TYPICAL Aaron, eating popcorn as the world burned! As the clips got worse, Kaylor's wails rose to what would unfortunately become her catchphrase: "*Fawk* Aaron!"

Aaron went from defensive—saying "Sorry" in a way that implied he wasn't—then seeming to disassociate, then insisting it was his "experience" and he was allowed to have it, then yelling at Liv for coming at him on Kaylor's behalf. "I have made mistakes," Aaron said. "But in the moment, that's how I felt!"

In an interaction that didn't make the edit, Thomas says, Aaron told Kaylor the producers had made him get together with Daniela. Kaylor responded with anger: "I have the same fucking producers that you do, and I didn't cheat on you!"

"Honestly, I feel like he didn't think it was really his fault because the show is unscripted, but it's pretty heavily produced," Rob says of Aaron. "No one can make you do anything, but they push you; I saw firsthand he was really pushed in Casa. But then watching it, I was like, 'Bro, I mean, you did it at the end of the day. It doesn't matter if someone you thought was your friend tried to talk you into doing this—you did it, and Kaylor is a real person with real feelings, and they're hurt. You have to be responsible for that. There's no blaming anyone else—it was you.'"

During Movie Night, Rob got his own moment of reconciliation. They played the clip of Leah scorning Rob for crying during his panic attack. Leah laughed nervously and made excuses—she'd seen him flirting with someone else and was upset—before she eventually apologized. "I'm deeply, deeply, deeply sorry for everything I said there," Leah said. Rob looked like he'd been punched. "It's not funny to me,"

Leah went on. "I don't think you're a bitch or a pussy or whatever I called you in there."

Rob accepted but told her, "People keep asking me, 'Would you ever get back with Leah?' And I'm like, 'I really like Leah, and I laugh with Leah, and I love being around her, but I don't trust [her] anymore.'" He explained how embarrassed he had been about crying and that it was because he knew he was going to hurt her or Andrea.

Leah never asked how he was doing, Rob said, even when he was sobbing—she just kept saying how *she* was feeling.

"I was like, 'How am I in a place with twelve people, and I feel more alone than I have in years?'" Rob said. "And I lost it, and I jumped in the pool like a dumbass."

Rob is grateful for the Movie Night experience. "That was one of the best moments in the show," he says. "It made me so happy that I stayed in the Villa to have that moment. I would've had just this uneasy feeling for so long if that had never happened . . . It was so good to just fully bury the hatchet with Leah and that just to be over and done with. At that point I thought we were gonna be friends—it didn't work out that way, but that's totally fine."

The conversation inspired Zapruder-footage-level dissection from fans and content creators. *Bachelor* alum Nick Viall's podcast, *The Viall Files*, started covering *Love Island USA* intensely in season 6, alternating reality recaps and cast interviews with episodes where he gives relationship advice that frequently invokes an advanced amateur take on attachment. For what it's worth, when people's attachment styles are disrupted—as they constantly and deliberately are on *Love Island*—they can have a strong emotional response that temporarily overrides their ability to consider and accommodate how another person is feeling. So if, for example, someone with an anxious attachment style were seeking reassurance from an avoidant person and not receiving it, the anxious party might be too upset to check in with the avoidant one, and the avoidant one might jump in a pool.

Fans of the show would start making their pop psychology diagnoses on the *Love Island* Subreddit.

Following Movie Night, Aaron admitted he'd kissed Daniela because he wanted to and that he hadn't been thinking about Kaylor when he was doing it. It was honest enough that it seemed to prove the larger point—that Aaron wanted to be with Kaylor and not Daniela, which is why he'd fobbed the latter off on Rob. Kaylor took Aaron back, despite Liv strongly advising her not to. "You've got to learn to shut the window and know that there'll be a sunset the next day," Liv told her. Liv says in a scene that was cut—perhaps because there were so many post-mortems covering Aaron's Casa performance—Kaylor said, "He told me everything. Why expect there's more?" Of course, there was more. At the reunion, Aaron disclosed the hand-in-the-panties story, belatedly taking accountability at a point when it was no longer productive.

"Bro, you're just putting salt in the wound now," Rob thought.

By the time they were dumped from the Villa just before the finale, fans were exhausted by Kaylor and Aaron, individually and as a couple. They were sick of Kaylor crying. They were over Aaron justifying his misconduct. The couple broke up after the season ended, got back together before the reunion, then ended things for good. Aaron moved back to the UK and disappeared for months. He didn't get anything close to the reported six-figure deals of the other Islanders because he was, to put it mildly, not a fan favorite. What Aaron was offered he turned down to avoid further association with the show that had dragged him into a depression. He would sleep all day to stop his brain from ruminating about what he'd done in the Villa, why he'd allowed himself to be persuaded, his hatred of his compliance, what everyone was writing about him online, what Ariana had said on *Aftersun* about him being unkind to women.

What viewers saw obviously doesn't reflect the totality of what happened or what Ariana witnessed on set and through the daily footage she had access to. "The show is quite often holding things back to protect people," Thomas says. "If we had shown more, we would've gained nothing, and they would've lost more. If, for example, Aaron says something in a conversation that Kaylor is hurt by, and then he says two more things that are offensive to her, and they're not different, what do you gain by showing all three of those? Nothing. You actually just make his life worse. He made a mistake. He does not deserve for his life to be over now."

Eventually, Aaron's mother convinced him to leave the house for short walks. He got rid of his internet connection. He kept seeing his therapist from *The Traitors*, who provided his services pro bono to the man he'd cautioned not to go on reality TV in the first place. Aaron's first post–*Love Island* feeling of happiness was raising money for the hospice in which his grandfather stayed by hitchhiking across the country, and for a mental health nonprofit by cycling the length of Spain. "It was the first time in ages that I had a goal in mind and I was trying to do something for someone else," he says. "I try not to be negative, but the overriding thoughts . . ." Aaron says of *Love Island*. "It's kind of all I think about."

And yet, somehow, despite *Love Island USA* consuming his mind, Aaron made the decision to go on the show's spin-off *Beyond the Villa*. The series premiered in 2025 and followed all of the main season 6 cast members besides Rob as they lived in (or, in Kaylor and Aaron's cases, stayed in) Los Angeles.

Beyond the Villa was, as the title suggests, about the group's post-Villa lives and might have filled the pop culture space vacated by Ariana's era of *Vanderpump Rules*. But it lacked *VPR*'s depravity and *Love Island*'s kinetic ephemerality—with the exception of Kaylor and Aaron's ongoing friction and evident attraction, it mostly showed the rest of the cast sitting in bars and talking, with occasional cameos from PPG in which they spoke about their anxiety. Aaron did it for the money, he says—he wanted a van to drive to Italy and Switzerland with his brother, with whom he makes YouTube videos.

But Aaron also got something like closure with Kaylor. He got to be the person he wished he'd been on *Love Island.* "I don't think I'll ever let anyone else ever influence me ever again," Aaron says. "I've had to learn through default to just take responsibility." When Kaylor invited him back to her place, producers told him he should go—they weren't able to keep filming at their current location. Aaron declined. His choices were, as ever, his own.

The producorial plotting and unnatural setting that seemed to push Aaron and Rob to emotional dysregulation was also responsible for creating season 6's winning love story. When Kordell Beckham first met Serena at the firepit, they were both auspiciously dressed entirely in *Brat* green. "We didn't necessarily go in going, 'These two are gonna be a couple,'" Thursby-Palmer says. "But from night one, the first time they looked at each other, we were like, 'There they are.'"

Kordell, a twenty-two-year-old aircraft fueler and the brother of NFL star Odell Beckham Jr., seemed to happily accept this reality. Serena remained a self-described "slow burn" who was open to talking to almost every bombshell who walked into the Villa, including Miguel. Serena grafted on him, asking if he got his brows done (no, they're just naturally perfect) and telling him she wasn't competitive over men. JaNa interrupted with eggs for Miguel, served three ways: scrambled, over easy, and as an omelet. "Now is not the time, JaNa," Serena said to her, utterly pissed off at a member of PPG for what would be one of their few moments of discord. "She knows I haven't really had that butterfly instant connection with somebody since I've been in here," Serena explained in the Beach Hut. She just seemed unenthusiastic about Kordell, who shared his ambition to act and get a Cheez-It sponsorship deal. That cracker sponcon was a dream was ick-inducing to Serena.

Still, after telling Kordell she didn't feel a romantic connection, then putting him "back on the radar," Serena informed him he was her number one—for now. It felt to viewers (and the other Islanders) that Serena was keeping Kordell as a reserve option, which she seemed to affirm right before Casa in the "Stick or Twist" challenge. Each couple stood on opposite sides of a closed door and were told to keep dancing if they wanted to stick in their couple or leave the dance floor if they wanted to "twist" to other options. Kordell stuck; Serena twisted. "I'm telling myself, 'Shit, I got nothing to worry about,'" he said in the Beach Hut afterward, visibly wilting. "I do feel stupid. I do feel like I was played. Fucking looking stupid. I'm over here giggling and shit about this girl. She don't even feel the same way."

That season, Thursby-Palmer came up with a novel entrée to Casa Amor: The men could choose whether they wanted to go or not. "Ben's idea was to say they have to take self-responsibility, because they can't blame us as much if they are in control," Thomas said. It may sound like a dangerous proposition to leave the season's most important (and expensive) set piece in the hands of the Islanders, but it proved to be a compelling plot element: All the men, including the dance-disrespected Kordell, decided to leave.

While they were gone, something shifted for Serena. It seemed like Kordell had been too close for her to see properly in the Villa, and the distance to Casa had given her the perspective she'd needed to appreciate a man who simply wanted her—and to be paid for his love of cheesy snacks. "I miss Kordell so much," Serena told Kaylor. "But I'm such a hard bitch, I don't want to show that . . . That man has been so patient with me, so attentive. It's like, I need him. I'm sorry. I want him."

PPG was typically sympathetic. "I will take these heels off and run," JaNa told her later. "Say the word and we'll go to Casa Amor right now, because you know I don't give a fuck."

Unlike Serena, Daia McGhee was not afraid to show Kordell that she wanted him. They made out all over Casa while the twenty-seven-year-old travel blogger affirmed him, from telling him he deserved someone who was all about him to complimenting the size of his penis.

Kordell was conflicted, but having someone say "I'm here for *you*" was enough to get him to get close enough with Daia that the footage appeared to show them dry-humping; then he brought her back to the Villa, where he thought he would continue to be able to explore both connections and choose between the woman who had twisted away from him and the one who had stuck it on him.

When they returned, Serena attempted the scoff of someone who just *knew* this was coming, clapping for them sarcastically and talking about Kordell getting his "petey-wacker wet." He understood Serena was masking her hurt, while the male Islanders viewed her vehement response as unreasonable; to them, she hadn't allowed Kordell to be happy with her, and now she was trying to prevent him from enjoying things with Daia. "The other guys were saying things like, 'Oh, I don't know, maybe she's too upset,' or 'We didn't like the way she was talking,'" Ariana says. "Kordell never bought into that. He was always like, 'No, she has a right to feel this way.' A lot of times guys will do or say whatever to impress other guys, and I feel like that was such a healthy thing."

This is why Kordell would fare so much better than Aaron on Movie Night. "Seeing what I did, where I fucked up, and how it affected Serena, dog . . ." Kordell said after he watched her respond to the footage of him. "That shit hurt."

Kordell kept trying to have an honest conversation with Serena, but she was too guarded to engage. Eventually, she broke. During a climactic scene in which the pair fought while Serena paced back and forth the entire length of the dock—which Thomas calls "Serena getting her steps in"—she let Kordell in on what millions of viewers already knew: that she had needed a different kind of test than he did to understand that she only wanted him. "It didn't take me a week to explore with another guy to know that it was always you," she said, weeping. Finally, the guy who'd been second best to the possibility of a better man and the woman who realized nearly too late that she'd overlooked the person she'd loved all along were on the same page. The effect was cinematic; an unscripted romantic comedy moment in an era with a paucity of great rom-coms.

Many viewers had initially felt like Serena was leading Kordell on, though the PPG stans would defend her by pointing out that she was always honest with him about her ambivalence. By the time they made it to the dock, the audience, Serena, and Kordell had reached consensus: They belonged together.

"Even though she's so much younger, Serena is just such a beautiful example of someone who grew so much in allowing herself to let her walls down," Ariana says. "Watching her be able to go through that journey was really inspiring, because I just felt like I could take a piece of that into my own life and be able to express my emotions that well."

Thursby-Palmer says, "It was actually only going through the journey and jumping over the obstacles"—the ones he and his team had set up—"that by the end they were like, 'Actually, I think you are my person.' And they were so much stronger for it than if they never actually went on *Love Island*."

The public was enchanted. Kordell got his Cheez-It brand deal. Serena got to be the heroine of the season, along with the other members of PPG; all three made it to the end. "Do you know how rare it is for a trio—a best friend trio—to be in the final?" Leah asked as they broke into a goofy three-way dance in lieu of a designated handshake.

"PPG for lifers," JaNa cried.

In addition to creating love, friendship, and intergenerational wealth–inducing endorsement money, the show had created memes. The images became shorthand: PPG gave Spice Girls girl power; Rob slipping into the pool was the new Homer Simpson disappearing into a bush; Kaylor honking "*Fawk* Aaron!" was the transference of loserdom that happens when you can't leave a relationship with someone who can't step up; Kordell's Cheez-Its were the triumph of an oversaturated influencer era; and Serena's was a journey from the "hard bitch" she told everyone she was at the beginning of the season to the secret softie she'd been worn down into by the ordeal of the series.

"You need some adversity," Thomas says of how to triumph on *Love Island*. "If you want to be on one of these shows, then you want to be Serena. Pray to the TV gods that you get an arc like that."

14

Standing on Business

FOR THE FIRST TIME, *Love Island USA* wasn't going into the summer as the unwanted American spin-off of a beloved British series. All of a sudden, after six seasons, their show was a hit. While Bergie had made $15,000 influencing in the entire year after season 5, people from the season 6 cast were making many multiples of that for one post. Every member of PPG, plus Kordell and Kaylor, were signed to star in commercials that would air during every episode of season 7 for those poor souls who weren't paying for Peacock Premium Plus with no ads. Maura Higgins was absent from most of the season of *Aftersun* because she was in Scotland filming *The Traitors* with Rob, who would don his signature no-shirt overalls look as he became the most beloved cast member on the show even after betraying Maura for the win, prompting her to say, "You're never gonna have a girlfriend after this. You're such a good liar." (She forgave him when he bought her a Birkin bag with his winnings.) Any season 6 cast member who had lasted more than a few weeks was now at the level of the biggest stars in the entirety of *Love Island UK*—except Molly-Mae, of course.

But there was the question of how *Love Island USA* could sustain that energy. There was no "next Leah." There is no "new Rob." You couldn't depend on producing the love story of Kordell and Serena, or the collision and implosion of Aaron and Kaylor, or anyone diving in a pool in a way that didn't feel derivative of what had come before.

"Every format has a life cycle," ITV's Huub van Ballegooy says. "There is no endless growth. This is not the official opinion, but after season six, I personally thought, 'Holy crap, [it] really took off. Wow, if that was the peak, it was already great.'"

Adding to the burden of these expectations was the fact that the team was breaking up: In spring, Vuong moved over to Peacock's parent company NBCU to run alternative programming, and Thomas went to Pantheon Media Group to develop new shows, though he was still present for much of casting. Thursby-Palmer was in charge, with NBCU unscripted executive Rachel Smith's team from Bravo working on the corporate side. "Ben will pick a different North Star every year," Thomas says of how Thursby-Palmer runs *Love Island USA*. "He's pretty unflappable in terms of audience discourse." (This contrasts with Thomas, who was reading every Subreddit post and watching every TikTok about the show.) "Ben is the least cynical and most assured producer I've ever met, who also will never do things for any other reason than he thinks it'll be the most satisfying, entertaining way for that thing to play out," Thomas says. "But he will change his mind if someone has a better idea."

A few items were given special attention on the casting wish list. The number of applications blew up, from sixty-two thousand the previous year to ninety-five thousand. Though this was great news about interest in the show, many of those people were already pursuing influencing careers; it would not work if too many cast members had the same, studied profession. Casting director Gervais's team was dispatched to find what she calls "normal people who just happen to be gorgeous." She was also looking for local specificity, which would scratch the itch the British weirdies had given Americans. "Regional accents for us are huge," Gervais says. Their holy grail is eight-time *Survivor* cast member Rob Mariano, who has a Boston accent so thick he's known exclusively as "Boston Rob." "We are always hunting," Gervais says. "We still haven't found our fricking Boston Rob." They would, however, find Taylor Williams, a twenty-five-year-old rodeo competitor and veterinary school student from Oklahoma City whose dropped-gerund drawl was so inscrutable that closed-captioning would often simply skip over his dialogue and move on to the next Islander's sentence, hoping viewers would get the gist.

Another casting goal was finding men who were the top female applicants' types. "I can't tell you how many girls in this casting phase mentioned Miguel," Gervais says of Leah's head-turning boyfriend. "We said, from season six, what boys would you be attracted to? Every single person said Miguel. Every. One."

There was also an increased focus on finding Islanders of Asian descent. "Just candidly, I don't think we've delivered on that like we need to be," Gervais told me while casting season 7. "It's a conversation we have every season, and I genuinely think it's an area where we have to do better. I don't think we've done it justice." There had previously been mixed-race Islanders with Asian heritage on *USA*, but bombshell Zak Srakaew was one of a tiny number of cast members of entirely Asian descent. Zak was ideal: a *Big Brother* alum and fast-talking friend of Miguel who had moved to Manchester after spending his early childhood in Thailand. During his casting process, Gervais told me, "This one guy, he got off [the call], and we were all like, 'Oh my God. Oh my God.' And the network exec was ready to go meet him then and there. It was one of those moments where you're like, 'Yeah, we nailed it.'"

There was another Islander producers were particularly excited about: Ace Greene, a twenty-two-year-old content creator with a million followers on TikTok who watched his viral videos, in which he taught people in Pakistan how to do hip-hop dances. The acolytes were each squared in a box like the opening credits of *The Brady Bunch*, and Ace would begin the video by quizzing them on the lyrics or artist they would be dancing to that session. “Tell me who Ice Cube is?” Ace asked, as a man mimed putting ice in a cup. Ace feigned exasperation while people's farm animals sounded in the background. (“Whose damn chicken is that?”) At the end of the clips, everyone danced somewhat in unison. It was consensually borderline-insensitive fun that showcased what would be Ace's primary qualities on the season: his awareness of what would be interesting to watch, and that people responded positively to him being plainspoken. “He does the thing that so many Islanders don't do, which is that he speaks truth whether you want to hear it or not,” Thomas says. Of course, being on a perpetually filmed television show versus a self-edited video platform would offer a different lens on Ace's unvarnished thoughts.

Jeremiah Brown, a twenty-five-year-old model from Los Angeles, was recruited after Thursby-Palmer saw him in a marketing video for a jewelry company in which Jeremiah demonstrated his ability to be sexy while working out and showering. He filled out the lengthy psych test, which he says one would have to be truly unwell, or what he considered foolishly honest, to fail. “People can just lie,” Jeremiah says, naming a sample land-mine question: “Do you hear voices?”

“Respectfully, even if I'm hearing things, I'm saying no,” Jeremiah says. He had been in therapy for several years; not for auditory hallucinations, but to address what caused him to cheat in a past relationship. Jeremiah received positive feedback about his mental health care from the show's psychiatrist, whom he says told him, “The work you've done as a guy your age in this society's amazing, because most people don't work on themselves till way later. [You're] family-oriented, always like to get better, low ego.”

Jeremiah admits, “It sounds weird, saying it about myself, because it sounds like I have a big ego, but this is just what she said.” He jokes, accurately: “‘Most handsome guy.’ I think I heard that in there.”

To introduce the opening lineup that had taken seven months to put together, the season opened on an intricate dance sequence set to a cover of Janelle Monáe's "Make Me Feel," which, among its many glitzy moments of choreographed mugging and bopping, highlighted Ace's TikTok moves. The display was a harbinger for the spectacle that season 7 would become.

The first coupling heightened the previous season's opening game, in which kisses were doled out under the pretext of the Islander being the answer to a cheeky question. For season 7, the women got to pick whom they coupled up with based on dueling make-outs with two male Islanders, which were dragged down to slow-mo speed by the editors. Many were delivered to a man standing directly next to a woman who had already picked him, infusing the gambit with both cringiness and a preview of the just-next-door sex acts that they'd experience all summer in the bedroom. Ariana provided respectful horndog commentary. Her role enjoying the hedonism of the show while playing master of ceremonies would continue throughout the season in between delivering news of challenges, votes, and the rest of the producers' demonic interventions. (On *Aftersun*, Ariana would brag that someone online called her "horny Jigsaw" in reference to the psychopathic horror sadist.)

The scene would provide miniature portraits of the OG Islanders which would prove accurate throughout the season. Chelley Bissainthe, a twenty-seven-year-old day trader from Orlando, was in exacting control of her reactions. Nic Vansteenberghe was a twenty-four-year-old with a nursing degree, and while he might not always understand what was going on, he would always be respectful in his cluelessness. Austin Shepard, a twenty-six-year-old pool cleaner from Michigan, was just hoping to hook up.

During the first coupling, Jeremiah was chosen by Huda Mustafa, a twenty-four-year-old fitness influencer with an inability to be inauthentic that was inflamed by a strong and often skewed self-perception. Huda immediately established a sniper/target dynamic between them that Jeremiah initially seemed into. During their time together—and in the aftermath of their coupledom—the pair would dominate nearly all *Love Island* conversations.

Huda is the mother of a then-five-year-old, a piece of crucial information that she relayed to the Villa in stages: first to some of the women, then to a shocked Jeremiah, then to Nic. "I have a secret to tell you," Huda said to the nurse-cum-model. "I'm a mommy."

"Mommy?" Nic repeated, bewildered.

"I'm a mom," Huda clarified.

"*Mamacita*," Nic said, prompting them both to laugh.

"No, I'm a mommy," Huda said.

"A mom of what, a dog?" Nic asked, trying to compute the information he was hearing like he was Robert Oppenheimer calculating the theoretical physics of the atom bomb. They eventually reached a shared understanding that Huda was the parent of a human child.

This was internet candy, a clip played endlessly in what would be the first of many canonical season 7 moments. Ariana and Megan Thee Stallion, who would soon have a bigger role on the season, re-created the conversation in a lip sync, as did *Las Culturistas* co-hosts Bowen Yang and Matt Rogers, Karol G and Jimmy Fallon, Derek Hough and Jennifer Lopez, Olivia Rodrigo and Ed Sheeran, and what felt like every woman who gave birth in June 2025.

Most seasons of *Love Island* take a few weeks to start hitting; viewers don't know any of these people yet, and the Islanders aren't familiar enough to hook up or have any meaningful disagreements. Huda bypassed any get-to-know-you period and settled comfortably into the dramatic heights of a coupledom where, on the outside, their neighbors would presumably be calling the police with noise complaints about how loud the sex and screaming were.

Huda's emotional poles ranged from "sweetly seductive" to "seemingly ready to light the Villa on fire with everyone inside." Within a week, her coupling with Jeremiah provided her with the material she needed to get to the latter. Jeremiah committed what Huda considered to be major indiscretions, including kissing someone other than her in a challenge, serving her partially raw pancakes then not being jealous when another man made her properly cooked ones, and, most unforgivably, going on a date with placidly nubile bombshell Iris Kendall, a twenty-five-year-old spray tan artist, in which they virtuously sat on a beach to chat. "My dream date," Huda said, unwittingly going viral once again. "Cute. And he knows that."

Huda interpreted this simple act of participating in the show as a casus belli. "Fuck you," she said, fuming. "He's a fucking bitch . . . He's using her as a fucking escape goat so he can stay in the fucking game."

Thomas was watching from home, during what would be the first summer he had ever spent with his five-year-old. *"Oh my god,"* he texted Vuong about the phrase "escape goat." *"Did you see this?"* Obviously, everyone had. Production was doing the opposite of what it called "the Bravo wink": a knowing sound effect or edit to make the audience aware production is in on the joke. "The show makes you feel like the editors and the people making the show didn't know that this was happening, that this is funny—but of course they fucking do," Thomas says. As a first-time viewer of *Love Island USA*, he'd fallen for the same trap he'd set for the last six seasons. "You feel like you discover it," he says of the unacknowledged hilarity. "It fires your brain in a different way—you are now excited because you are finding this humor in something that's being treated really sincerely."

It did not feel funny in the Villa, however. "You're a fucking bitch!" Huda screamed at Jeremiah across the property. "You're a pussy-ass bitch!"

At that point, Jeremiah says the other Islanders became concerned. "Everyone was scared to leave her with Iris," he says of Huda.

While Huda was having a crashout—her default status during this period—Ace was turning it to his advantage. He'd been poking at Jeremiah all season, which at this point was only a week and a half long. During the "State Your Case" challenge, Huda said she'd once slept with two men in one day because "the first guy didn't satisfy me." (Other much more alarming revelations came from Austin. By his own self-reported data, he had cheated on six partners and sent more than a thousand nude photos.) After the game, the boys asked Jeremiah about Huda's admission. Jeremiah said he'd also had sex with two people in one day and that he always made sure his partners got to "the finish line," so he wasn't worried about Huda seeking out someone else. Ace questioned him five different times in five different ways in what seemed like an attempt to get him to crack and admit "the truth."

Ace's inconsistent aggression was confusing to Jeremiah, who says, "There was never no beef really when we were off cam. We're just cooking, eating, laughing, joking every lunch and dinner. Just having a blast. We would rap battle together, play basketball, water volleyball—it was all love. We were all best friends, I feel like. And sometimes the cameras come on and it's, 'You need to do this,' and getting called a scammer and him yelling at me at the firepit." Ace's allegations of Jeremiah's "scamming" centered on his strong and vocal initial attraction to Huda, which had cooled as Jeremiah decided that getting berated at high volume was not his preferred communication style.

Jeremiah recoupled with Iris, prompting Huda to flip out in a way that cratered the spirit of the Villa. It felt like every word from Huda was about Jeremiah, who had the audacity to move on and explore another connection. Huda couldn't stay away from him either, often cornering him for conversations. Each interaction between them ended in a conflict that amounted to a version of this exchange:

Huda: "Why are you doing this to me?"

Jeremiah: "Please, I do not want to hook up or fight with you anymore."

To exist in the Villa means accepting when a decision is fully final. While the schemes of the producers might sometimes reverse a schism that seemed irreparable, the offending party is not going to convince a former partner that they should still be together when the former partner explicitly doesn't want to be—especially if that person has other options. During an elimination where the Islanders could have ended the entire thing, they instead kept Huda from being dumped—with the caveat that she stop killing the mood with her outrage. "I can't do it anymore, bro," Nic said. Huda could. After she was benevolently saved by her peers, she went right back to her antics, eavesdropping outside the (relatively) sheltered Speakeasy lounge as Iris and Jeremiah discussed how glad he was to have exited a "toxic" affair.

"Huda promised the other Islanders she'd stop shouting at Jeremiah," Iain said in voice-over. "But she didn't say anything about creepily whispering at him. I smell a loophole!" Huda walked in in a way that appeared contrite and nonthreatening; Iris, never one for drama, got up and left without any issue. The conversation was a tennis match of blame and accountability. In a hushed voice, Huda reiterated her anguish and how much she cared about Jeremiah, then took responsibility for her actions, then told him the situation was partially *his* fault, then said her bad behavior was due to his actions.

Cowboy Taylor stood outside the door with his mouth dropped open before stopping in the Speakeasy entrance to make a face that silently said, no closed-captioning required, "Huda! What are you doing?"

Everyone watching seemed to have an opinion about them: Huda's already passionate fandom accused Jeremiah of love bombing her, while the majority of viewers felt her actions were out of proportion to any supposed wrongdoing. Everyone but Huda agreed they shouldn't be together. To fans, the relationship was toxic but also intoxicating. Thomas compares it to the World Cup. "We're all together in the moment," he says, citing a post he saw that read, "America hasn't been this united since Kelly Clarkson won *American Idol*."

Still, after fifteen episodes of operatic drama, the desolation of Huda and Jeremiah's relationship had become a fog of doom over the Villa. The cloud dissipated the moment Megan Thee Stallion stepped onto the show with a true fan's knowledge. "Huda, my friend," she said. "First of all, I just want to say, the face card is so crazy. We want to see more smiles, though. I feel like it's been a rough couple of days, and I don't like that for you." Meg pointed at Huda and told the other women, "She's standing on business. If she had twenty toes, they would all be down."

Then Meg hosted a twerking contest, in which the women wore Hot Girl Summer swimsuits from the rapper's line and had dance-offs with the boys. Everyone gamely participated in the challenge, but it was Huda's moment of glory; she might not be able to temper her responses, but she could drop ass. Huda bent over and started oscillating hypnotically, her thighs undulating like a wave pool filled with mercury. The move transitioned to the ground, where Huda's cheeks alternated in slapping the floor. "I wouldn't suggest that's because it's now operated by the Bravo team," ITV's Mike Beale says of the move toward more sexual content on *USA*, with a sarcasm as dry and British as an unsteeped tea bag.

Though the date of Megan's visit had been long planned, it fortuitously shifted the rancid energy in the Villa—producers didn't have to plan an additional party or challenge that would lighten things up. Huda was momentarily sanguine, bolstered by the win and Megan's words of affirmation.

Jeremiah's dumping three episodes later also helped Huda move past what was clearly a relationship of no return. The voting process had a touch of machinating: Ace led the boys in removing Jeremiah from the Villa based on him being too closed off with Iris instead of pursuing other connections—never mind that Nic, one of Ace's closest friends in the Villa, had been coupled with twenty-five-year-old influencer Cierra Ortega for longer. Though Ace subsequently claimed producers pressured him to vote this way and apologized to Jeremiah, this would be the beginning of the audience's unshakable feeling that Ace was an operator.

"They tried to villainize me liking someone, and just one person,"

Jeremiah says. "It's like, 'Bro, I don't have to explore three girls if I don't want to. If I'm not attracted to the three girls the same, I'm not gonna hoop when I don't wanna hoop.'" Jeremiah says producers also encouraged him to explore people he wasn't interested in. "There were sometimes where it's like, 'Pull this person or that person,' where I wasn't really feeling them," Jeremiah says, though he notes, "You could definitely say no." He left the Villa alongside Hannah Fields, a twenty-three-year-old medical student from Tucson. Huda stayed in Fiji.

Iris seemed to be the season 7 Islander who *Love Island*'s gameplay tried hardest—and succeeded least—at rattling. She'd been developing something with Jeremiah before he was sent home; when she subsequently got serious with TJ Palma, a twenty-three-year-old Airbnb rental entrepreneur from Pleasantville, New York, he was voted into the bottom by America and dumped when the Islanders saved mealy-mouthed Taylor. TJ had not engendered much audience support after a series of moves that included giving the women low scores in the kissing challenge.

Despite the way the public felt, Iris very much liked TJ. "When TJ left, I was devastated," she says. They'd been an official couple for four days, during which they displayed very visible chemistry. After he left, Iris found herself bawling, which she tells me was the most she's wept since her grandmother passed away. Then she revises the statement: She realizes she'd cried more tears over TJ, which astonishes her still. "I didn't think that I was gonna feel that way," she says. "I don't cry." *Love Island* had *Love Island*–ed Iris—she was feeling heretofore unexperienced feelings at warp speed.

When TJ left, Iris briefly thought about following him, then stayed, without any seeming urgency to recouple. A single Islander tends to latch on to others to avoid vulnerability—the kind that leaves them feeling like no one wants them or the type that puts them up for dumping. "If it doesn't work, then I'm not going to *make* it work," Iris says of her laissez-faire approach to love and television. "It's not meant to be that way. Every single time there was a recoupling, every single time there was an elimination, I was okay with going home."

Two days after her heartbreak, Iris got together with Pepe Garcia, a twenty-seven-year-old personal trainer and former professional basketball player who had shielded Iris from being alone with Huda during one of her crashouts. They had a conversation in which Iris said she hates sleeping alone; Pepe's pupils dilated before Iris explained that meant she aways co-slept with her female roommates or dog. The two immediately recoupled. Iris remained eminently chill and yet still totally open to play the game; she'd had three boyfriends in her entire life, then found two more honest-to-god connections in less than a month on *Love Island.* America would vote her one of most genuine women in the Villa on her way to the finale with Pepe.

"Every single person I was with—Jeremiah, TJ, Pepe—I really gave a hundred percent of myself to those people," Iris says. "I tried to see it through with everybody because they were giving me the same energy. I was like, 'I'm going to make things work and see why I'm here.'" (If this is confusing given Iris's previous stance against "making it work," she is discerning between a situation that is viable and one that is not.)

In addition to creating a fresh start for Iris, Jeremiah's dumping put him in an interesting position: He was ousted near the beginning of the season, which, obviously, is normally bad. But he left with a tremendous amount of goodwill and was able to enjoy the love audiences felt for him while the season was still going on. He turned down a spot on *Love Island Games* season 2, opting to use the public's interest in continuing to watch him to convert forty-four TikTok followers to millions, many of whom tune in for Jeremiah's monthly book club. "I love it," he says. "It brings me joy. It helps people. I had so many people tell me, 'I haven't read in X amount of years. Now you got me reading again.'" Leaving early and watching the rest of the season live also gave him a unique frame of reference; because producers and his castmates were no longer acting upon him, he achieved a level of objectivity that usually takes a lot longer to reach, if it ever is. (It helped that his therapist watched the season.)

Cierra had a very different trajectory. The influencer came in as a bombshell, recoupled with Nic, and had a very cute relationship that featured two extremely brief sexual encounters. She was sweetly unobjectionable to the other women and tended to display a positive-neutral head-tilting physicality, like a video game character waiting in a virtual lobby for the other players to arrive.

In early July screenshots of old Instagram stories surfaced in which Cierra used a slur against people of Asian heritage in reference to how her eyes looked when she smiled without Botox, as well as an apology she sent to someone who told her the word was offensive. It was the kind of thing that couldn't be found on a background check but that would emerge in this new era of digital detective work. Unbeknownst to the Islanders, a furor was developing among viewers.

Ariana found out about the post while in glam for the "Hate to Burst Your Bubble" challenge, in which the audience had ranked the Islanders from most to least embodying of each category. According to Ariana's timeline, several people tagged her in comments about Cierra on the evening of Wednesday, July 2, which was morning in America and around the time the story was becoming mainstream. Ariana is frequently sent posts featuring incorrect or unhinged content, but after seeing the same thing pop up multiple times, she forwarded the messages to what she describes as the authorities "above me" and was told, "It's already being assessed above *them*." By the time she, Cely, *Games*' dairy expert Callum, and *Love Island Australia* host Sophie Monk sat down to film *Aftersun* on Friday, Cierra was gone. But because *Aftersun* would air before the episode that explained Cierra leaving, Ariana wasn't able to address it, even though viewers were expecting her to. "Unfortunately, I'm the only person that is kind of front-facing," she says. "I can't speak for Peacock—they have to handle things the way they have to handle things because they have their own legalities and things like that."

The next regular episode showed Cierra disappearing in the middle of the day, with a voice-over from Iain stating she'd "left the Villa due to a personal situation." Because so much of the audience was aware of what was happening, *Love Island USA* didn't feel it needed to provide further explanation. After Cierra was pulled, the season 7 Islanders were brought in to have a conversation with Thursby-Palmer, as well as ITV America and NBCU. Islanders were told "the bare minimum" of what needed to be explained so that Nic knew Cierra had done something wrong and didn't try to follow her out of the Villa.

Suddenly, with one week left to go, it was a new season. Cierra leaving meant Nic could guiltlessly pursue Olandria Carthen, a twenty-seven-year-old elevator salesperson with a face that looked like it was created by AI to catfish people and an ass that Megan Thee Stallion told her she'd been saving screenshots of. Nic had secretly kissed Olandria when she was blindfolded on day one during a challenge, and it felt like production had been pushing them together to fulfill the audience's desire to see them become what fans had termed "Nicolandria."

People were yearning in the comments and making TikTok montages of moments they felt revealed the Islanders' true feelings for each other. Even Nic's parents weighed in and said they hoped the pair would get together. "The thing with Olandria is she really is like a queen vibe," Nic's mom said. "I'd like to see what she brings out of him, and I think he can bring out in her a playfulness that we haven't seen yet." The revelation that they had apparently been destined to be together seemed bewildering to Nic and Olandria, who hadn't been clued in to the audience's projection of their relationship. They were still in the exploratory phase, while fans were all but planning their wedding.

During the same period they were forgetting she existed, Cierra gave an apology in which she took accountability for using the derogatory word and pledged to educate herself. Cierra—who is of Mexican and Puerto Rican descent—asked the people who were sending her death threats and calling ICE on her family to please stop. She did not, however, address the underlying implication of her posts: that it was undesirable to have Asian features. The uproar subsided, but there would be no short-term return to grace for her.

Cierra, evidently done expressing contrition, posted a bikini video with the meme prompt "You look happier" and the text "I booked a flight to Mykonos after surviving the villain edit on reality TV"—though she hadn't gotten a villain edit—"and I didn't end up with the guy who never actually liked me and wanted my friend the entire time."

Meanwhile, Ace receded after finding out that America was not responding well to his Villa leadership during the Burst Your Bubble challenge. Going into it, he announced, "I'm feeling great! This is the first time I'm finna have a conversation with America." In that conversation, he discovered that he had been voted among the Islanders who were least genuine and possessing of boyfriend material, and, with Chelley, one of the couples viewers would least like to vacation with.

"I was surprised how fans saw him because he is so charismatic," Thursby-Palmer said. "Fans are allowed whatever opinions they want, but sometimes these thoughts or comments start to build traction, and then suddenly that becomes the narrative. He was doing the *Love Island* experience. He was being authentically himself."

Part of Ace being himself appeared to be that he wanted to keep the Islanders he was close with in the Villa, going to lengths to protect Taylor, Nic, and Chelley during internal votes. "Of course you want to be there at the end with your friends," Ariana says. "I feel like that's a very natural thing. And right out of the gate, he was one of my favorites this past season because he was really *seeing* things." Like Curtis, Ace clearly has high emotional intelligence, and, like Curtis, it can read as overly shrewd. Ariana relates. "I'll do an interview and somebody will say, 'Oh, media trained,'" she says. "I've never been media trained. I'm that person that overthinks everything. So, me, as an overthinker, I would be horrible in the Villa." (There is another reason why Ariana feels she would be a bad Islander: "I nap too much," she says.)

As Nicolandria completed their friends-to-lovers plot and Ace turtled as he tried not to do as much as the audience seemed to think he was doing, the Age of Amaya began.

When Amaya Espinal entered as a bombshell, the self-termed "Dominican Princess" from New York City was a slow grower for the audience and her fellow Islanders. Quickly, the twenty-five-year-old cardiac nurse became the first American Islander to give viewers the kind of linguistic fanny flutters they'd experienced watching *UK*. She had a penchant for malapropism—"gratitually" for gratefully, "dieskyving" for skydiving—and an openness that Ace tried to cast as a lack of boundaries to the other Islanders. "No offense to Ace, but we got the rundown of what happened between them in a different sense of how it happened," Jeremiah said of an interaction where Ace effectively accused Amaya of being weird and aggressive because she tended to touch conversational partners and call people "babe."

Amaya would eventually become the sweetheart of the season by being the kind of person who would sing a motivational song alone to herself after another day of getting turned down. "I never said I was perfect," she vocalized tonelessly in the makeup room while putting on moisturizer. "I never said I didn't have any flaws. But at least I'm pretty. And at least I'm a little funny. And at least I'm my own best friend." Amaya had no romantic prospects yet, but she had accidentally seduced the audience.

After many weeping sessions and learning she was the most popular Islander, Amaya let the men of the house know she was no longer willing to be the Villa buffoon; actually, she was a deeply empathic person with a facility for language that she finally felt confident enough to deploy after being gaslit for twenty-three episodes. "I'm not gonna have a sugar rush anymore from the word candy you're feeding me," Amaya said to the camera in the Beach Hut when Zak came simpering back after announcing during a challenge that the first time they kissed, he hadn't wanted to but did it anyway. (Zak's newfound openness to the relationship followed the same public vote that clued Amaya in to her power on the outside.) It was an arc that mirrored Bergie's, except the size of the platforms was wildly different: Amaya was being courted by every brand from IHOP to JetBlue before she even got out of the Villa, while Bergie was posting for comped supplement drinks.

Producers were aware of Amaya's commercial potency. She was featured in sponsored segments with Coffee Mate and the skincare brand CeraVe, which ran in between commercials where Leah, Kordell, Serena, Kaylor, and JaNa were being paid to promote the latter brand, as well as Jose Cuervo and Maybelline. Islanders are not compensated for using partner products inside the Villa, but Thomas says the proof of concept of an Islander being associated with the brand is worth the free labor. "With Amaya, I think using Coffee Mate in the show is a small price to pay as long as ITV and NBC hold up the deal at the other end," Thomas says. "Which is to say, 'Go get your money'" and approve any sponsorships she wanted to pursue once she got out of the Villa.

Amaya coupled with twenty-eight-year-old Bostonian Bryan Arenales in episode 30, the same episode as Cierra's departure. After her outcast-to-victor journey, Amaya's win with the late-breaking love interest was foretold, which usually makes for a dull finale.

But when you're dealing with Huda, the unexpected is inevitable. Since Jeremiah's exit, she had been on the most extreme redemption arc to air on *Love Island*. Thursby-Palmer says it was unintended. "We don't sit there and go, 'Right, what's the master plan for you? How are we gonna turn this around?'" he says.

After mostly making amends with her castmates, Huda recoupled with twenty-seven-year-old professional basketball player Chris Seeley at Casa, a pairing that seemed like a more stable base for her. There were some potential hurdles; for one, it pissed off Chelley, who was coupled up with Ace but interested in Chris. Also, when Huda asked what Chris's type was, he said, "I always attract emotionally unstable women," as if he were a honey pot with no top and these emotionally unstable women were just falling into him and getting stuck there like Winnie-the-Pooh. This was the same loose read on reality that Chris would later bring with him to *Games* season 2. "My name's Chris. I'm sure you guys probably know who I am," he said as he introduced himself.

"Why would we know who you are?" *UK* season 7 Islander Lucinda Strafford responded.

Despite his awareness of what had drawn him to her, Chris seemed confused by Huda's behavior. They'd have sex at night, but then she'd refuse to kiss in public because the other cast members had been clear that they didn't want to get involved in her relationships anymore. Still, Huda got upset and told him she wanted more public affirmation from him. Chris visibly withdrew when Huda sought comfort because her nose got bopped in a pillow fight. "Hey, hello," she said, trying to wake him up to comfort her. "I'm going to give you three seconds, I'm dead-ass. Three, two . . . Hello?"

Without turning over, Chris grunted, "I want to get some sleep."

Huda said, "Just snuggle me then. If not cuddling is worth me being upset tomorrow, that's the battle you're picking, so congratulations."

As a Casa boy, Chris had watched all the previous episodes, so none of this should have been at all surprising; Huda was the person she'd been the whole season—and presumably her entire life. Like Ekin or Leah, she is a person who can only be herself, which even Jeremiah sort-of appreciates. Chris's growing antipathy for getting exactly what he'd bargained for was palpable.

Their final date was on a platform in the middle of a body of water. After a singer appeared mid-conversation to perform the world's most witheringly awkward rendition of "Moon River" for the miserable couple, Chris goaded Huda into breaking up with him, presumably to spare him from having to end it with her.

Huda was wearing heels, and the path back to land involved a trek through a few inches of water. "Do you want to carry me, or do you want me to walk?" Huda asked.

Chris, who is six-foot-eight and could have lifted the teeny Huda like a throw pillow, took her by the hand and said, "I'm not gonna carry you." He left, and Huda stayed behind to pour herself another glass of champagne and take off her shoes.

While Chris moped through the finale, Huda maintained a seraphic smile—since Ace and Chelley had just been dumped, she, Nic, and Olandria were the only Islanders from the original lineup who remained to celebrate Amaya's victory and collect the spoils of headlining the biggest season of *Love Island* ever.

15
A Greater Duty

BRAVO OVERLORD AND *Watch What Happens Live* host Andy Cohen was brought in to co-host the season 7 reunion on the strength of his monomaniacal attraction to drama and ability to dissect it. (He had also co-hosted season 6's reunion.) He was the counterbalance to Ariana's less sensational, more empathic approach, which she grants results in little of the tea that viewers tune in to see. "I don't wanna say good cop, bad cop," Ariana says of her and Andy's roles. "But I do think that there is a bit of that. He's so fun. Every time I'm on *Watch What Happens Live*—even if he is being messy—I'm laughing about it."

The reunion didn't so much build on the season as expose its flaws. During the two-hour episode, the stars of the season mostly sat quietly—the pairings hadn't spent enough time coupled on-screen to produce drama that needed rehashing weeks later. Jeremiah and Huda's relationship was long in the rearview and had already been litigated on separate podcasts. Thomas also notes that the moderated confrontations of the show don't suit the strengths of *Love Island*'s best cast members. "What makes an amazing Islander is very rarely what makes an amazing reality TV personality," he says. This left the season's "who?" players to squabble among themselves while more familiar Islanders like Nic and Olandria were barely featured. Cierra wasn't invited. Huda, of course, would deliver. In one of the most enjoyable moments of the episode, Andy asked about her new boyfriend, who had appeared on the Netflix dating shows *Perfect Match* and *Too Hot to Handle*. By that time, the couple was Instagram official and had attended a red-carpet event together. "I can't speak about my relationships outside the Villa," Huda said. "Legal reasons. I'm not allowed to speak. It's Netflix. I'm not allowed to talk about it." (Netflix says this is not accurate.)

"Tell Netflix this was the number one streaming show of the summer," Andy replied. This was by a factor of nearly 100 percent—*Love Island USA* was watched for more than 13.6 billion minutes between June 1 and September 1, according to Luminate Data, while the number two most-viewed show, *Ginny & Georgia*, had a little over 7.5 billion minutes of view time.

The fact that most of the couples were just a few weeks old, along with the mind-boggling increase in interest, made the return to their new reality hit the relationships harder than in an average season of *Love Island*. Days after the reunion aired, Bryan and Amaya and Pepe and Iris, the only remaining couples besides Nic and Olandria, announced their breakups. Iris got back together with TJ and says she's still friends with Hannah, Jeremiah, Amaya, and Clarke Carraway, who recoupled with Taylor at Casa. This group would make up the core cast of *Beyond the Villa* season 2. Iris also vouches for the true heart of Huda, though no one but Chris seems to think anyone could keep up a false persona for that long, under that level of observation. While people can obviously feign chummier friendships, Thomas says that in his experience, people who are putting on an act on a closed-set television series with constant monitoring can keep it up for about twelve days. If someone acts consistently for six weeks, that's probably how they are in real life.

"She was just real to herself," says Iris.

By the reunion, it was clear Huda was one of the big winners of *Love Island*. She appeared in an NFL commercial, as well as a partnership with the unrelated but fortuitously named Huda Beauty. The deal lasted only a month, until Huda and her new boyfriend did a live stream during which one of Huda's fans called Olandria, who is a Black woman, the N-word. In the moment, Huda giggled, then later argued about her responsibility to respond to a "bad word" that someone else said, and eventually, under much pressure, apologized to Olandria. Huda's fan base had previously attacked Olandria, who was the season's runner-up and a rare crossover star of mainstream fashion and media, working as a model with embraces from the Council of Fashion Designers of America, *Vogue*, and *Glamour*, which featured her and Nic on the cover of the magazine's 2025 Holiday issue.

When Olandria informed Huda she and Chelley were being racially harassed by Huda's fans, including being sent an image of George Floyd with Olandria's face edited over it, Huda declined Olandria's request to intervene and post about it. "I was getting hated on as well, racially," said Huda, who is Palestinian American, by way of defense.

It wasn't the first time that a *Love Island USA* fan base had fomented against the supposed enemies of their favorite. Most members of Leah's coven—her name for her followers—simply enjoy watching Leah make food for Miguel at home or show off her horseback riding. But some express their adoration for her by attacking anyone whom they perceive has wronged her.

"Honestly, I'm terrified to talk about anything that has to do with that," Rob says about his altercations with Leah on the show, "just because I just don't want any drama there."

Jeremiah said something similar about Huda's stans. "Her fans are OD, so I have to watch what I say," he said, using a slang term for *over the top*. "Her fans are, like, scary."

Ariana has no patience for this type of viewer. "If that warrants you sending death threats to them, you need help, because that is disgusting," she says. "Sometimes I feel like those people's privileges of even being able to watch the show should be taken away."

In 2023 in the UK, Parliament passed the Online Safety Act, intended to keep people from experiencing trolling from unverified accounts and to hold social media platforms accountable for the content on their platforms. No such law exists in America.

Pile-ons can happen for the most minor slights. When Cely made a scripted G-spot joke on season 7 of *Aftersun* that the coven interpreted as implying Leah shouldn't be in PPG—it's too stupid to explain further—Cely's DMs were inundated. "Fuck you, you ugly cunt jealous bitch," people wrote to her. "Kill yourself. If I see you, I'm gonna kill you." Rogue fans sent the producers death threats because they perceived them to be responsible for Leah's "bad" depiction on the show—the same depiction that had made them root for her in the first place.

"The fandom around Leah in particular is so passionate, so fresh to the show, that they would get really mad at us for the hero's journey that she was on," Thomas says. "They would say that we would set her up to fail. Part of the thing that made people love her was the way that she dealt with the problems she faced. Of course, we're going to throw obstacles and problems in front of people. That's drama, that's narrative. How you deal with those problems and overcome them or don't overcome them—that's on you. But that's what makes it compelling—that's why they love her, and it's interesting that they hate us sometimes for that."

The attacks on Olandria felt different. They weren't just violent, inappropriate reactions to an actual *Love Island* conflict; they were removing the hate from the context of the show and placing it solely on her race, in the grossest, most terrifying way possible. It underscored a problem that had arguably been part of *Love Island* from the beginning.

* * *

In 2019, two years after Marcel Somerville's first appearance on the show, he testified in front of the House of Commons about reality television alongside season 5 star Yewande Biala. Both stars had experiences on the show that reflected the challenges of being Black on *Love Island.* The inquiry followed the deaths of Mike, Sophie, and the person who had failed a lie detector test on *The Jeremy Kyle Show*, and aimed to identify potentially harmful elements of filming a reality series and becoming a public personality. At *Love Island*'s then-highest point, increased visibility had come with corresponding responsibility.

Marcel's opening commentary focused on his reluctance to be a bombshell on season 2, which aired the year prior to his. Marcel was conscious of being "the first fully Black contestant to appear on the show." On a series that lacked diversity, he said it would be negative representation for a Black man to come in and steal someone's girlfriend. He also discussed the initial coupling ceremony, which he felt ended up in humiliation for those who weren't picked—particularly for people of color. In each of the first couplings in the first three seasons of *Love Island UK*, people of color were "left on the bench"—*Love Island*–ese for being deemed a temporary pariah based on sight alone. This would continue to be a challenge in the UK, especially for dark-skinned Islanders, until season 5, when production began more consciously integrating the cast. A couple with no white Islanders would not win until season 9's Kai Fagan and Sanam Harrinanan were voted favorite couple. It followed a season where the public got to do the first coupling and basically matched everyone by their closest skin tone. (Production would repeat that opening move in a regular season only once more, with the same results.)

Coco Jackson, who began as a runner in *Love Island UK* season 2 and is now a senior producer, acknowledges the issue. "People have felt that they haven't been picked because of being a person of color," she says.

There were other, less overt issues in their handling of race and diversity that didn't seem to factor into production until Islanders and people online started calling them out. When Marcel went on season 3 in 2017, Superdrug was the toiletry sponsor. There were no products specifically for people of color; further, the barber they brought in was not experienced with cutting textured hair. (Marcel, never one to throw someone under the bus, assures me Carlos did an okay job.) At a show with a mostly white executive team who was working without rest to make a blockbuster daily show, trying to accommodate needs they weren't even aware existed was not yet a top priority.

The House of Commons hearing coincided with a pronounced shift in what considerations were taken to accommodate the distinct needs of diverse Islanders, from casting in a way that didn't set them up to fail, to giving the cast training about microaggressions as part of the Duty of Care, to making sure their grooming needs were taken care of. When Marcel came back for *All Stars* in 2024, the Villa was in a different echelon of sensitivity: Boots provided all of the toiletries and products he needed, and production found a "sick" stylist in Cape Town who knew how to work with different types of Black hair.

"From the early stages, if we know they're going in, we will have that frank conversation with them, like, 'What is your routine? How do you want to walk in there and feel your best?'" says Jackson of the shift toward inclusivity. The commercial team, she says, now ensures "the sponsorships that we have are inclusive of Afro hair and mixed-race hair, making sure that we've got beauty experts so when people get maintenance"—the extensions, dye jobs, and manicures Islanders get on their days off—"that we cater to our Islanders and make sure that it's not just an afterthought." One of Jackson's responsibilities is importing hair. "I'm forever flying in wigs," she says.

Pinning down UK executives and producers on things that may not have been handled appropriately at the time mostly results in them demurring—in their eyes, they're just the means of production, rather than perpetuators of any outside issues. *Love Island* originated in the land of a white monarchy and has, at this point, expanded to reflect the makeup of the entire Commonwealth. It is made up of a cast and watched by a population who live in a world that is suffused with racism—and misogyny and the stigmatization of body diversity—and occasionally that seeps into the program. "It's a tricky one, isn't it?" executive producer Lewis Evans said when I asked about the initial couplings historically disadvantaging people of color, among other such issues. The casting team now tries to look at whom applicants have dated and make sure their supposed "type on paper" aligns with their actions; they will make sure, for example, that people have actually been in interracial relationships. Though people may not even realize their unconscious biases, Evans says, "the minute they get in the Villa, their stated type seems to go out the window."

The people who make *Love Island USA* say they're still striving to improve the way they deal with race, which resulted in the two slur-related eliminations from season 7. By the time Cierra was removed, the show had already dealt with an off-camera moment of racist language, when cast member Yulissa Escobar was taken out of the Villa by production after someone found a podcast in which she repeatedly used the N-word, establishing the zero-tolerance policy for hate speech.

The reverberations of Cierra also forced the show to contend with its bad history with Islanders of Asian descent—specifically East Asian cast members. (Sanam would be the first and, so far, only winner of South Asian heritage of *UK*, in season 9.) Filipina Islander Sharon Gaffka of season 7 was dumped after two weeks and said she felt like she was there to "tick the boxes" of diversity. It's an ongoing problem: The first person dumped from the Villa on *Love Island UK* season 12 was Sophie Lee, a twenty-eight-year-old motivational speaker who would be the only Islander of entirely Asian heritage featured on the show that summer. Her castmate Shakira Khan, who is of Pakistani descent, pointed out that season 12's women of color were ostracized by the central clique.

As to whether Cierra's racist language could have been addressed within the text of the show, Ariana says, "I do think that it is a good question of 'Where is the appropriate place for that conversation?' because I do feel like there is a lot of nuance. It's not a quick conversation either, and it's not necessarily a conversation that I'm even equipped to be a part of in my position. But at the same time, I do think *Love Island* is sometimes such a microcosm for things like this that do come up in the real world."

So far Peacock is keeping *Aftersun* as a gossipy romp rather than a forum for serious discussion. Still, Ariana has tried to discuss racism and misogyny on the show in the past. "Some of the things I said made it to air," Ariana says. "Some of them, Peacock was like, 'That's too harsh. We're gonna cut that out.' I do agree with the 'be kind' rhetoric, but sometimes people just don't listen when you tell them nicely."

Love Island's ethical code is one in which ignorance or bad behavior is not called out by the show itself unless it could harm the Islanders, but rather is left to be judged by the players and public. Like Ariana, Thomas wishes there was a way to integrate these lessons into the actual series. "I wish that we could have people on shows who behave badly, and then we could talk about it and hold people accountable and get to the end point rather than just pretending like it doesn't exist," Thomas says. He also recognizes this has gone poorly on reality television before, with the disastrous *Bachelor* reunion that followed the first Black Bachelor, Matt James, picking as his winner Rachael Kirkconnell. Rachael had gone to an antebellum South–themed costume party in college and appeared in photos that were posted online. She was also reported to have liked TikToks about the Confederate flag.

That "After the Final Rose" episode was hosted by Emmanuel Acho, a sports analyst, host of the anti-racism digital series *Uncomfortable Conversations with a Black Man*, and author of a book by the same name. Acho seemed ill-equipped to handle an hour-long reunion special capping off nineteen years of what could generously be called "white-skewed" programming. This two-decade-long run culminated in longtime host Chris Harrison getting fired after a patronizing interview with Rachel Lindsay, the first Black Bachelorette. Thomas says that unlike *The Bachelor* under that regime, "I think we've proven with the show that *Love Island* is not racist—or trying not to be racist. It's working in good faith."

"I think this is the best show of multicultural representation on television in the dating space," Thomas insists. "And it's still probably only halfway there."

16 Villains

THE VILLAIN MIGHT BE the most important archetype on *Love Island*—there is no force more galvanizing in a group setting than having a person whom everyone can agree is the problem. A villain focuses energy away from other conflicts and allows Islanders and viewers to bond over their agreed-upon opinion that *that guy sucks*. They give people permission to have fun being mean; the villain brought this upon themself with their own behavior, after all.

Love Island's unreality allows us to enjoy what psychologists call "everyday sadism": the little tickle of joy we feel when the men of *Jackass* shoot fireworks out of their asses or a local newsperson slips while stomping grapes. "We find it acceptable because this feels both real and at the same time slightly not real," says David Taylor, literature and culture professor at Oxford University, about *Love Island*. "It's beautifully sunny. These are absurdly beautiful people. So that sense of the hurt and the humiliation, we can swallow that if it's a set instead of a council flat somewhere with people struggling to make ends meet."

No one goes on *Love Island* thinking they'll be a villain. While anyone cast would be at least faintly conscious of the fact that there always is one, new Islanders step into the Villa with the ingrained entitlement of a healthy person born to a wealthy family in a G7 country; it's a shame others aren't as lucky, but this just happens to be what God had planned for them. Just by participating in the show, an Islander is admitting they think they could win a likability contest, that they're compelling and fanciable and hot. Even a cast member as self-lacerating as Cely, who cried with regret for not having gotten her boobs done before the first coupling, had been trying to get on TV for years before *Love Island.* She and all the other Islanders, in the most benign way possible, have committed one of the seven deadly sins: vanity. It's seen in every season. On *All Stars* season 1, Georgia Steel cried because two men wanted to couple with her. One of them was Toby, who tried to cheer her up with an affirmation practice. "What are you grateful for?" he asked.

"I'm grateful for my natural long hair," Georgia said, sniffling.

If *Love Island* is a morality tale—and all reality television is, to some degree—then that means the audience is waiting for comeuppance and willing to deliver it, even as we also want cast members to do the right things and fall in love.

The point of the show is to elicit deep feelings; you won't watch seven hours of TV weekly for two months if you don't care about the casts you see on-screen. "You invest in people, and you love and you hate people," Spencer-Hayter says. "You're loving to hate them."

UK Season 11's Joey Essex might be the Islander viewers most delighted in hating. He also went back on the deal that Cowles had made when he first floated the reboot. On *Love Island*, there were not supposed to be celebrities, just people who hopefully could be transformed into them through the show. The thirty-three-year-old was a career reality personality who had been on *The Only Way Is Essex* in the show's salad days of 2011–2013, when Kate Middleton was a fan and Spencer-

Hayter was a producer. Joey's surname actually is Essex, though changing it to the name of a show is not beyond the realm of something he'd do. He successfully exploited his hot, dumb, confident persona, coining the phrase "reem" to describe the state of his hair when it was looking particularly good, then releasing a song called "Reem" and product line called D'reem Hair. Joey subsequently appeared on *I'm a Celebrity . . . Get Me Out of Here!*, *Celebs Go Dating*, and *Celebrity Ex on the Beach*. Reality TV seemed to follow Joey wherever he went, to the point where he was walking down the street in Los Angeles and a former *TOWIE* producer spotted him and asked if he would appear on the Netflix real estate series *Selling Sunset*. He played the role of someone looking to buy a place in town with charm, as the agents masterfully pretended to be dazzled by his stardom.

But *Love Island* eluded Joey. In 2022 Joey's agent Dave Read saw that his former client Adam Collard had returned to *Love Island* season 8 after previously appearing on season 4. Though he knew big names were not allowed to be cast on the show, Read felt like an Islander returning as a now–public figure had changed the parameters of what was permissible. Read picked up his phone and sent Spencer-Hayter a video message. "Hi Mike, great show last night," Read said. "I hope you'll get the pay rise—bringin' Adam back is genius. I'm sat with someone who thinks if you want a real bombshell, this is how to bombshell." Then Read turned the camera to his client's pretty, veneer-filled face so he could deliver what he clearly considered a scorching invitation: "If you want a bombshell, you've got Dave's number, you've got my number, let's do it," Joey said. (He followed this with a hand motion where he pretended to drop a bomb.) Spencer-Hayter wrote back and said network executive Amanda Stavri "would never have it." Joey was too well-known.

Two years later, Spencer-Hayter was watching a casting tape in the same room as his now-husband, who is a social worker. On-screen was Grace Jackson, a twenty-five-year-old model from Manchester who mentioned that she'd dated Joey. "Oh, so you've got Joey coming in," Spencer-Hayter's fiancé said, as if it were obvious. Spencer-Hayter was disappointed with himself. "How the hell did I not think of that?" he asked. Joey's history with Grace meant that he was technically part of the *Love Island* universe, making his appearance on the show legal by its ever-shifting bylaws.

Spencer-Hayter called Read and asked if Joey still wanted to do *Love Island*—assuming he passed all of his tests and Stavri signed off. Joey very much did, and Stavri relented in the face of Spencer-Hayter's dual hopes for the casting. "It's a great press headline," he says. "And for viewers, it's like, 'Joey Essex in the *Love Island* Villa? *What?*'" Spencer-Hayter had found a new way to surprise UK viewers after ten seasons and progressively softer ratings compared to their US counterpart.

While Joey was going through the process, he read paper of record the *Daily Mail* and saw it had leaked that Grace was going into the Villa. Spencer-Hayter hadn't mentioned to him that she'd be there. *"Effing hell,"* Joey texted Read, along with a screen grab of the article. Because Joey's appearance would be a secret, Grace wasn't aware that he would be on the season.

Getting Joey to Mallorca without the press finding out became, as Read says, "a military procedure." Even in what was a period of waning relevance for *Love Island UK*, the tabloids camped out at Palma de Mallorca Airport to see who was going into the Villa, so Joey couldn't fly direct. Production got him to Ibiza, then put him on an overnight car ferry to Mallorca with a boatload of elderly Spanish people who weren't likely to recognize a celebrity of Joey's caliber.

Joey showed up at the Villa on the first night as the first bombshell. Islanders were awestruck, as Spencer-Hayter had hoped. Though some of the younger cast members were unaware of who exactly Joey was because his tenure on *TOWIE* had ended eleven years earlier, their relative elder castmates' reactions let them understand his status in the Villa. "Obviously, Joey coming in, the boys are scrambling," thirty-year-old recruitment manager Munveer Jabbal said. "We're all shitting ourselves, to be honest."

"I want people just to get to know me on a level as well, just for who I am as a person," Joey said, as if coming onto *Love Island* after getting second place on the celebrity figure skating series *Dancing on Ice* was like Brad Pitt trying to make a connection on Raya. It sounded ridiculous to viewers, especially those watching in America. But at the beginning of season 11, Joey basically *was* the Brad Pitt of the Villa. Even discounting his fame, he was the best-looking Islander of the season, with azure eyes and abs as distinct as Venetian blind slats. The Islanders were merely as tickled as women Joey encountered in the wild, including the formidable Grace. Ronnie Vint, twenty-seven-year-old semiprofessional footballer who looks and sounds like a used coffin salesman, would become Joey's closest confidant after the jolt of his fame wore off. "At first it was like, 'Oh my God, it's Joey,'" Ronnie says, "but then the next day it's like, 'Joey, he's one of us.'"

This is not strictly true; Joey was certainly one of the Islanders, but he was also the leader of the Villa. Stavri's concerns about having a famous person on *Love Island* were soon borne out. "He didn't quite follow by the same rules as the Islanders because he's a celebrity," she says of Joey, who was disrespectful to the ex who got him on *Love Island* and attempted to instigate fights and hookups among those he clearly considered his supporting cast. Viewers, she says, "get quite outraged if you don't follow the etiquette. There can be some quite big fallouts from that."

Though Spencer-Hayter says producers worked very hard to build other stories, bringing Joey Essex on had the intended effect of drawing attention to his conspicuous and disruptive presence. "He made it *The Joey Show*," Spencer-Hayter says of behavior like Joey quoting his old *The Only Way Is Essex* lines about his hair looking reem. "Maybe as a viewer, it was quite heavy Joey. And it's a big commitment: fifty-seven nights. So you had a lot of Joey, and then by the end maybe the audience were thinking, 'Hmm, you know, we want to give these other people we've fallen in love with a chance.'"

Mimii Ngulube won the season after a terrace scene that was as mortifying as Ekin's was seminal. Naturally, Joey facilitated her humiliation. Mimii, a twenty-four-year-old mental health nurse, wanted to have a chat to resolve things with Ayo Odukoya, a twenty-five-year-old model with whom she'd previously been coupled and still had a lingering coquetry. She asked Joey to discreetly ask Ayo to come up and have a private conversation on the terrace, which she unfortunately entered into upright on her knees, so she was lower than the sightline but not in the kind of alluring crawl that would make the encounter read as untoward. Mimii walked—"walked"—to the couch, taking teeny-tiny knee steps, like she was knelt in prayer and needed to scooch over to let a large party into a pew without interrupting Sunday service.

Joey immediately began making a huge deal about the "secret mission," loudly mentioning there was something he couldn't talk about in an effort to get Islanders' attention and artlessly creating a scene for viewers. Ayo declined Mimii's invitation because he was in a new couple after Casa, and a rule so obvious it hardly bears mentioning is "if you don't want to fuck up your current couple, don't go on the terrace for a secret conversation with your ex who is open to rekindling things." Joey began cajoling Ayo, telling him if he wouldn't have a conversation with Mimii on the terrace, he should at least go to the terrace and have a conversation about *why* he couldn't have a conversation on the terrace. Joey then tried dragging Ayo up the stairs. Ayo wouldn't join him and instead had a tearful talk with his current partner about her insecurities around Mimii. Joey hid in a fake plant and cartoonishly motioned to Ayo, trying to summon him to meet his ex. "No," Ayo shouted, waving Joey away with his hand. "That's all dead, bro."

As the season lurched toward its conclusion, Joey's star power was burning off his tolerability. This seemed especially true for Grace, whom Joey kept accusing of being obsessed with him as she pursued relationships with other men. By the end of the season, she had gone from a person for whom her association with Joey was an asset for getting cast on the show to being visibly disgusted that she'd ever entertained him as a partner. "Bore off, man," Grace said as Joey told her to shut her mouth and claimed she was bitter.

For his talent show performance the day after the terrace debacle, Joey performed a rhythm-free rap, mostly recapping all the times the other Islanders were annoyed with him. Though his castmates laughed along in reminiscence of Joey's most irritating hits, the song ended with a call and no response. "When I say, 'secret,' you say, 'mission!'" Joey shouted. "Secret!" Silence. "Misson!" Nothing.

When Joey was dumped from the Island before the finale, the cast and audience's initial awe had already curdled into antipathy. "I've done it for too long, because nothing's personal for me," he said about reality TV in an interview with *The Sun*. "Everyone in there took things very personal, but that's on them."[1] Joey broke the ultimate rule of *Love Island*: using the fakeness to prevent himself from caring. "It's a TV show, innit?" he said. It was, but it didn't feel like *Love Island*. And Joey leaving so late gave viewers only a few episodes to spend time with all the Islanders *The Joey Show* had been distracting them from.

Joey's presence felt like a season-long gimmick, or an experiment to see how long C-list fame would sustain his status in the Villa before the other Islanders accepted Ronnie's words that he was just "one of us"—which meant that they had the power to get rid of him.

Ronnie would become the unexpected trailblazer of the summer. He was the first Islander with advanced male pattern baldness to come on *Love Island* without plugs, which was inadvertently revealed in a quick night vision shot that exposed his real hairline and became one of the few non-Joey flash points of the season. Producers made the decision not to feature Ronnie's daily hair-in-a-can routine, which he hadn't been hiding. "They was protecting me," Ronnie says. "If anything, I would rather it be out there. But obviously I just didn't realize how big of a deal it was, because I was thinking, 'Girls'll put makeup on—I'll put hair on.'" When Ronnie got out of the Villa, he got a brand deal with Toppik hair fibers, along with some free golf clubs, which he was using to play a round with friends during the entirety of our conversation. "I've turned something that could be an insecurity into a big opportunity and a brand deal at the end of the day," Ronnie says.

Despite becoming the villain of a season he clearly thought he'd be the star of, Joey also got sponsorships off the back of it, Read says, and his appearance fees went up—he made good money playing Joey Essex on TV. Joey also fulfilled Spencer-Hayter's wish for a shake-up come true, though it was like he'd made it on a monkey's paw. The show got press—bad press. And the audience was certainly shocked. It was the least watched season ever.

17

Vegas, Baby

TONI LAITES HAD BEEN propositioned before. As a twenty-four-year-old pool cabana server at the Fontainebleau Las Vegas, Toni had been offered jobs, (very) early retirement, and other less fiduciarily minded requests. On a Monday afternoon in spring 2025, a married man in his late thirties asked Toni what was a standard workplace question for her: "Are you single?" This time, it changed her life.

The question came from Mike Spencer-Hayter, who was in Las Vegas for his honeymoon. Like the ceremony, this vacation was slotted in between production for *All Stars* and *UK* season 12. Spencer-Hayter realized their server wasn't what he "would class as your average American." Toni had the craic. A decade past the Sugar Hut days, Spencer-Hayter says he almost never does this anymore—but that day, he wondered if he should chat up Toni. His husband said yes.

So Spencer-Hayter asked if Toni was available. She was suspicious: "I thought you were on your honeymoon, with a man," she said. He affirmed he was and asked again. Toni was unencumbered romantically and by any knowledge of *Love Island*, which she'd heard of but had never seen—plus, she didn't really believe this person *ran* the show. A few days later, the casting team reached out and began the process of making sure Toni was psychologically, medically, and entertainingly sound to be on TV. Despite Spencer-Hayter's repeated insistence over multiple conversations with me that he wasn't interested in bringing over anyone from the US, he had his first American Islander for *Love Island UK* in its twelfth season. Spencer-Hayter thought it would be a bold, risky choice—hopefully one that would go better than the bet on Joey.

Toni presented big looks to accentuate the kind of confidence that had made her stand out at the Fontainebleau pool: huge earrings, sparkles, lavishly overlined lips. During the Duty of Care, the team asked Toni what she wanted hair- and makeup-wise. (Yes, glam is considered essential for the well-being of Islanders.) The team always does their best—Jackson would be flying in wigs, as always—but they made it clear they might not be able to provide *exactly* what Toni asked for. Toni has the supreme ability to know precisely what she needs and would not count on the *Love Island* glam team to get an approximation of those items. Toni brought her own clip-in hair extensions and four sets of ostentatious press-on nails that were custom-made by her tech. The effect was Gen Z Adriana-from–*The Sopranos* styling with Paulie Walnuts's attitude.

Toni walked into the Villa as the first bombshell of the season and took twenty-three-year-old cabbie Ben Holbrough from twenty-two-year-old Shakira Khan, a dry beauty with a clenched-jaw Northern accent and an uncommon directness that drew Toni to her. Toni was doing Shakira a favor with the steal; Ben had a rank masculinity and dire need for attention that caused him to do things like end an argument by breaking the fourth wall and yelling across the yard, "You've just given *Love Island* loads of content. Well done. Ey! She's made content for the next three weeks, lads." (He would later apologize.)

Toni was cast as a big swing but also as an outsider. She would feel the status keenly. "The first week I wanted to get the fuck out of there," Toni says. "I almost feel as though the Islanders weren't trying to help me interact with them or understand what they were talking about." Having never seen the show, Toni didn't even have a cursory knowledge of British slang. "It's not like we're speaking a different language. I didn't go in thinking, 'Oh my God, these people are so different from me,' but that's the way they felt about me."

There was a general feeling of distrust in the Villa in season 12 that was encouraged by an early date in which Ben, twenty-six-year-old personal trainer Dejon Noel-Williams, Harry Cooksley, and the other men met three bombshells while the women watched a stream of the encounter. During it, Harry, a thirty-year-old semiprofessional football player, revealed he was concerned Helena Ford was a "good-time girl" and mentioned the twenty-nine-year-old flight attendant had confided that she had had a threesome. Most of the other boys said the women they were coupled with weren't their usual types. The women were aghast. It was Movie Night in real time.

Spencer-Hayter and Stavri had come up with the idea to show the footage as part of an overall revamp for the show to emphasize its evolution. "Oh wow, they're doing that on day three," they imagined the audience thinking about showing the women men's dates while they were still on them. "What the hell are they gonna do in week two?" Other new elements were an initial coupling based on written descriptions of the other Islanders with no visuals, as well as the somewhat less impactful excision of the beanbags and the introduction of a redesigned water bottle.

But the central drama of the season was pure old-school *Love Island* and would suck the Villa back to a time that was both more innocent and more licentious; horniness needs no bells and whistles. Harry was an apparently perma-tumesced figure who would split audience opinion and prompt a level of debate that *Love Island UK* hadn't had in years. While he was coupled with the mink-voiced Helena, Harry took twenty-four-year-old banker bombshell Yasmin Pettet to the Hideaway for a private chat, which is now permissible without invitation in the UK for those who aren't in a couple. Yasmin's hyper-erect spinal position and endless appetite for talking about sex were an appealing juxtaposition, giving her an almost prim affect while she did things like ask the coupled-up Dejon if he would have a three-way with her and Toni. "When you're on top, is it still like . . ." twenty-six-year-old electrical engineer Jamie Rhodes asked after they got together. "Do you maintain posture?"

"Yeah, my posture's always really good," Yasmin said, confirming her cowgirl would sit like the queen.

"You're making me want to take some risks right now," Harry told Yasmin in the Hideaway.

"I'm just sort of waiting for you to shut the fuck up and kiss me," Yasmin replied.

Yasmin would be divisive in a positive way. "I felt like in all my years of casting, Yas was one of the most interesting people I've ever met," Spencer-Hayter says. "I wasn't sure whether she would be loved and celebrated or whether she wouldn't go down as well with the audience. But the public were obsessed."

Changes in who was interested in whom were happening so quickly that the show had become appointment viewing once again—if you missed an episode, you'd get spoiled on the night's surprises. Helena knew Harry and Yasmin had kissed, but rather than put up a fight out in the open, she went on a trench warfare–style mission to win him over, alternating explicit seduction and emotional avoidance as shields and weapons. When Harry coupled up with Shakira, Helena appeared coolly removed, telling him it was fine in her posh purr. Then she whispered "I can't wait to fuck you" in Harry's ear during the Heart Rate Challenge before pulling him out of bed with Shakira to go sleep in the Hideaway together.

Their pattern was complicated when Harry's former girlfriend of three years, thirty-year-old accredited hydrogeologist and uncredentialed chaos agent Emma Munro, returned from Casa with the intention of either fucking up Harry's game, recoupling with him and winning the show, getting back together, or just giving him a whiff of her underarm. As Helena spied on the pair, she witnessed Emma lift her elbow, exposing her glorious pit to Harry. He reacted like Gollum getting a glimpse of the ring. "You wanna sniff?" Emma said. "I know you like to smell them."

"That took everything not to sniff your armpit there," Harry said, visibly restraining himself from lunging into it.

Harry disrespected Helena yet again by repeatedly sitting down with Shakira to emit the kind of sexual charge that can only come from conversations where the dialogue is about how much the two people don't want to be together. This time, Helena had had enough—for the minute. Until that point, she had been larking around to prove just how alluringly unbothered she was. Now she was finally turning away from Harry. This rejection germinated a tiny sprout of empathy in the footballer. Harry began to cry to Dejon as he realized that following his predilections actually wounded the people who incited them, something he had never considered prior. More selfishly, Harry also gleaned that his actions unintentionally damaged the situations he might want to return to in the Villa once he'd gotten bored of all those shiny new glands. "It'll never be the same now after the way I've acted," Harry lamented, realizing for the first time that *he* was the problem, not his relationships.

Spencer-Hayter was elated. "He's a fantastic character," he says of Harry. "I love him. Some of the people didn't like him or didn't agree with the way he went about things, and it's holding a little bit of a mirror to society. Like, there is a Harry in every town"—someone whose charisma allows them to overplay their advantage. Being on the show, Spencer-Hayter says, allowed Harry to learn more about himself and also provide viewers with a situation that could allow themselves to discern what they find acceptable in relationships. "That's why the show is so brilliant," Spencer-Hayter says. "Because you can identify behaviors you might like or dislike, or you should or shouldn't do."

"He's thirty years old," Toni says of Harry. "You figure out who you are at that point in your life, and he said himself that he's a very self-destructive person. When things are going well in his life, he sabotages them, and he admits to that flaw and says he's gone to therapy and worked on it. And I think he still has work to do, but he's one person I can say is just unapologetically himself. That's why I resonate with him." This acceptance was easier won after Harry stopped messing around and focused on Toni's best friend Shakira.

That settling down did not stop Harry from oozing Harryness. After humiliating Helena throughout the season, he met her parents on Family Day. Harry apologized for his pillage of the Villa at Helena's expense—and, to his delight, his contrition was accepted. Helena's father relayed a customer's comment that Harry "wears his dick on his sleeve" but also that he looked good.

"Why are you complimenting him?" Helena said through not-yet-dry tears. "He's just broken my heart!"

"He can talk his way out of anything," construction project manager Blu Chegini marveled during his own visit with his mother. (She was introduced by Iain as the "legend of the sex shop," in one of the narrators' many references to her lingerie and adult product store.)

Another Islander's mother called Harry a "lovable villain." Viewers appreciated the antihero for driving the season.

Before Harry and Shakira succumbed to their love-hate relationship and recoupled, the four people running the Villa were Harry, Dejon, Helena, and Meg Moore, a twenty-five-year-old payroll specialist from Southampton with seventies blonde highlights and an insistence, less and less convincing each time it was uttered, that "My name's Meg, not mug." This crew explicitly directed the action by encouraging people within the inner circle (along with their JV squad member Harrison

Solomon) to pursue relationships with their own preferred picks. They also had high school energy, with the boys egging each other on and the women turning their distress about their own relationship dysfunction toward easy targets. It was unattractive to viewers, who seemed to want to keep the bullies around to see them get their comeuppance—or to watch them convert, as Harry did.

The brunt of hotties facing sudden onset hotness relativity was primarily borne by Toni and Shakira, whom Meg and Helena accused of grafting desperately. "Go on, strut your stuff, walk down your fucking catwalk," Meg said about the pair. Toni and Shakira responded in kind, with Shakira calling Harrison "cockroach number one" and Harry "cockroach number two."

"It's not that I didn't care, because everyone wants to be liked of course," Toni says. "But I'm very confident in who I am as a person. So at least in the beginning, I didn't question myself. But it's hard when you spend eight weeks in that environment. You almost do sort of question, 'Am I the problem?'"

This new feeling of not trusting herself was underlined by her back-and-forth relationship with Harrison, a twenty-two-year-old professional footballer who, like *USA* season 6's Liv and season 5's Marco, had attended Florida Atlantic University—as had Toni, though their matriculations didn't overlap. Toni grew increasingly irritable as Harrison toggled between her and Casa girl Lauren Wood, a twenty-six-year-old dog walker from York. Toni landed in the bottom of a public vote with Shakira, who was at that point still unreconciled with the pit-snuffling Harry.

Harrison was delighted to have two women vying for him and began showing off. "Do you have a condom?" Harrison stage-whispered to Harry and Helena, who sniggered as Harrison and Lauren pumped away and Meg and Dejon watched. All the Islanders have access to contraception, so Harrison didn't need to involve the popular kids in the act.

"I think deep down inside of him, the way that he acted on the show is not really him," Toni says. "The circumstances shaped him, and he was trying to be cool in front of the other boys, who were the ringleaders. And he thought that it would work in his favor to be the player and go back and forth between girls, but it wasn't received well by viewers, obviously."

Now, six weeks into the season and two from the finale, Harrison was at the bottom with Toni on top. (Not in that way—Toni maintained a steadfast "no sex in the common bedroom" policy throughout the season.)

After sleeping with Lauren but not informing Toni of that critical piece of information, Harrison met Toni on the terrace and pitched her the idea that the two of them should recouple. Toni smiled, looking like the Grinch when he came up with the plan to steal Christmas from Whoville.

Their reunion blindsided the rest of the Villa—Lauren despondent, the rest of the cast whispering among themselves. Harrison had the look of a man realizing he'd made a terrible mistake, and Toni, while maintaining her standard defiance, had clearly lost the heady elation she'd had in the planning of this coup. Her former partner Cach Mercer shut down, the normally unflappable dancer standing by the firepit dejectedly. Once he was out of sight of Toni, he began weeping on Ty Isherwood's shoulder. "I haven't cried in years," twenty-four-year-old Cach said, shocked at what this routine part of the *Love Island* formula could induce when it happened to *him*.

Spencer-Hayter was back in the UK, and by the time the team had called to tell him that Harrison had changed his mind and picked Toni over Lauren, Harrison already regretted the decision and wanted to change it. His compunction grew after he realized he had to inform Toni about what had happened with Lauren the night before he and Toni recoupled. "I think for once I'm at a loss for words here," Toni said when he revealed he and Lauren had sex. "And you still left her? You're so stupid. See, now you're really the bad guy." That was it for Toni.

"Free me from the shackles of this boy-child," Toni said in the Beach Hut. "I feel nothing at this point."

"Harrison could not make a decision," Spencer-Hayter says. "So one minute, he was like, 'I'm a hundred percent all into Toni.' The next minute, 'I'm a hundred percent all into Lauren.' Then the next time he'd speak to our producers, it was, 'No, I'm a hundred percent into Toni.'" It was as maddening for the crew as it was for Toni and Lauren. Eventually, Lauren got dumped, and they told Harrison if he wanted to leave, he should. He did.

"We were so reactive this year," Spencer-Hayter says. "Myself, the execs and the channel, and Amanda [Stavri] would sit and make a plan for that day based on the story. The next day, we'd have morning viewing."

The morning viewing is that 8:30 screening when the top producers and network executives watch a cut of the show made from yesterday's footage. Then, depending on what they see and how much it comports with the Islanders' projected behavior, they overhaul plans for what they thought they were going to film in the subsequent hours. In season 12, Spencer-Hayter says, "At least eighty percent of the episodes were changed on this series. I'd say, out of fifty-seven shows"—the regular episodes, not inclusive of *Unseen Bits*—"realistically, forty-seven were changed."

Instead of following through on their season-long master plan to upend both the formula of *Love Island UK* and the audience's expectations of it, Spencer-Hayter says they wound up doing almost none of the format-busting challenges they'd planned. "The drama was forefront," he says. It was back to basics—with the exception of the new water bottle—and would result in the most viewers *Love Island* had earned in seven seasons, including *All Stars*.

The truth was, before season 12, *Love Island UK*'s dip in cultural significance helped create the conditions for its renaissance. "It's the reality paradox," van Ballegooy says. "If you amass a huge success, it means everyone is also very aware of the success. That means people are becoming more self-aware and self-producing, and then you have to carry this weight." In its fourteenth season overall, with no massive Islanders to materialize from the Villa in some time, it would have been crazy for cast members to assume that suddenly that was going to happen again. In season 1, scenes aired of the cast talking about who would win the £50,000 prize. Subsequently, that pot had become irrelevant compared to the vast sum that could be waiting on the outside. Toni says during season 12, Islanders were once again open about their desire for the prize money, which was all they could hope for at this point in the run. But then, through the miracle of casting and some fuck-ass maneuvers from the boys, viewers were locked back in. It felt like that shedding of expectation let the show be the freaky free-for-all it had been in the early seasons.

As with the greatest heights of *Love Island*—or Charles Dickens or Nora Ephron—a delicious turn in fortune became the engine of season 12's conclusion.

Harry was now with Shakira, Helena was out of the Villa, and Harrison had skulked out after Lauren. The coterie was disbanded, and Dejon and Meg were increasingly marooned while Toni, Shakira, and Yasmin reigned as Villa queens. Dejon had, seemingly unintentionally, spent the entire season trying to prove Meg wrong about not being a mug, and the tension between them was driving the audience further away. On one occasion before she was dumped, even Helena turned on her bestie, clawing for status by talking shit about the woman she and Dejon were closest with in the Villa. "Meg's always just going to be angry with you," Helena cackled with Dejon. "You can't win." The latter sentence would prove prescient.

While Harry had traversed myriad armpits and made many trips to the Hideaway when he was still unattached, Dejon made the critical mistake of "testing" and "exploring" while being in a day-one couple. Whenever this discrepancy was discussed, Dejon would ruefully say they still weren't official, as if that designation were out of his hands. Soon after her arrival but well after Dejon had been steadily coupled with the woman he called "My Meg," Yasmin asked Dejon, "What are your biggest turn-ons?"

Dejon's response was simple and would explain at least half of the decisions he made: "I just love sex. I love it all." It was high-cringe to see the Villa Dad talking dirty, and Dejon was maddeningly watchable as he justified his coexisting urges.

He tried to offset the sins of his early *Love Island* days with a series of grand gestures. "I believe what's meant for you will always be for you," Dejon read off his phone as he asked Meg to be exclusive. "And I feel like the fact that you picked me when we first came in on the first day without you knowing who I was or what I looked like, I believe that was fate."

Hours later, the short film *Good Dejon Hunting* made its debut at Movie Night. A litany of flattery and innuendo with multiple Casa women culminated with Dejon suggesting a game of truth or dare and making out with twenty-seven-year-old nail technician Andrada Pop in Casa Amor. It was technically within a challenge but not nice to see for his Meg. It was worsened by Andrada telling Dejon he gave her "a little tingle," to which he responded, "Where's it tingling?"

Toni also got a shock at Movie Night: Producers played a scene of her crying over Harrison. "That conversation I knew would be seen by the public," she explains of the cognitive dissonance of *Love Island* filming logic. "I never thought it would be seen by everyone else"—as in, everyone else in the Villa, who were her equals, not her audience. "I felt very exposed," Toni says of not being able to choose how she was presenting herself to the other Islanders in that moment.

Movie Night played out with most of the women coming after Dejon, questioning the stated strength of his feelings for Meg and the options he concomitantly entertained. Meg had initially been pissed off at him, too, demanding why he'd used his secondary pet name for her, "baby girl," on another girl in Casa. But as the other Islanders' opinion of Dejon as a player congealed, Meg started getting defensive of him and what their partnership reflected about herself.

Dejon and Meg's status was further degraded during the game "Couple Goals," wherein the Islanders were asked to sit around the firepit in their bathing suits and name the pair who best fit prompts like "Which couple cares most about how they are perceived?" Meg, warily frowning before anyone had even named them, said, "I don't feel like we care; we say it how it is." Toni, Cach, Helena, Blu, Shakira, Dejon's former best friend Harry, and two other couples voted for them, citing Dejon wondering openly about how they were being depicted on the series. Meg and Dejon also took first place for the question "Which couple is the most fake?"

"Do you want me to pick someone else?" Toni asked with sarcastic innocence after the couple started fighting against the charge.

Islanders also noted that relationship markers like exclusivity and the exchange of I love yous that were meted out by the formerly withholding Dejon in the last several weeks of the show were suspect in their timing. Meg hoisted an omnipresent but not-quite-convincing smile that lingered queasily for the next few days.

Their castmates were onto something, even if they didn't have all the information viewers did. The footage that Dejon was so worried about seemed damning, showing that during an argument, he focused on what was being shown of him on-screen—which, in fairness to Dejon, would naturally impact their relationship once they were off-screen. In a scene where the couple was bickering away from the rest of the Villa, Dejon told Meg to be careful with what she said about him because, he said, "We're on a TV show, and they can literally put highlights of you—"

Meg cut him off, saying, "I don't care if we're on a TV show."

"I don't know if the cameras are around and you're trying to make me look bad," Dejon said.

Meta-textual conversations about the edit are on the list of material that would never make said edit. They made an exception in this case. "There was an air that he was maybe fake from the other Islanders," Spencer-Hayter says. "When he talks about the cameras to Meg, we left the edit running so you could see there was no cut." They wanted no room for accusations that this conversation had been manipulated, which might be forthcoming from someone who was so conscious of television production.

In the penultimate episode of the season, all of the ex-Islanders lined up to explain who should go home out of the bottom couples. These cast members—this time not the remaining couples' direct competitors for the prize but rather people who had left the Villa—had watched the whole show and witnessed how the country was turning on Meg and Dejon. They pointed out their many arguments, asserting that Meg liked Dejon more than he liked her, and implied that Dejon was a horndog who wouldn't be able to resist the many temptations that awaited when there was an entire country of women who might be tingling for him. Dejon felt compelled to debate every criticism, saying that it didn't matter what anybody thought because they knew they would work on the outside and were so happy. This mantra was delivered not with the vehemence of his past protestations, but the resignation of a man using his final words to insist on innocence. To the surprise of no one and the elation of the public, Dejon and Meg were dumped.

While Dejon was digging himself into a hole, Toni was clawing her way out of one with the help of her two-inch neon press-ons.

Recoupling with Harrison in front of Cach had humiliated him, and Toni had to deal with that in ways she normally never would have contended with. "In real life, a block button is very useful," Toni says. "I think our generation is quick to just delete, goodbye, and never see you again. But *Love Island* forces you to do the opposite. In the Villa you can't block people you spend twenty-four hours a day with, and you're forced to confront issues you have with people and get over things more quickly than you would."

Cach had previously been a relaxed, quirky presence in the Villa, playing pranks such as pretending he had been a member of the boy band JLS. When the other Islanders excitedly started questioning him and realized he didn't know anything—not even who the "other" members were—Cach said that management had made him sign an NDA, so he couldn't reveal their names. It was this sort of easygoing presence that added levity in the Villa during the more heated days of mean-girl plotting and the Toni and Harrison quagmire.

After the ambush at the recoupling ceremony, Cach was cordial with Toni but unwilling to open himself to a second public humiliation. Then she did something she'd never done before. "I would never usually chase a boy, ever, ever, ever," Toni says. "But me being the emotionally intelligent person I am, I knew where I had gone wrong and that it was stupid and it was hurtful. So I had to pick up the pieces and fix things, because I know Cach deserves it."

Toni, who had spent so much of the season with her arms crossed telling people to fuck off, realized she needed to be vulnerable. Or rather, she had to embrace that she'd already been made vulnerable by the situation she (and Spencer-Hayter) had put herself in and the things she could not control about it. "I felt very exposed," Toni says. "Being in the bottom of the first public vote was really hard, because there wasn't another vote for weeks and weeks and weeks and weeks." The break in time paid off with the audience—the kind of shift in opinion that Spencer-Hayter and his team monitor as they schedule vote-based dumpings. "It wasn't until the last public vote, where I was voted favorite girl, that I started to really realize, 'Maybe I am doing the right thing,'" Toni says. "It's a nice feeling to come out with that same attitude because I don't have to keep up a persona. I can still be me, because that's what people loved me for."

Toni maintained her self-assuredness throughout, but now she was using it in service of making a relationship work, rather than wrestling with one that didn't. "The way you treat me has made this whole wacky-ass experience worth it," Toni said to Cach during a final toast, facing her fears of being earnest in any context. "I think everyone has seen how happy you've made me." Toni began crying as she told Cach, "I feel like a different person. I don't think anyone's ever treated me as good as you do."

Cach gathered her in his arms and began stroking her as he explained how he had come around. "You're so unapologetically yourself," he said. "It makes it so easy for me to operate the way I operate—your emotions are literally on a platter."

This was true but did not fully honor the fact that in eight weeks, Toni had expanded the spectrum of what she would display from states that made her feel high status—anger, sexiness, derision—to include ones that made her feel unprotected. Her shambling into sensitivity had allowed that a nice person love her and the audience root for her in a different way than she had expected.

The first American to appear on *Love Island UK* would also be its first American winner. Toni and Cach had won over the UK viewers in a season that brought new charm to the things that had made *Love Island* special in the first place. Season 12 would garner the most press the show had had in years—the comms team hadn't anticipated the interest and found that, for the only time since season 3, they were understaffed to handle the number of requests for the Islanders. And the all-American group of bombshells that would function as a de facto Casa Amor in the season of *All Stars* that aired five months later seemed to concede the rise of the US, even in *Love Island*'s motherland.

Toni had always felt like a star and took to her newfound notoriety with the expectance of someone stepping into a car they'd called for themself. She began the process of permanently moving to the UK to be with Cach and to take advantage of brand deals she was offered there, from Asos to Google. As of this writing, the couple is still together. She, Cach, Shakira, Yas, and Harry enjoy the outside together, doing karaoke and playing Toni's favorite game, bingo.

Toni credits Spencer-Hayter—and his husband—with giving her a non-cabana career and the love she found on a show where she experienced a crisis of confidence and also competed in a blindfolded kissing contest against six other women.

Toni misses one thing about being on the show: "When you're in the Villa, you don't think about the millions of people that are watching you," Toni says. "Now it's all I can think about."

While Toni was grateful for the time she had on *Love Island*, she also wanted to impress upon us the one aspect that we often forget as we watch these very real people navigate a very constructed environment for our viewing pleasure: "Please remember that we're all human beings."

18 The Outside

BEING ON *LOVE ISLAND* alters people on a molecular level. Islanders' biomes are introduced to bacteria from mouths they never would have kissed. Brand-new neural pathways are carved by traumas and loves they never would have had. Their perspectives shift as they go from being the subjects of their own lives to being objects in a game that doesn't end at the finale.

People will often tell Islanders they signed up for this. But a person can only intellectually understand the bargain they're making before they go through it. They can only imagine what their own season might be like by watching previous ones—and even if they do, the show changes every year and within most episodes at the whims of production. Nor does it fully penetrate to hear former cast members explain what it's like to become an Islander as part of the Duty of Care. Spencer-Hayter insists potential cast members are urged to think about how their lives will change because of the experience. He says they can't be told enough to "look publicly and see the positive and negative impact of the show over the last ten years. You can see that information, you're briefed, you're fully supported. Are you ready to give up control and do the show? Because it will catapult you regardless." The problem is that when people look at the potential downsides, they think, "Sure . . . but it will probably work out for me."

Multi-franchise star Toby Aromolaran applied to the series with what he thought were eyes wide-open. "You've seen the Molly-Maes, the Tommy Furys," Toby says. "You know going onto the show, 'Okay, cool. I'm on national TV. I'm giving up my privacy.' But as nice as ITV is to have the best of the best tell you all of these things, nothing in the world can prepare you for what you experience when you come out of the Villa."

"It's not a natural thing to have fame overnight," season 5 cast member Chris Taylor says of walking into the outside. "Even people like Sabrina Carpenter or whoever you think got famous overnight, she's been doing this shit for ten years," Chris says. "She's grafted for it. We've just been on TV for a couple of weeks."

Islanders clearly want to be part of a successful TV show. But when they sign their contracts, whether they've read them or not, they can't comprehend what they have to sacrifice as tribute to that success, both during the process and in perpetuity.

After an Islander leaves *Love Island*, they go to a hotel and are given a fast-forward version of what the world thought of them over their time on the show: *This moment you completely forgot became an internet fixation, then this happened and your family got death threats, but now basically everyone likes you.* They sit through the briefing about their professional futures and are told that they should be prepared to have press show up at their homes. They are informed of the therapeutic resources available for them, of which they are expected to avail themselves. "It's like a rehabilitation back into the real world," Toby says, "but the whole world has changed." Many Islanders expressed similar feelings of disconnect with familiar surroundings that were now changed by a context that no one from their old lives shared. "I can explain it to my mom and my family and whatever," Maura says. "But unless you've experienced it, you really don't know." Maya Jama has seen the whiplash many times: "You're working at Tesco, and then people want to know who you're snogging," she says.

Comms head Jeffreys is one of the people who fills Islanders in about their press coverage before they are given their phones back and return to the outside. He says that whom viewers turn on depends on a number of factors: how popular the season is, how firmly the audience feels about the cast members around a specific Islander. Sometimes the audience is having so much fun that they'll blow past something that in another season would necessitate the removal of an Islander from the Villa; sometimes who gets punished seems correlated to their race. During season 5, for instance, an old photo of Anton dressed in blackface at a party was released. Anticipating major repercussions, ITV helped craft an apology statement with his mother, and producers were ready to act. To the publicity team's surprise, there was little public outcry. The leak had happened during week one, when people didn't know or care enough about Anton to be outraged by his teenage racism, and then the season took off. Anton would make it to the final and mostly avoid blowback. Meanwhile, his season 5 costar Michael, who is a Black man, says he got death threats and violent, racist messages from people who were upset that he'd flirted with Amber again. People DMed him his parents' address to show they knew where they lived. One person sent him a photo of his license plate.

Once they get their phones back, Islanders finally see firsthand what everyone made of their time in the Villa, unfiltered by a gentle PR team or a refracted reveal through a challenge. They are suddenly aware how the public has perceived their own experience. Follower counts increase exponentially; their DMs are flooded with curses and propositions, both business-related and carnal. Starting in season 3 of *UK*, it became so competitive to sign Islanders that when they came back from the airport, Read says, they found potential representatives "sat around their mum's and dad's house with a cup of tea waiting for them to come home to say, 'Please, can I be your agent?'"

Islanders appear on *Aftersun* to discuss their time on the show, and then a series of media appearances are set up (or at least approved) by ITV or Peacock. The UK team gets one month of say over where an Islander can speak or appear and what business opportunities they take on, while USA gets a year, though they tend to be very permissive; Islanders are free to talk shit about the show—and do—as long as they don't say anything that violates an NDA, which covers specific details of production. Thomas says, "The way that we treat that is very much, 'You gave us your summer, and your lives, and your hearts, and your openness, you should make your money now.'" OnlyFans accounts and sex toy sponsorships are acceptable, while diet products, microtransaction services, gambling, and anything else that might prey on young viewers are forbidden.

Islanders can enter partnerships with fashion companies, go to clubs and bars for personal appearances, appear on podcasts or start their own, write memoirs, make deals that align with their fitness/thirst trap/vacation content, and go on brand trips where they're paid to hang out with other influencers in front of the public and drink shots while the hoi polloi take photos of them. Some will make it onto the cast of *The Only Way Is Essex*, and a rarer bunch will continue to appear on higher profile reality show gigs with celebrity casts, including *All Stars* or *Games*. A much smaller number will get spin-offs that follow their post-Villa coupledom. A teeny percentage become presenters—Olivia Attwood is a panelist on the chat show *Loose Women*, and her castmate Kem Cetinay has a radio program. Some paths are singular: Kem's ex Amber Davies starred as Jordan Baker in a 2025 West End production of *The Great Gatsby*. Season 1's Zoe Brown managed to disappear entirely after sobbing with regret over having sex in the Villa.

The transition from being someone having an experience to *being* experienced by the people who watched you is jarring. "You walk in as one person, then walk out another," Dani Dyer says of *Love Island*. When she was sequestered in the Villa, her sun exposure and fluids were monitored in what was effectively an open-air biodome. "You're just so protected, and then all of a sudden you walk out and you're like, 'I'm scared now,'" Dani says.

The paparazzi were constantly filming Dani. She'd been able to forget about the cameras in the Villa; here, they were a sign that everything had shifted. Dani and Jack would regularly be approached by fans telling her they voted for her—and, she emphasizes, they were so affirming, so *nice*—but Dani always worried about how she was being processed. "What if someone meets me and they're disappointed?" she thought. "What if they're like, 'Oh God, like, she doesn't look how she looks on TV'?" What if they had a conversation with her and were dissatisfied? "Fame is great, and it gives you amazing opportunities, but you can't just turn that off," Dani says. Nearly every Islander I spoke with described people taking their picture or filming them without asking, anywhere from the Tube to Waitrose, as if the photo taker still had a one-way relationship with a person who was on TV and that Islander couldn't see them.

Amy Hart always follows her father's rule: "You must never say no to a picture . . . unless you are eating your dinner." The first part was no problem; it's actually more difficult to get Amy to stop engaging with a fan. Someone asked her for a photo at the 9/11 Memorial & Museum, and Amy happily obliged, asking if the person was excited for the winter season of *Love Island*. Another visitor, likely there in somber remembrance, asked them to lower the volume of their conversation about reality television.

The second part of Ian Hart's directive was harder for Amy. One of her first meals outside the Villa was at a TGI Fridays in London, and at the summit of *Love Island UK*'s acclaim, people kept stopping by to say hi and ask for a photo. Amy initially stuck to the plan of saying she was eating and offering to find them afterward, but she couldn't handle their dejected looks. She'd feel terrible and say, "No, let's do it now!" Then *that* person would tell someone else Amy was in the restaurant. "I ate cold food for the first year," she says.

"There are only two times I can actually pinpoint if anyone could ever say they'd had a bad experience," Amy says. One incident was when it was her turn to buy a round during a pub crawl, and she asked if they could wait until after she paid, and they told her to fuck off. The other was ten days after she got out of the Villa, at her twenty-sixth birthday party at STK Steakhouse in London. Fans kept coming up to her, to the point where Amy was interacting with them instead of the people who had traveled into town to see her. She was starving, so a couple of her girlfriends stood up and chatted with their backs to her, shielding Amy while she plowed through her steak. A year later, an angry hoard member messaged Amy: "I was in STK when you were there for your birthday and you were so rude. You didn't even acknowledge us. You didn't even look at us."

Right before I talked with him, Chris Taylor attended a friend's stag do at a sports bar in Dublin. "I literally did like a four-hour meet and greet with everyone that was in there," Chris says. "I didn't really speak to any of the lads I was with because I physically couldn't. People would literally just get their phone up and point it at your face whilst you're doing whatever you're doing, which is kind of weird. But at the end of the day, what I appreciate about this situation is the people that come up to me and want to speak to me are also the people that put me in this position in the first place. It's just a bit ungrateful really, to be like, 'I don't give a fuck about who got me here.'" As for whether it was a bit ungrateful to his old friends from college to not spend time with them at the bachelor party, well, that's what it's like to be friends with an Islander. "I haven't had an uninterrupted night out" since the Villa, Chris says.

The kind of fame *Love Island* generates is rare—in its speed, in its intensity. As Chris said, the public is responsible for the Islanders' new station, and after all the time they invested in the journey, they don't want it to end just because the season is over. They've seen more intimate moments than most people's closest friends have in real life. The fans have also been having a collective communal experience that is rare in a post-monoculture world—a simultaneous viewership that occasionally delivered simultaneous orgasms. (The Super Bowl could never.) During the summer of 2025, massive viewing parties started popping up for screenings of *USA* season 7 and *UK* season 12—people wanted to go through this phenomenon together, which swelled already outsized feelings about strangers they now felt they knew so well.

Almost no Islanders can translate their *Love Island* celebrity to an arena totally separate from the show. Molly-Mae has, of course, and Olandria seems poised to—she and Maura attended the 2026 Golden Globes. A few months after he left the Villa, Chris was invited to the premiere party for the DC movie *Birds of Prey* with season 5 castmates Danny Williams, Michael Griffiths, and Lucie Rose Donlan. When he got there, the film's star Margot Robbie ran up to him and called, "Chris!" opening her arms for a hug. "This is fucking weird," Chris thought. "The fuck is going on here?"

Robbie is a *Love Island* superfan. Her thirty-first birthday party was *Love Island* themed and featured a heart-shaped martini luge. When Dr. Alex George said that Megan Barton-Hanson looked like Robbie during season 4, Robbie freaked out. "We were like, 'Oh my God, they know who I am on *Love Island*!'" she told the British newspaper *Metro* in 2018.[1] "We'd just finished drinking beer and eating crisps and saying, 'We're so disgusting. We could never be on *Love Island*. We're such fatties. They would never let us on.' They all have some amazing bodies, and they are so gorgeous and are always so done up and looking incredible." The statement is both blatantly untrue and a testament to the impossibly high physical standards of the show.

About eighteen months after Robbie's starstruck encounter with

Chris, he got an email from Warner Bros. asking if he wanted to self-tape for *Barbie*.

Chris was stupefied. He'd spent the last year on various unscripted television programs with the general aim of getting hosting or acting work but without clear direction on how to accomplish that. "I could never have even perceived that I'd be in a Hollywood film," Chris says. "If I was writing a goals list, like, 'Get in a Hollywood . . .' How would I have even achieved that? And then it just kind of happens."

When I met Maya in 2025, her hope was to be known for theatrical work that doesn't rely on wearing revealing dresses. "Something that shows I can act," Maya says, her face beatifically still. "No teeth, crawling on the floor." She would star on season 2 of Guy Ritchie's Netflix series *The Gentlemen* just over a year later.

Ariana would call this "manifesting." "I think it's important that you have an idea of where you'd like to go," she says, "so that new attention and the new eyeballs that are on you are working for you, and you're not working for them. You put the puzzle pieces together so that five, ten years from now you're still able to build something for yourself. Because if you say yes to things you don't really believe in or you're not really sure where you're going with everything, then they drop you, and it's kind of like, 'Well, now what?'"

Think of Bergie. He was the season's breakout star and a standout on the (at the time) much more highly viewed *The Traitors* a few months later. (When he was eliminated from a challenge, Real Housewife of Atlanta Phaedra Parks would wail, "Not my Bergielicious! Not my baby!" As one of the titular traitors, Phaedra would eventually murder her Bergielicious.) After a year of attempting and failing to influence, the ever-sensible Taylor convinced Bergie to stop trying to be a reality star and pursue the thing he'd wanted before *Love Island*, other than finding a girlfriend to give his old diary entries to. He is in school for a medical degree in physical therapy, which he will complete in 2027. Taylor also got him to start going by his real first name: Carsten.

Ariana knows she can't depend on *Love Island.* No one should. "I love working with the show, and I love working with ITV, and I love working with Peacock," she says. "But when you think about it, [Peacock's parent company] NBCUniversal is a multi-million-million-million-dollar company. They're always gonna be okay. So you kind of have to make sure you're taking care of yourself as well, in your heart as well as in your career."

The reality of that is that Islanders are agreeing to enter a system designed to cause disharmony on the way to evolvement and, hopefully, eventually, acceptance. What happens within that disorder is up to people who will inherently look silly for our pleasure as they work it out. Generally, the more genuinely dramatic things are, the more people watch, and the greater the consequences, good and bad, for cast members.

Though it's understood the core viewership of *Love Island* is young adults, several Islanders were shocked to find out that *children* were watching their exploits on the show, too. When Jeremiah was being mobbed by Huda's fans for what they alleged was gaslighting, he was disturbed—first by the charges against him, then by the fact that when he looked at a poster's account, they were usually "a little ass kid." Ariana had gone through this before when she was on *Vanderpump Rules.* "People would come up and they'd say, 'You are my daughter's favorite,' and the daughter's maybe eight years old. In my heart, I would just be like, 'Why is your daughter watching *Vanderpump Rules*? That is wrong.' So I feel pretty similar about children watching *Love Island.*"

In its own way, the series provides an opportunity for discussion. Like many parents—including Michelle Obama—Huub van Ballegooy watches the show with his kids. He finds it offers a way into serious conversations that might otherwise be uncomfortable. "If I sit my twenty-year-old daughter down like, 'Oh, let's have a talk about how you should be treated or how you should treat people,' she's like, 'Dad, shut up,'" he says. "But if you're watching an episode where this guy is being very toxic to this girl and then you hear her say, 'Yeah, that's not great,' then you have an opening. And I think that's also a part of the success of this show."

For Islanders like Amy and Dani and Chris and Bergie—sorry, *Carsten*—and Ekin and Maura and Molly-Mae and Molly and a few dozen others, there may be negative side effects, but *Love Island* has given them much more than it has taken, for now. There are many, many Islanders who may be less obvious success stories but still met their partner, or made some money, or learned about themself. Even Aaron, who experienced true psychic harm, says he doesn't regret going on *Love Island* because of the changes it caused him to make.

Whether they consider this or not, every cast member constructs a permanent, semi-clothed monument to the person who thought it would be a good idea to go on *Love Island*. They can control to what extent they take advantage of that image and what they decide to do after those short, hot weeks and how they respond to people's judgments or plaudits of them. But they can never change what viewers saw: the version of them that will always be naïve enough to believe they understood what it would mean to be an Islander forever. That's why we love them.

Epilogue

IN WALKER PERCY'S 1958 ESSAY "The Loss of the Creature," the writer laments that cultural framework keeps us from authentically experiencing things.[1] According to Percy, the only person to ever *really* see the Grand Canyon was the first guy; the rest of us show up and go, "Wow, it looks just like it does on postcards!" or "This isn't as great as everyone made it sound." But the Villa would be nothing without its signifiers, rendered in neon on clear Perspex placards that can be moved around the Villa and stored in between seasons. "Crack on," they prompt the contestants, which also serves to remind them that the words they say could become apostolic catchphrases. The show's enduring aesthetics—faux plants, the show's ethe laid out in semi-cursive, monogrammed bottles handed to every Islander on arrival, heart-shaped archways, garishly colored swimsuits on surgically-enhanced bodies—are so iconic because they are a physical representation of the pull of *Love Island*: It is an artificial environment that creates true feelings.

I know firsthand. To be in the Villa, as I was in January 2025, is to be transported by many items lovingly surveilled in the hundreds of hours of the show that have aired since its debut more than a decade ago.

The first thing you do after arriving at the Villa is take inventory of all the things you've seen on TV. When you're there, you understand how the set's open-concept claustrophobia encourages interaction and eliminates the ability to keep long-term secrets. On the far side of the garden—which, like everything else, is very near—is the firepit, where every Islander will learn again and again if they've been dumped by the public, or their castmates, or via the designs of producers. The cushions in the semicircular sofa around the pit have little heaters and air conditioners built in for deliberations that can last hours with reshoots for coverage. It is thrillingly false and cheery, like a Barbie Dreamhouse with only slightly more human proportions and about the same amount of pink decor.

You can see the sleeping arrangement in which everyone's beds are lined up in a row, like the orphanage in *The Cider House Rules* but with full-sized Ikea bed frames close enough so that would-be sleepers can hear a midnight handy a bed or two over.

The bedroom, like almost every other indoor space, has no windows—if natural light were let in, that would impact the ability of the more than seventy unmanned cameras to capture action without resetting to accommodate for the sun's shifting position. There are only two bathrooms on the main property for a cast that can balloon to nearly twenty people, with a toilet behind the shower and one downstairs, necessitating elaborately timed and executed coordination.

When you walk around the Villa, you see all the places in the yard where Islanders have had a "private" conversation that will be parsed by producers, viewers, and their castmates, who turn their heads to openly snoop. You cannot appreciate the dearth of peace until you're in the space where nothing is safely out of earshot.

Love Island is filmed on luxurious properties—the Fijian resort that *USA* has commandeered, Sa Vinyassa with its infinity pool in Mallorca. *All Stars* will begin one week after my visit. Set at Ludus Magnus, the South African estate is aptly named for an ancient Roman gladiatorial training school and rents for $10,000 a night. The drive from the front gates to the Villa takes about fifteen minutes; on the way, you pass by a sign for a horse jumping arena and a curated stream that charmingly overtakes the road. The Villa is stunning at a distance, with stonework and what feels like endless grounds laden with palm trees and mountain views. Up close, the opulence is obscured by a patina of plastic—all the plants on-site are replicas, from the Astroturf to the potted flowers. Familiar fluorescents and metallics are stapled to every surface to re-create the *Love Island* look, and as I walk through the space days before filming begins, lurid pillows are being set on synthetic upholstery, transforming a villa into the Villa.

Because, of course, this has all been set up. *Love Island* is fabricated to incite its characters to passion. It works. And the hundreds of real people who create all of this are right outside the Villa, in the dozens of Portakabin containers that have been assembled as a base camp that is run by Mike Spencer-Hayter. The thirty-nine-year-old paces in the sand between barracks like an impish General Patton with a vape and a knit button-down. He is ready to make love happen, not war, but the level of planning is commensurate. During the five-week *All Stars* season, Spencer-Hayter will produce six new hour-long episodes a week that will air hours after the events depicted within them occurred, plus *Unseen Bits*.

Spencer-Hayter walks me around the offices where this will all be planned, reacted to when it doesn't go as planned, and cataloged. One container houses the C-suite of the setup, a grim vessel for executive producers that has cages over the windows. Another box is lined with bright plastic and lights set up to film intro videos for bombshells. The command center is one of the largest spaces, all darkness and LEDs. At the front of the room are eight massive monitors, each documenting a different area of the Villa from sixteen different vantage points.

In the middle of the control room, a large vertical screen shows a floating, golden, glitter-filled heart—*Love Island*'s snow globe (beach globe?) logo. It is the "Island Chat Control," from which the team drafts messages that are beamed to the Islanders' phones, which cannot receive outside communication. "I've got a text!" is among the most commonly used phrases on *Love Island*. These texts can deliver news ranging from who is getting dumped from the Villa to an alert that the Islanders will be participating in a challenge called "Piss Artist." There is, naturally, a wall covered in laminated cards representing every possible game, from Piss Artist to the Heart Rate Challenge.

Right now, as I stand in the Villa, Marcel Somerville is in an apartment in Cape Town, and he believes he and Gabby Allen are in a good place seven years after a cordial, air-clearing conversation that took place after their breakup. He assumes she will be in the Villa because he has been asked what he would do if she were in every press interview ITV had arranged for him before the season. "Never say never," he said when the *Daily Mail* asked if they could get back together if they were both in there.[2]

The public knows they will both be on the show because the cast list has just been announced, and they voted on whom they'd like to see coupled up before filming began. Knowing the results of this vote, and that Gabby does not feel as sanguine about their breakup as Marcel does, Spencer-Hayter devised a devious plan, which he lays out for me as we sit in the indoor lounge on a sofa.

"Our first game that we're doing this year is called 'Red Flag,'" Spencer-Hayter says. "So Maya's going to go in the Villa first. She's going to mingle with everyone, then say to the girls, 'Line up, girls. You've each got a red flag in your hand. It's now time to give it to the boy you think is the biggest red flag and say why.' So Gabby might go to Marcel and go, 'There, it's for cheating on me. I'm still pissed off.' But then later that night, it will be revealed that the public put them together. So it should be fantastic."

"You just can't write this shit," Gabby will tell me a few months later, though Spencer-Hayter basically had. "Like, what the hell? I never thought I would be sharing a bed with him." After what she calls her "initial fuck you" of handing Marcel the flag and revealing he'd had sex with another woman in the hotel where they were vacationing, the pair reached *Love Island*'s version of catharsis. They started talking to each other at night, like they'd done their first time on the show—but this time with reminiscence instead of anticipation. "How's your mum?" they asked each other. "How's your brother?"

Gabby told Marcel. "I remember us doing this."

This was a balm for viewers—who, despite what Marcel thought, did not harbor the same longing for his reunion with Gabby that they'd had for Molly and Callum. Being forced to restore relations was also good for Marcel and Gabby. "It was kind of a peace that I wouldn't have got if we didn't do the show," Gabby says.

Two months later, the finalists will be standing at the same firepit that I had, their fates shaped by obstructions of Spencer-Hayter and the crew. Their choices will play out on the dozens of computers lined up across the control room, where editors would transform the live footage into stories on the whiteboards, not knowing where any of them will lead. Ekin-Su will go from volatile bombshell to joining Curtis in a sustainably simmering couple that will take third place. Fishmonger and "really funny guy who maybe doesn't have the muscles" Luca Bish will break his feigned indifference and cry under the firm hand of season 11's Grace, finally released from her past relationship with Joey Essex and free to have her own arc. They will be runners-up to unlikely champions Casey and Gabby, who will break up in a few months before both joining the cast of *Games* season 2.

As the other storylines resolved while the season built to these absolutions, Chris Taylor and Elma Pazar and Messy Mitch and Marcel were erased from the board. Then Ekin and Casey and all the rest were, too, leaving to go be Islanders on the outside, where there is no way to re-edit the footage that will shape who they are to everyone else.

"It's drama that engineers transformations, because that's what we want to see," Oxford's Professor Taylor says of British pantomime, the unlikely inspiration for this show. Characters evolve, whether they want to or not, through situations they can't control. The machinations of the play—and its producers—force them to adapt to those situations. "We both anticipate those changes and also are surprised when they happen," Taylor says. "Pantomime has to tread this fine line between something that feels very familiar to us as a formula we immediately recognize and that we can immediately engage with emotionally, and quite strategically placed surprise in order to keep us coming back to it. We've seen it all before, and we've also never seen it before."

"The perfect episode you are belly laughing at something, you are crying at something, you're getting cross with something," Thursby-Palmer says of *Love Island*. "But there's always hopefully a happy ending, just like a rom-com."

At least, that's how it's supposed to be—as always, the Islanders make their own decisions. In December 2025, during the final days of *Love Island Australia*'s season 7, something happened that had never previously occurred on any season of *Love Island* in any country. Host Sophie Monk offered the remaining contestants $20,000 to walk away single. Dylan Towolawi, a twenty-five-year-old Irish construction worker who had appeared on the previous season, took the money, which was removed from the $50,000 prize for the pure of heart. Dylan's fellow Islanders quite fairly labeled him a cunt. He had possibly, and seemingly accidentally, broken the season and the show.

Without the implicit understanding that no one is playing to steal the cash that has been present since *UK* premiered in 2015, it's easy to see how *Love Island* could become a strategic game of deception. That worked for *Love Island*'s successor in appointment viewing, *The Traitors*. But imagine someone you had lain next to in bed, whispering to for weeks, whom you were intimate with either visibly, so the world knew, or secretly, so it was the only thing you didn't reveal on a TV series where everything is shown. Maybe you told each other you loved each other. And imagine that person revealing they'd humiliate you for the equivalent of a few months' salary. It would just feel gross to have the potential bedrock dishonesty in a game that's supposed to be played with real feelings and actions—even ones that are prompted by and rewarded with completely unnatural mechanisms, in the Villa and on the outside.

Despite the fact that I was on the set of a TV show I've seen hundreds and hundreds of hours of, looking at the devices used to record it and then the live feeds they were transmitting around the Villa, it did not occur to me that I had been filmed until I was watching the finale of *Love Island: All Stars* weeks later. On-screen, I noticed the same cameras I'd seen in person tucked in the frames of shots of the same places I had explored, documented by other cameras that were off-screen. I remembered being in the control center, looking at footage of the places that I had just been without any thought that whoever had been in the control room would have seen me and everything I was writing about this uncanny experience in my notebook: "Maya, white dress ruched, peach toenails, smells amazing." In the Villa, I lost object permanence of myself. Sure, when *I* was looking at the feeds, I could watch everyone else milling about the Villa. But the me who had walked through the set no longer existed after that moment; I had left that behind when I went into that dark room, where I was the one writing the story. How many cast members had told me they forgot the cameras were there, or at least what it meant that they were? How many had I actually believed before the instant I understood that I'd done the same thing?

Love Island's magic is making all the effort behind it seem like nothing. It's having Iain constantly pointing out how cheap a show is that employs thousands of people around the world for productions that are twenty-four hours a day, seven days a week. It's undercutting the proceedings by dressing cast members up like cats and clowns and lulling them and us into thinking the whole thing is just a silly TV series that might get them enough followers to monetize their workouts or contouring routines. If there's a better bombshell waiting for their partner in the first few days, they certainly don't care enough to get upset about any of these people they just met, and we definitely haven't formed attachments to characters on a TV show whose season just started. Maybe they should bring in some new Islanders to shake things up. But when the banana peels the producers have been placing around the Villa bring these ridiculous people crashing to their perfect asses, suddenly we want to take into our arms the Islanders who just weeks ago were unknown to us and have them cry thick, foundation-melting rivers for the first time in years, or throw more fruit at them for hurting the Islanders we love, even if someone suggested they do it, even if they didn't really mean it and weren't trying to hurt anybody.

"You want to try and do this in the best way possible," Thomas says. I truly believe they are, especially because of the reality he acknowledges about that goal. "Maybe there's no way to actually do that," Thomas says. "Maybe there is no actual free-range chicken version of fucking reality TV. Maybe by definition, we are burning all of these people."

And then we wait for them to make another season.

Acknowledgments

Thank you to the Islanders who shared themselves with us on-screen and in the many conversations that made up this book.

To Caroline, Sophie, and Mike.

To the geniuses who gave us *Love Island*; in particular Richard Cowles, Mike Spencer, Simon Thomas, Ben Thursby-Palmer, Amanda Stavri, Angela Jain, Tom Gould, Danielle Gervais, Coco Jackson, Lewis Evans, Billy Bowers, Mike Beale, Huub van Ballegooy, Sharon Vuong, and, I guess, Les Moonves.

To the team at Atria, including the brilliant Kate Napolitano, Jimmy Iacobelli, Hannah Frankel, Chelsey Drysdale, Rebecca Munro, Erin Kibby, Alison Hinchcliffe, Jessica Laino, Sara Kitchen, and Carolyn Levin.

To our shepherds Ariana Madix, Iain Stirling, and Maya Jama.

To Gary Morris at David Black Literary Agency, who sent an email in August 2024 that read, "Do you think there's a book in *Love Island*?"

To the editors who made me a writer, and the ones who I have the privilege of working with today: the deeply adored Claire Howorth, who is responsible for the *Vanity Fair* story that this book came from; Mark Guiducci; Peter Griffin, who gave me my entire career in collaboration with Tom Junod and Don Draper; Ross McCammon; David Granger;

Lisa Hintelmann; Richard Dorment; Maria Fontoura; Sasha Weiss; Nitsuh Abebe; Kat Stoeffel; Nick Catucci; Leah Carroll; Whitney Joiner; and Richard Just.

To my mom, for watching every minute of this show and transcribing every piece of British slang in every interview, and to the rest of my family, who mostly do not know what *Love Island* is: Haley, Jackie, Marcellus, Cassius, Imogen, and the Clothier-Clatterbuck-Levitas-Pawloski clan.

To Audrey Fromson, for her contributions to fact-checking. Any errors are mine.

To the skill and expertise of Ivana Cruz, who designed the Villa map and archetypes chart; Mike Schur; Jen Celotta; Professor David Taylor; Tony Thorne; Dr. Daniel Campbell-Meiklejohn; and Gallatin's Dr. Karen Hornick.

To Justin Jeffreys and Jason Tolbert, without whom this couldn't have happened, and to Ryan McCormick.

To the friends I would take to the Villa: the Soulmates, Emilia LaPenta, Bennett Jackson, linguistics adviser Ali Dawkins, Steve Baust, Alex Wintz, Francesca Fanelli, Alex Stewart, and brother Oresti Tsonopoulos; A.A.A.A., Angie Martoccio and Andy Greene; the GC, Brennan Carley and street team leader Megan Zehmer; James Chat, my Laura Larocca and Ben Phillips; and Alex Richanbach, a one-person Do Bits Society.

To Nelly Tsonopoulos, whose generosity made it possible to complete this, and to the Bausts and Wintzes.

To Alex, always.

And to Carsten Bergersen, who went on *Love Island* to find love and did.

Notes

Introduction

1. Walter Benjamin, "The Work of Art in the Age of Mechanical Reproduction," *Illuminations* (1935): 4, https://web.mit.edu/allanmc/www/benjamin.pdf.
2. Anna Peele, "How *Love Island* Became a TV Reality of Sex, Fame, and Sometimes Tragedy," *Vanity Fair*, June 2, 2022, https://www.vanityfair.com/style/2022/06/how-love-island-became-a-tv-reality-of-sex-fame-and-sometimes-tragedy.

Chapter 1: Early Days

1. Sean Hayes, Will Arnett, Jason Bateman, hosts, *Smartless*, "Ricky Gervais," SiriusXM, December 7, 2020, https://podcasts.apple.com/us/podcast/ricky-gervais/id1521578868?i=1000501584798.
2. Charlie Brooker, "Island of Lost Hope," *The Guardian*, May 27, 2005, https://www.theguardian.com/culture/2005/may/28/screenburn.features16.
3. Frances Kindon, "Harry Styles' Poignant Way of Remembering 'First Big Love' Caroline Flack," *Mirror*, August 6, 2020, https://www.mirror.co.uk/3am/celebrity-news/harry-styles-poignant-way-remembering-22467522.
4. Caroline Flack, *Storm in a C Cup: My Autobiography* (London: Simon & Schuster UK, 2015), 100.
5. Prince Harry, The Duke of Sussex, *Spare* (New York: Penguin Random House, 2023), 109.
6. Peele, "*Love Island*."
7. Rebecca Davison and Colette Fahy, "'It's totally innocent!' Lauren Richardson's Friend Leaps to Her Defence Amid Reports of Cheating with Zayn Malik," *Daily Mail*, March 19, 2015, https://www.dailymail.co.uk/tvshowbiz/article-3002359/Friends-Lauren-Richardson-defend-Zayn-Malik-cheating-rumours.html.

Chapter 2: Doing Bits

1. Peele, "*Love Island*."

Chapter 3: Once Again with Feeling

1. Kimberley Bond, "Love Island Boss on Body Diversity: We Want to Be Representative but We Also Want Them to Fancy Each Other," *Radio Times,* June 26, 2019, https://www.radiotimes.com/tv/entertainment/reality-tv/love-island-body-diversity/.
2. Peele, "*Love Island*."
3. "LOVE VILE LAND Fury as ITV Show Full Uncovered Sex Scene at 9pm," *The Sun*, July 1, 2016, https://www.thesun.co.uk/tvandshowbiz/1377199/fury-as-itvs-love-island-shows-full-uncovered-sex-scene-at-9pm/.

Chapter 4: Game On

1. Peele, "*Love Island*."
2. Peele, "*Love Island*."
3. "IT'S OVER Love Island's Gabby Allen DUMPS Marcel Somerville after discovering he bedded another woman behind her back while they were on holiday TOGETHER," *The Sun,* April 30, 2018, https://www.thesun.co.uk/tvandshowbiz/6177174/love-island-gabby-allen-dumps-marcel-somerville-cheated-holiday-hotel-guest/.

Chapter 5: Where's Your Head At?

1. Carl Greenwood, "Love Island Lesbian Couple SPLIT After Just One Night as a Couple as It Becomes Too Much for Sophie," *Mirror*, July 5, 2016, https://www.mirror.co.uk/tv/tv-news/love-island-lesbian-couple-split-8353991.
2. "I DON'T TRUST HER 'I Don't Want to Hear Any Bullsh*t Lies': Love Island's Tom Reveals Whether He'll Take Sophie Back After She Quits Villa for Him," *The Sun*, July 7, 2016, https://www.thesun.co.uk/tvandshowbiz/1400746/i-dont-want-to-hear-any-bullsht-lies-love-islands-tom-reveals-whether-hell-take-sophie-back-after-she-quits-villa-for-him/.
3. "Sophie Gradon on Internet Trolls," Radio Aire, posted June 22, 2018, by Pulse 1 News, YouTube, https://www.youtube.com/watch?v=N4V7rNx_pWw.
4. "Sophie Gradon: Love Island Star Took Own Life," BBC, April 18, 2019, https://www.bbc.com/news/uk-england-tyne-47933722.
5. Alex Green, "ITV Chief Condemns 'Absolutely Disgusting' Abuse Aimed at Love Island Stars," *Belfast Telegraph*, August 22, 2019, https://www.belfasttelegraph.co.uk/news/itv-chief-condemns-absolutely-disgusting-abuse-aimed-at-love-island-stars/a/116762730.html.
6. Emma Pryer, "Love Island Star Sophie Gradon's Mum Says Tragic Death Has Left Her with Brain Tumour," *Mirror*, April 3, 2021, https://www.mirror.co.uk/tv/tv-news/love-island-star-sophie-gradons-23848146.

7. Peele, "*Love Island*."
8. Saskia Rowlands, "Parents of Tragic Love Island Star Mike Thalassitis Open to Meeting Caroline Flack's Family," *Mirror*, March 23, 2024, https://www.mirror.co.uk/3am/celebrity-news/parents-tragic-love-island-star-32426745.
9. Peele, "*Love Island*."

Chapter 6: Buzzing

1. "LOVE ISLAND INTERVIEW WITH WINNER AMBER SPILLING BIG LOVE ISLAND SECRETS, MOLLY MAE, BIG NEWS, BEEF!," posted May 9, 2022, by Murad Merali, YouTube, https://www.youtube.com/watch?v=qfRihrxmIJs&t=1s.

Chapter 7: USA! USA!

1. Alex Marshall, "If It's on 'Love Island,' Britain's Talking About It," *The New York Times*, July 6, 2018, https://www.nytimes.com/2018/07/06/arts/television/love-island.html.
2. "Love Island - SNL," posted October 5, 2019, by *Saturday Night Live*, YouTube, https://www.youtube.com/watch?v=xj65JgmJBYc.

Chapter 8: The Flack

1. Peele, "*Love Island*."
2. Anna Peele, "In *Caroline Flack: Search for the Truth*, a Grieving Mother Tries to Clear Her Daughter's Name," *Vanity Fair*, November 10, 2025, https://www.vanityfair.com/hollywood/story/caroline-flack-docuseries-love-island.
3. Christine Flack, self, *Caroline Flack: Search for the Truth*, documentary series, Christian Collerton, director, Disney+, A Hulu Original Series, November 10, 2025, https://www.hulu.com/series/1dea5842-c77e-4b57-bcf8-4cef879daa26.
4. Vicki Newman, "Photo of 'Caroline Flack's Bloodied Bed' Emerges After She Pleads Not Guilty to Assault," *Mirror*, December 31, 2019, https://www.mirror.co.uk/3am/celebrity-news/photo-caroline-flacks-bloodied-bed-21192679.
5. Jim Waterson, "The Sun Takes Down Article About Caroline Flack from Website," *The Guardian*, February 16, 2020, https://www.theguardian.com/media/2020/feb/15/the-sun-takes-down-article-about-caroline-flack-from-website.
6. Prince Harry, *Spare*, 109.
7. "Caroline Flack Inquest: 'No Doubt' Presenter Intended to Take Own Life," BBC, August 6, 2020, https://www.bbc.com/news/uk-england-london-53676793.

Chapter 16: Villains

1. Felicity Cross, "ACTING UP Joey Essex Admits He WAS a Love Island Producer Plant and Says 'There Needed to Be Drama—I Had to Be That Guy,'"

The Sun, July 31, 2024, https://www.thesun.co.uk/tv/29602064/joey-essex-love-island-producer-plant/.

Chapter 18: The Outside

1. Rebecca Lewis, "Margot Robbie Is Rooting for Jack and Dani on Love Island—But She Doesn't See a Resemblance to Megan," *Metro*, July 5, 2018, https://metro.co.uk/2018/07/05/margot-robbie-rooting-jack-dani-love-island-doesnt-see-resemblance-megan-7685816/.

Epilogue

1. Walker Percy, *The Message in the Bottle: How Queer Man Is, How Queer Language Is, and What One Has to Do with the Other* (Farrar, Straus and Giroux, 1975).
2. Niomi Harris, "Love Island: All Stars' Marcel Somerville Responds After Gabby Allen Detailed Her Hopes of Reconciliation Despite His Cheating—But He IS Still Married to His Unfaithful Ex," *Daily Mail*, January 9, 2025, https://www.dailymail.co.uk/tvshowbiz/article-14267335/Love-Island-Marcel-Somerville-responds-Gabby-Allen-reconciliation-reunion-cheating-married-ex.html.

About the Author

ANNA PEELE is a contributing editor at *Vanity Fair*. She spent the first eight years of her career as an editor at men's magazines and received the ASME NEXT Award at the 2016 National Magazine Awards. She has also written for *The New York Times*, *The New York Times Magazine*, *New York* magazine, and ESPN. Her feature on Bravo was *Vanity Fair*'s most read story of 2023, and her February 2025 cover story on Prince Harry and Meghan Markle broke traffic records for the publication. Peele graduated with a BA from New York University in 2010 and lives in Manhattan with her husband. She can be found watching astonishing amounts of reality TV or walking in Central Park. Find out more on AnnaPeele.com.

About the Author

ATRIA BOOKS, an imprint of Simon & Schuster, fosters an open environment where ideas flourish, bestselling authors soar to new heights, and tomorrow's finest voices are discovered and nurtured. Since its launch in 2002, Atria has published hundreds of bestsellers and extraordinary books, which would not have been possible without the invaluable support and expertise of its team and publishing partners. Thank you to the Atria Books colleagues who collaborated on *Enter the Villa: The (Unauthorized) Reality Behind Love Island*, as well as to the hundreds of professionals in the Simon & Schuster advertising, audio, communications, design, ebook, finance, human resources, legal, marketing, operations, production, sales, supply chain, subsidiary rights, and warehouse departments who help Atria bring great books to light.

Editorial
Kate Napolitano
Hannah Frankel

Jacket Design
James Iacobelli

Marketing
Erin Kibby
Morgan Pager
Ebony LaDelle

Managing Editorial
Paige Lytle
Shelby Pumphrey
Sofia Echeverry
Abby Borchers

Production
Sara Kitchen
Brigid Black
Chelsey Drysdale
Jill Putorti

Publicity
Ali Hinchcliffe
Jessica Laino

Publishing Office
Suzanne Donahue
Dana Trocker
Abby Velasco

Subsidiary Rights
Nicole Bond
Sara Bowne
Rebecca Justiniano
Germanie Louis